From War to Cold War

From War to Cold War

The Education of Harry S. Truman

ROBERT JAMES MADDOX

Westview Press
BOULDER & LONDON

Copyright © 1988 by Westview Press, Inc.

Published in 1988 in the United States of America by Westview Press, Inc., 5500 Central Avenue, Boulder, Colorado 80301

Library of Congress Cataloging-in-Publication Data
Maddox, Robert James.
  From war to cold war.
  Bibliography: p.
  Includes index.
  1. Truman, Harry S., 1884–1972. 2. United States—
Foreign relations—1945–1953. 3. World politics—
1945–1955. I. Title.
E814.M33 1988   973.918′092′4   88-5487
ISBN 0-8133-0443-1

Printed and bound in the United States of America

The paper used in this publication meets the requirements of the American National Standard for Permanence of Paper for Printed Library Materials Z39.48-1984.

10   9   8   7   6   5   4   3   2   1

Contents

Acknowledgments

I am grateful to the unfailingly helpful staffs of the libraries I visited during the course of research. I also wish to thank the Intercollegiate Studies Institute, Inc., for permission to use, in somewhat different form, material from my article "Roosevelt and Stalin: The Final Days," which appeared in *Continuity: A Journal of History* 6 (Spring 1983), and the Center for the Study of the Presidency for permission to use material from "Truman, Poland, and the Origins of the Cold War," *Presidential Studies Quarterly* XVII (Winter 1987). I am grateful to Robert H. Ferrell and John Lukacs for interrupting their own work to read the manuscript and to Ida May B. Norton at Westview Press for her many suggestions.

Robert James Maddox

CHAPTER ONE

Introduction:
The Grand Alliance

The United States and the Soviet Union became allies when Adolf Hitler declared war against the United States four days after the Japanese attack on Pearl Harbor. As allies, they dominated the anti-German coalition, along with Great Britain, and later bludgeoned Japan into surrender. The Grand Alliance was a strange partnership because the two Western nations had little in common with the Soviet Union beyond the necessity to defeat their enemies, and many Soviet wartime aims conflicted with those of its allies. That strains should have developed within such a relationship was inevitable; they existed already between the United States and Great Britain. That these strains led to the condition known as the Cold War was the result of personal characteristics of the leaders of the three nations as well as of historical and ideological forces.

Past U.S. relations with the Soviet Union provided an inauspicious foundation for collaboration. In 1917, President Woodrow Wilson had refused to recognize the revolutionary Bolshevik government on the grounds that it had seized power illegally and did not represent the will of the Russian people. In the early summer of 1918, he authorized a military intervention in Siberia through which he hoped to unseat the Bolsheviks. He did not intend the operation to accomplish this task directly. Rather, he wanted to secure the trans-Siberian railway for use as a pipeline to supply and equip anti-Bolshevik groups in the interior. He hoped that, nourished and trained, they would become strong enough to overthrow the radicals and establish a "responsible" government. His primary motive was to reopen the Eastern front, deactivated by the Brest-Litovsk Treaty in March 1918, but his dislike of bolshevism caused him to continue the operation for more than a year after the armistice of November 1918. Josef Stalin alluded to the intervention several times during World War II conferences; it no doubt strengthened the suspicions of a naturally suspicious man.[1]

Wilson contributed to U.S. distrust of the Soviet Union with his anti-Bolshevik rhetoric during the fight over the League of Nations and his toleration of witch-hunting subordinates, both of which helped create the "Red Scare." His nonrecognition policy was continued by Republican presidents, who periodically issued condemnations of Soviet activities within Russia and abroad.

As Democratic candidate for the presidency in 1932, Franklin Delano Roosevelt indicated he meant to reverse this policy. Nonrecognition had failed to produce any discernible changes in the Soviet regime, as its supporters had claimed it would, and many saw it as contrary to U.S. interests. Further, Soviet-U.S. rapprochement might curb Japanese aspirations in the Far East and might provide new markets for a U.S. economy mired in depression. Roosevelt began negotiations during his first months in office, but the benefits expected from recognition proved illusory. Disputes over Soviet payment of debts contracted during the war, legislation prohibiting loans to nations defaulting on such debts, and Comintern activity within the United States ruined chances of a working relationship.

During the depression years, Americans on the left generally regarded the Soviet government favorably. Many shared journalist Lincoln Steffens's frequently quoted view that the Soviet Union represented the future and "it works." The Soviet image was enhanced during the Popular Front period of the mid-1930s, when Communist parties in the West cooperated with liberals, because the USSR seemed an ally against fascism. Later, however, revelations of Stalin's purges convinced previous admirers that the Soviet government was a tyranny scarcely less onerous than Nazi Germany.

Events of 1939–1940 made matters worse. The USSR's antiaggression pact with Germany in August 1939 shocked even the remaining faithful, as did its occupation of eastern Poland two weeks after the Nazi invasion in September. Its invasion of Finland later that year made it appear that the Soviet Union was Hitler's partner in crime. Arguments in behalf of Soviet security needs did little to alter depictions of the struggle as one between tiny, brave Finland and the insatiable Russian bear. Soviet conduct after Hitler invaded the West did not change U.S. perceptions. As France collapsed and Great Britain struggled on alone, the USSR lived up to its commitments by providing foodstuffs and raw materials for the Nazi war machine. While doing so, it seized the three Baltic states of Latvia, Lithuania, and Estonia.

Germany's invasion of the USSR in June 1941 radically altered the situation. The then relatively unknown Sen. Harry S. Truman stated a popular view when he said that the United States should let the dictatorships fight it out and only help whichever side was losing. President Roosevelt understood, however, that the fate of Europe hinged on the outcome. If Russia collapsed, Hitler would have at his disposal virtually all the resources of the continent to use against the British. Roosevelt extended Lend-Lease Act benefits to provide war materials to the Soviets despite predictions that they could hold out only a few months at most. Attitudes changed later in the year when they not only slowed the Nazi onslaught, but fought it to a standstill before Moscow and Leningrad.[2]

The enormous struggle on the Eastern front led to two conclusions after the United States entered the war. The USSR would have to bear the brunt against Germany until Anglo-American power could be mobilized and, if victory were achieved, would play a major role in postwar Europe. These assumptions in turn posed two interrelated tasks for the United States, in Roosevelt's view. The first was to do everything possible to sustain Russia by providing badly needed supplies and equipment. The second was to convince Soviet leaders that past enmity and distrust must be put behind to create a lasting peace. FDR pushed his subordinates to fulfill the first obligation; the second he took upon himself.[3]

Having been assistant secretary of the Navy during World War I and president through most of the 1930s, Roosevelt understood Soviet suspicion of the Western powers. He sought to overcome it by convincing Stalin that the United States wanted cooperation to continue into the postwar world. To Roosevelt, success was necessary to maintain peace because, although he endorsed an international organization, he believed only a large power condominium would be effective. Finally, Soviet-U.S. collaboration during the war would make the American people more receptive to playing an active part in world affairs during peacetime.

FDR damaged his cause only a few months after Pearl Harbor. He approved a plan, drawn up by General George C. Marshall's staff, for a 1943 invasion of France across the English Channel. But the plan also contained provisions for an emergency assault in 1942 if that appeared necessary to stave off Soviet collapse. FDR became so enamored of the latter proposal that he cabled Stalin, asking him to send Foreign Minister V. M. Molotov to Washington to discuss a "very important military proposal involving the utilization of our armed forces in a manner to relieve your critical western front." Molotov arrived in Washington during late May after talks with the British in

London. Responding to his direct question, Roosevelt assured him he could "inform Mr. Stalin that we expect the formation of a second front this year."[4]

It was a major blunder. British leaders regarded the plan as folly, and Winston Churchill hurried to Washington to persuade Roosevelt that North Africa was the only feasible place to open a second front. This was not what FDR had led the Soviets to expect, but he agreed because it would divert some German forces and because he believed it critical for American morale to take the offensive against Germany. In this instance, the British surely were right. Troops lacked training in amphibious operations, landing craft were in short supply, and long-range fighters to provide air cover were not yet operational. Considering the difficulties encountered when the cross-channel invasion did take place, landings in 1942 almost certainly would have led to disaster and prolonged the war. It is ironic that Roosevelt's zeal to encourage the Soviets and show them he was a good ally led him to make a promise he could not keep, thereby feeding their mistrust.[5]

The Soviets were disappointed again by the Casablanca Conference of January 1943. Stalin declined to attend, saying he was needed at home to direct the war effort. At the conference, Roosevelt and Churchill agreed to the invasion of Sicily. Although preparations for a cross-channel invasion were stepped up, it was put off for another year. The decision was made within the context of conflicting views between the United States and Britain over strategy, but it must have seemed to Stalin that his Western allies were leaving the Soviet Union to bear the burden while they waited to pick up the pieces.

At Casablanca, Roosevelt proclaimed one of the most controversial policies of the war: the doctrine of "unconditional surrender." He said the idea simply popped into his mind at the time, and Churchill later wrote that FDR's statement astonished and appalled him. Neither told the truth. Roosevelt had decided on unconditional surrender weeks earlier and secured Churchill's assent before making the announcement. Critics have charged that the policy prolonged the war because Nazi and Japanese propagandists used it as proof that the Allies meant to destroy their nations. FDR adopted the doctrine to avoid what he regarded as a mistake of the last war, when a negotiated peace permitted extremists to claim that Germany had not been defeated in the field, but had been "stabbed in the back" at home. He also wanted to compensate for failure to open a second front by assuring Stalin that his Western partners would not negotiate separately with the enemy. In so doing, he hoped to dispel any notion the Soviets might have of making terms with Hitler.[6]

Roosevelt had a chance to win over Stalin in person at the Teheran Conference, which met in late November 1943. Convinced of his persuasiveness, the president believed he could convince the Soviet leader of American goodwill. The fabled Roosevelt charm does not translate well in conference notes. It consisted largely of jokes and quips, often at Churchill's expense. Stalin responded indulgently, thereby leading Roosevelt to think he had succeeded. He later told an aide that the more he teased the prime minister the more Stalin warmed up, until at last he "broke into a deep, heavy guffaw. . . . The ice was broken and we talked like men and brothers." That FDR accomplished anything more than encourage Stalin to exploit Anglo-American differences is unlikely. Yet Churchill shared Roosevelt's illusion. "If only I could dine with Stalin once a week," he boasted shortly after Teheran, "there would be no trouble at all. We get on like a house on fire."[7]

Aside from an Anglo-American promise to launch the long-delayed cross-channel invasion by late spring of 1944, most of the discussions at Teheran were exploratory. They established positions on issues that would provide the basis for negotiation at Yalta. Postwar treatment of Germany was an exception. Both Stalin and Roosevelt inclined toward radical dismemberment of Germany to prevent repetition of what had happened after the last war. FDR offered a plan for dividing Germany into five parts and for establishing a trusteeship over the Ruhr and Saar region. Even Churchill, who opposed such a drastic approach as likely to produce chaos, recommended that Prussia be detached from the rest of Germany. All three leaders, for reasons of their own, retreated from this concept in the months following and showed little enthusiasm for it at Yalta.

Talks about Poland revealed a dilemma that would plague Roosevelt. The Atlantic Charter he and Churchill had issued in August 1941 condemned territorial changes imposed by force and endorsed the right of all peoples to choose their form of government. Although Stalin had given a hedged endorsement of the charter, Roosevelt understood he was adamant about retaining Polish territory occupied in 1939— roughly corresponding to the Curzon Line—and also meant to establish a "friendly" government.[8] How could FDR agree without incurring the criticism, particularly from voters of Polish extraction, that he had betrayed the charter to placate Stalin?

Roosevelt took refuge in silence. He said little in discussions during which Churchill and Stalin agreed that Poland should be compensated for losses in the east by gaining German territory up to the Oder River. They were far apart on who would govern Poland. Churchill hoped to work out an arrangement between the London-based Polish government in exile and the Soviets, but their relations had been poisoned six months earlier when the former publicly accused the USSR of murdering nearly 5,000 Polish officers in the Katyn Forest in 1940. FDR told Stalin privately that he was sympathetic to Soviet desires, but that he could not be a party to any agreements until after the 1944 elections because he was afraid of alienating the Polish vote. Stalin said he understood.[9]

Roosevelt's success in trying to resolve the contradictions between idealistic wartime statements and his realistic assessment of Soviet goals depended on Stalin's cooperation in Eastern Europe. It helps explain why he so ardently courted the Soviet leader's trust. If Stalin were convinced of America's goodwill, FDR reasoned, his apprehension about security might be sufficiently eased to permit him to treat this area with a light hand. If he valued partnership, furthermore, he would spare Roosevelt domestic embarrassment by at least going through the motions of holding plebiscites and relatively free elections. FDR was a bit cynical perhaps, but what was the alternative? If he pressed matters over which he had no control, he would justify Stalin's fears and probably cause him to choke occupied nations into submission. No one would benefit.

Roosevelt explained to Stalin his ideas about a United Nations. He saw it as a three-tiered affair: an assembly of all nations, limited to debate; a council composed of the Big Four (the United States, Great Britain, the USSR, and China, which FDR included despite its weakness and internal divisions) and six regional representatives, which could decide nonmilitary issues; and finally, what he called the "four policemen." Only the latter, he said, had power to enforce peace. When Stalin suggested separate organizations for Europe and Asia, to be dominated by the United States, Great Britain, and the Soviet Union, Roosevelt said he doubted Congress would approve an arrangement that might involve sending U.S. troops to Europe. As one scholar has written, Stalin "must have been delighted to learn that Roosevelt planned to permit the Russian and British armies to dominate the continent after the war."[10] Roosevelt said he wanted to study the issue further, so it was not discussed in formal session nor mentioned in the communiqué. He later abandoned the phrase "four policemen" as too blatant, but they would dominate the Security Council as permanent members with veto power.

Asian affairs were discussed briefly at Teheran. Although the United States had taken the offensive in the Pacific more than a year earlier, it was assumed that many months of fighting lay ahead and that an invasion of the Japanese home islands would be necessary. The atomic bomb was only a possibility that could not figure in military calculations. Roosevelt believed it crucial that the Soviets engage Japanese forces on the mainland so they could not be employed against U.S. landings. Stalin repeated a promise he had made to Secretary of State Cordell Hull in Moscow a few weeks before the conference: The USSR would declare war on Japan two or three months after Germany's defeat. When he said he expected compensation for such assistance, Roosevelt proposed that Dairen in Manchuria be made a free port to provide the Soviets a warm-water outlet on the Pacific. FDR did not object to Stalin's mention of special rights on Manchurian railways providing access to Dairen nor to acquisition of the Kurile Islands and the southern half of Sakhalin Island. As FDR reported these conversations to the Pacific War Council in Washington, on which a Chinese member sat, it is inconceivable that the Chinese government was not informed of Stalin's objectives. No protest was raised.[11]

FDR's conduct during the Teheran Conference symbolized his approach throughout the war. Determined that differences among the Allies should not impede military operations, he was reluctant to grapple with divisive issues. Partly this was his style: He was inclined to put off hard decisions in hopes a solution would turn up. It may also have reflected a peculiarly American naïveté about separating military and political goals. But FDR was motivated by another consideration. He believed public support for an active role in postwar affairs, including membership in the United Nations, was a fragile commodity. Remembering the Senate's rejection of the League of Nations, he was afraid this support would collapse if the United States became involved in open disputes with the Soviets. He failed to appreciate that maintaining the fiction of smooth cooperation during the war might produce a stronger negative sentiment when divisions no longer could be disguised by statements of solidarity.

The Polish question provides a case in point. As mentioned, FDR understood that Stalin meant to have a "friendly" government, but hoped he would have enough regard for his allies to permit the appearance of an autonomous regime. Unwilling either to antagonize Stalin or Polish voters, Roosevelt simply let matters slide through most of 1944, leaving Churchill the task of trying to work out a compromise. FDR met with Polish Prime Minister Stanlislaw Mikolajczyk in June, but provided nothing beyond encouraging words. When the Soviets crossed the Curzon Line in midsummer, they announced that liberated Poland would be administered by the Committee of National Liberation based in Lublin. The Lublin Committee was a Moscow puppet, and it appeared the London Poles might be excluded from any role.

On July 31, as Soviet troops reached the Vistula River a few miles away, an uprising in Warsaw began. The exile government and the Polish Home Army operating under its command wanted to liberate the city as a demonstration of strength, hoping it would encourage Great Britain and the United States to stand behind them against Lublin's flimsy claims to legitimacy. The Soviets stood in place for two months while German units destroyed the stubborn resistance. Whether this was deliberate or due to tactical and logistical considerations, as the Soviets claimed, is unclear. In any case, the anti-Lublin underground in Warsaw was crushed. When Stalin, who referred to the Polish rebels as "criminals," refused to permit U.S. and British aircraft to land behind Soviet lines after dropping supplies, Roosevelt spurned Churchill's plea to act more boldly. To the prime minister's suggestion that they send the planes with or without permission, FDR alluded to the need for Soviet help in the war against Japan.[12]

By the end of 1944, prospects for a democratic government in Poland were nonexistent. Stalin recognized Lublin as the provisional government over FDR's protests, claiming it enjoyed broad support among the people. Churchill and Roosevelt knew its strength rested upon the Red Army and the People's Commissariat of Internal Affairs (NKVD). The most they could expect was that Stalin would support the formation of a government that would include sufficient representation of other political parties to gain a measure of independence from Moscow.

The president remained similarly aloof from affairs of other East European nations. In October 1944, Churchill flew to Moscow where he worked out the famed "percentages" deal with Stalin. According to this agreement, Great Britain acknowledged Soviet predominance in Bulgaria and Romania in return for a similar position in Greece—influence in Yugoslavia and Hungary would be split fifty-fifty. The prime minister's action ran against U.S. statements opposing spheres of influence, but he wanted to make the best deal he could while there was time. Roosevelt did not denounce the agreement; he merely said he would consider it a temporary wartime arrangement. He was less willing to offend the Soviets over nations such as Bulgaria and Romania than he was over Poland. Stalin may have regarded FDR's conduct at Teheran and his failure to repudiate the percentages agreement as acquiescence.[13]

The German question remained in flux after Teheran, but raised controversy within the administration. The State and War departments advocated moderate treatment of Germany once its war-making potential had been eliminated. Secretaries Hull and Stimson believed the German people should be accorded a modest standard of living and their nation reintegrated into the European economy. Dismemberment and harsh treatment, they reasoned, would spawn hatred and the desire for revenge that would preclude lasting peace.

Secretary of the Treasury Henry Morgenthau, Jr., whose friendship with FDR gave him considerable influence, was appalled at what was coming out of State and War. He argued vehemently to Roosevelt that the policies Hull and Stimson advocated would leave Germany intact and capable of future aggression. He played upon FDR's belief that the German people were inherently warlike and would not change just because the Nazis were removed. FDR agreed. "We have got to be tough with Germany," he told Morgenthau, "and I mean the German people, not just the Nazis."[14]

Morgenthau had his aides draw up a program even more punitive than that Roosevelt had proposed at Teheran. It called for heavy reparations in the form of plant removals and forced labor, large-scale destruction of industrial and mining operations, and drastic dismemberment of Germany, with portions parceled out to her neighbors. It would have left Germany impoverished. Hull and Stimson remonstrated without success.

When Churchill and Roosevelt met at the second Quebec Conference in September 1944, FDR sent for Morgenthau. Churchill at first opposed the secretary's ideas, saying he did not wish to chain Great Britain to a dead body. Whether he succumbed to Morgenthau's argument or the offer of $6.5 billion in postwar aid is debatable, but he and Roosevelt initialed the Morgenthau plan on September 15. FDR reneged when details of the plan leaked, arousing heavy criticism. He denied he wanted to turn Germany into an agrarian nation and claimed his views had been misrepresented. To Stimson he said he scarcely remembered reading the plan, and he attempted to shift blame by declaring that "Henry Morgenthau pulled a boner."[15]

Roosevelt never decided what to do about Germany. As usual, he considered the issue within the context of U.S.-Soviet relations. The USSR had sent mixed signals as to its position, but two weeks before the Yalta Conference, Assistant People's Commissar for Foreign Affairs I. M. Maisky told Ambassador W. Averell Harriman the Soviets wanted reparations out of current production for a period of ten years, in addition to plant removals. This meant that substantial German industry would have to be retained to produce the goods. FDR was firm on one point. He did not want Germany reduced to starvation through reparations, thereby necessitating U.S. relief. Such a situation, he knew, would be condemned as obliging the United States to pay reparations indirectly to the USSR.

The 1944 elections that Roosevelt professed to fear in his talks with Stalin revealed no dramatic shifts among voters. FDR, taking care to emphasize his role as commander in chief of U.S. forces advancing on all fronts, handily defeated Thomas E. Dewey, and the Democrats picked up a few seats in both houses of Congress. In retrospect, and to some people at the time, the most significant factor in the campaign was FDR's selection of his running mate. His badly deteriorating health was reflected in his ravaged face, weight loss, and diminished vitality. Although still capable of winding himself up for public occasions, his condition was widely discussed in Washington. Few insiders believed he could survive another four years.[16]

The leading contenders for the vice presidency were the incumbent, Henry A. Wallace, and James F. Byrnes of South Carolina. Wallace's liberal views made him anathema to conservative Democrats, especially southerners, and many important urban political bosses. Byrnes, former senator and Supreme Court justice and at the time director of the Office of War Mobilization (OWM), was equally obnoxious to blacks and organized labor. FDR led both men to believe he favored them and that he was equivocating only for the sake of party unity. Then, at the last moment, he announced his preference for Sen. Harry S. Truman of Missouri. Bringing in a compromise candidate to avoid alienating opposing factions was an astute political move, but would have unforeseen consequences upon Roosevelt's death.

Byrnes was an old friend of FDR and exercised such broad powers as head of OWM that he became known as "Assistant President for the homefront." Confident of receiving the nomination, he was shocked and angered by what he regarded as Roosevelt's betrayal. His relationship with Truman added to his distress. Truman had entered the Senate in 1935 with a reputation soiled by association with the Pendergast machine of Kansas City. He had lived that down by hard work and his personal demeanor, but faced a difficult fight for reelection in 1940. Byrnes helped him by first seeking Roosevelt's endorsement, then soliciting badly needed campaign money. Later, as chairman of the Senate Audit and Control Committee, he made funds available for what became known as the "Truman Committee" to investigate corruption in the defense industry. As chairman, Truman achieved national attention as a watchdog who saved taxpayers billions of dollars. Truman not only promised to support Byrnes at the convention, but agreed to make his nominating speech.[17]

No one can tell how these events influenced each man's feelings about the other, consciously or otherwise. Truman truthfully assured Byrnes he had played no part in FDR's political maneuvering and that he had accepted the decision reluctantly. The South Carolinian professed to believe him. Still, it produced an awkward situation. To the proud and ambitious Byrnes, he had been denied a position he deserved in favor of a younger person of fewer attainments. Truman, on the other hand, knew he was a compromise candidate of lesser stature and was aware of his indebtedness to the older man. Both realized that more than the vice presidency probably was at stake because of FDR's physical condition. Outwardly, their relationship remained unchanged during Roosevelt's lifetime. Truman was in the administration but not of it: FDR neither solicited his opinions nor kept him informed. Byrnes, though no longer on intimate terms with FDR, continued to be the more influential figure—especially when he was invited to attend the Yalta Conference.[18]

In July 1944, Roosevelt had proposed that another meeting of the Big Three be held in September. Stalin first claimed he had to remain in Moscow to conduct military operations, then said his doctors had warned him against any "big trips." He relented in October, informing the president he would be willing to attend a conference the next month provided it was held in the Black Sea area. He turned down alternatives suggested by Churchill and FDR that would be more accessible to them. After several weeks of jockeying over location, Roosevelt requested postponement until after his inauguration in January. Finally, the two Western leaders bowed to Stalin's wish, as they had for Teheran, and the conference was scheduled at Yalta in the Crimea for early February.[19]

Churchill from the start wanted a meeting held as quickly as possible. He warned Roosevelt that there were "many matters awaiting settlement . . . which ought not be left to moulder." His apprehension was justified, as time worked in Stalin's favor. Every military success bolstered the USSR's claim to primacy in defeating the Germans. And the Soviets used the additional time to crush potential opposition through arrests and deportations in areas they occupied. What Churchill could not have foreseen was that Hitler would launch a surprise December attack against the Alliles in the Ardennes. Although this thrust was halted two weeks before the Soviet Union mounted its own offensive in mid-January, Anglo-American forces still were west of the Rhine when the Yalta Conference met. Russian spearheads were only forty miles from Berlin.

There were two issues Roosevelt chose not to raise at the meeting: a postwar loan for the Soviet Union and the Anglo-American atomic bomb program. In early January, Molotov handed Ambassador Harriman a request for a $6-billion loan at the low interest rate of 2.25 percent. The stated purpose of the loan was to help the United States through its anticipated postwar depression! After recovering from "my surprise at Molotov's strange procedure," Harriman reported that the foreign minister had implied that "the development of our friendly relations would depend upon a generous credit." Roosevelt wanted it the other way around. He hoped prospects of securing a loan would cause the Soviets to cooperate during and after the conference. Unwilling to incur a commitment, FDR preferred not to haggle. When Molotov at Yalta mentioned the issue to Secretary of State Edward R. Stettinius, Jr., he merely replied "that he personally was ready to discuss it at any time." No one brought it up again during the conference.[20]

FDR's decision not to tell Stalin about the atomic program may have had more significant impact on relations. Scientists estimated at least one bomb would be ready during the summer of 1945, although no one could guarantee when or whether it would work. The previous August, scientist Niels Bohr had tried to convince Churchill and Roosevelt that the Soviets should be informed before nuclear weapons were operational to avoid the appearance of using them as a threat. There was no way to prevent the Soviets from building bombs within a few years, he argued, and to prevent an arms race the USSR should be invited to participate in a system of international control.[21]

Churchill dismissed Bohr's proposal as foolish and dangerous. The prime minister, aware of Britain's diminishing status as a conventional power, saw the bomb as an asset that should not be squandered courting goodwill. Roosevelt gave the scientist a more sympathetic hearing, or so it appeared, but disregarded his advice. In September, FDR and Churchill signed a memorandum at Hyde Park stating that "the matter should continue to be regarded as of the utmost secrecy" and calling for surveillance of Bohr to ensure he revealed no information, "particularly to the Russians."[22]

FDR's reasoning is difficult to understand. Perhaps the rush of events and his poor health prevented him from thinking through the ramifications. Or he may have feared domestic repercussions later if relations with the Soviets turned hostile. He appears to have agreed with Stimson that no disclosure be made until it could be bartered for a quid pro quo. Yet Stimson also told Roosevelt it was almost certain the USSR knew about the program through espionage. What would be lost by informing Stalin of a development he assumed the latter knew about? If he feared Stalin would seek admission to partnership, surely he could have put him off with some excuse. He could have replied that the presence of Soviet atomic scientists in the United States would compromise security, for instance, or that he could not act without congressional approval. He seems not to have considered that his efforts to gain Stalin's trust might be canceled by the enormity of the "secret" he and Churchill had agreed to keep between them.

Roosevelt left Washington on January 22, 1945, for Norfolk, Virginia, where he boarded the heavy cruiser USS *Quincy.* His destination was the island of Malta in the Mediterranean, a trip of almost 5,000 miles.

Stettinius and others had flown ahead for preliminary talks with Churchill and British Foreign Secretary Anthony Eden. FDR intended to stay only briefly at Malta because he wished to afford no grounds for suspicion that he and Churchill were conspiring behind Stalin's back. He arrived on February 2, the day before delegations were scheduled to fly to Saki airfield and then proceed by automobile to Yalta about ninety miles away. Stettinius later wrote that FDR looked calm and rested when he arrived at Malta, whereas on inauguration day less than two weeks earlier "he had seemed to tremble all over." A British official who had not seen him for several months, on the other hand, told Stettinius he was "shocked" by the president's appearance.[23]

NOTES

1. Robert J. Maddox, *The Unknown War with Russia: Wilson's Siberian Intervention* (San Rafael, Calif.: Presidio Press, 1977). George F. Kennan's *The Decision to Intervene* (Princeton, N.J.: Princeton University Press, 1958) and Betty Miller Unterberger's *America's Siberian Intervention, 1918–1920* (Durham, N.C.: Duke University Press, 1956) stress other reasons for the intervention.

2. Robert Dallek, *Franklin D. Roosevelt and American Foreign Policy, 1932–1945* (New York: Oxford, 1979), pp. 278–281, 295–299.

3. Dallek, *Roosevelt,* pp. 337–338.

4. Roosevelt's message to Stalin is in *Foreign Relations of the United States, 1942* (Washington, D.C.: Government Printing Office, 1960), III, p. 543; his conversation with Molotov, pp. 575–577.

5. Robert A. Divine, *Roosevelt and World War II* (Baltimore, Md.: The Johns Hopkins University Press, 1969), pp. 90–91.

6. John L. Chase, "Unconditional Surrender Reconsidered," in Robert A. Divine, ed., *Causes and Consequences of World War II* (Chicago: Quadrangle, 1969), pp. 183–201.

7. Roosevelt's account is in Frances Perkins, *The Roosevelt I Knew* (New York: Viking, 1946), p. 84; Churchill's remark is quoted in Timothy Garton Ash, "From World War to Cold War," *The New York Review of Books* XXXIV (June 11, 1987), p. 47.

8. British Foreign Secretary Lord George Curzon at the Paris Peace Conference suggested this line, based on ethnic considerations, as the Russo-Polish frontier. Polish victories against Soviet troops resulted in the Treaty of Riga (1921), which fixed the boundary about 150 miles east of the Curzon Line.

9. The best account of the Katyn Forest massacre and its implications is Robert Szymczak, "The Unquiet Dead: The Katyn Forest as an Issue in American Diplomacy and Politics," unpublished doctoral dissertation, Carnegie-Mellon University, 1980. The Roosevelt-Stalin conversation is in *FRUS, The Conferences at Cairo and Teheran, 1943* (Washington, D.C., 1961), p. 594.

10. Divine, *Roosevelt,* p. 64.

11. Herbert Feis, *The China Tangle* (New York: Atheneum, 1965), p. 113.

12. Dallek, *Roosevelt,* pp. 463–465.

13. Vojtech Mastny, *Russia's Road to the Cold War: Diplomacy, Warfare, and the Politics of Communism, 1941–1945* (New York: Columbia University Press, 1979), pp. 207–209, and see Briefing Book Paper "American Policy Toward Spheres of Influence," *FRUS, The Conferences at Malta and Yalta, 1945* (Washington, D.C., 1955), pp. 103–106.

14. John Morton Blum, *From the Morgenthau Diaries: Years of War, 1941–1945* (Boston: Houghton Mifflin, 1967), p. 342.

15. John Lewis Gaddis, *The United States and the Origins of the Cold War, 1941–1947* (New York: Columbia University Press, 1972), pp. 118–122. Roosevelt's remark is in a dictation Stimson made after talking with FDR, attached to a memorandum from John J. McCloy to H. Freeman Matthews, October 4, 1944, in James F. Byrnes Papers, Folder 613(1).

16. Dallek, *Roosevelt,* p. 481; and Robert L. Messer, *The End of an Alliance: James F. Byrnes, Roosevelt, Truman, and the Origins of the Cold War* (Chapel Hill: University of North Carolina Press, 1982), p. 15.

17. Messer, *Alliance,* p. 26.

18. Why Roosevelt invited Byrnes to Yalta is unknown. In addition to denying him the vice presidency, FDR passed him over in favor of Edward R. Stettinius, Jr. for secretary of state when Cordell Hull resigned in November 1944. When Stettinius asked whether he did so because Byrnes "might question who was boss," Roosevelt replied, "That's exactly it." Calendar notes for 27 November, 1944, Stettinius Diary. Roosevelt may have extended the invitation as compensation or, as Messer suggests in *Alliance,* p. 37, hoped to use Byrnes's political connections to prepare a favorable reception for the conference.

19. *FRUS, Yalta,* pp. 3–21.

20. *FRUS, 1945* (Washington, D.C., 1967) V, pp. 942ff.; Stettinius's statement is in *FRUS, Yalta,* p. 610.

21. Martin J. Sherwin, *A World Destroyed: The Atomic Bomb and the Grand Alliance* (New York: Knopf, 1975), pp. 107–109.

22. The Hyde Park memorandum is reprinted in Sherwin, *World,* p. 284.

23. Edward R. Stettinius, Jr., *Roosevelt and the Russians: The Yalta Conference* (New York: Doubleday, 1949), p. 72.

CHAPTER TWO

Yalta

———————◆———————

The Yalta Conference began on February 4, 1945, the day after the U.S. and British delegations arrived from Malta. Housed in impressive if antiquated buildings, members of both groups complained about the shortage of bathrooms and the surplus of bedbugs. Whatever the inadequacies of accommodation, few could have been unaware that this meeting would have momentous consequences. With the war in Europe grinding to its end, the time for exploratory talks such as had taken place at Teheran was over. Decisions would have to be made about the postwar treatment of Germany and the liberated areas. Although much preliminary work had been done about the proposed structure of the United Nations, several important issues remained unsettled. The struggle in the Pacific was far from over, and from the U.S. standpoint, it was crucial to formalize Soviet promises to enter the war after Germany's defeat. Important as these matters were, they were subsumed by an even larger question: whether the wartime coalition would continue after the fighting. If it did, chances of another large-scale conflict would be small. If it began breaking down over one or more issues, prospects would be bleak.[1]

Of the three leaders, Stalin remains the most enigmatic. His stated objectives are clear, as are his cabled messages before and after the conference. Beyond that little is known. What did he mean when he said he wanted "friendly" nations on the USSR's borders? Would it be sufficient that they not be anti-Soviet, or did he intend all along to dominate them as eventually happened? What were his thoughts about the United Nations? Without access to internal Soviet memoranda, records of conversations, and recollections by associates, the answers can only be guessed. In the sets of notes taken during the discussions at Yalta, Stalin comes across as well-prepared, economical with words, and adept at pointing out inconsistencies in the arguments of others. Above all, one is struck by his apparent moderation. Adamant on certain matters, on others he seemed ready to accept compromise for the sake of Allied unity. Stalin's conduct at Yalta strengthened the belief, held by some U.S. officials, that he represented the "soft" faction in Moscow while Molotov spoke for the more militant group.[2]

Churchill was the most learned of the three and by far the most eloquent. However, his rhetoric sometimes carried him away from positions agreed upon within the British delegation, to the dismay of his subordinates.[3] In any case, he played from a weak hand, which words could not surmount. By this time, Britain was the junior partner in Anglo-American relations and alone could have little influence. Although it must have pained him, considering his feelings about the glories of the British Empire, Churchill understood his reliance upon Roosevelt's support.

Roosevelt's performance compares unfavorably with those of his counterparts. Lacking either Churchill's mastery of language or Stalin's command of facts, he often resorted to vague generalities or quips in place of reasoned arguments. One must remember how tenuous FDR's positions were on several critical issues. Soviet armies were in Poland and other East European countries; failure to reach agreements about these areas would eliminate any restraints on Soviet behavior. With regard to the Far East, Roosevelt was the supplicant—he and his military advisers believed Soviet participation in the war against Japan would shorten the war by months and save tens of thousands of lives. Finally, there were domestic considerations: Roosevelt believed that if cleavages developed between the Soviet Union and the West, the American people and Congress would reject the United Nations and retreat into isolationism, losing the chance of constructing a lasting peace.

Almost every account of the Yalta Conference includes discussion of FDR's health. Pictures show a haggard, at times slack-jawed, man obviously in poor health. Participants disagree over how much his physical and mental impairment affected his conduct during the conference.[4] The issue probably has been exaggerated. Had Roosevelt been in better condition, he may well have argued more cogently or been more adamant on one or another point. But that this would have changed events is a dubious proposition. And that even a healthy Roosevelt, to use his earlier boast, could have "handled" Stalin better than others is highly unlikely.[5]

The first plenary session of the conference was held at 5:00 P.M. on February 4. It was given over to reports of military progress and plans, and everyone praised one another's efforts. An hour before the session began, Roosevelt, accompanied only by his interpreter, met with Stalin and Molotov. Little of substance was discussed, but the talks provided another example of Roosevelt's desire to ingratiate himself with the Soviet leader by distancing himself from the British. At one point, FDR joked that he was feeling more "bloodthirsty" than at Teheran and hoped Stalin again would propose a toast to the execution of 50,000 German officers, to which Churchill had protested. A bit later, Roosevelt said that he was going to tell the Soviets something "indiscreet," which he would not say in front of the prime minister. For several years, the British had the idea of "artificially" building France so as to enable it to maintain large forces on the eastern frontiers and thus "hold the line" for the period necessary to create a strong British army. The British were "a peculiar people," he said, who "wished to have their cake and eat it too." The minutes do not record Stalin's reply, and one wonders what he made of such talk.[6]

Germany was the topic of discussion during the second plenary session on February 5. First on the agenda was dismemberment of Germany, a matter the three men had talked about for some time at Teheran. All still seemed to favor it, but no one showed enthusiasm for any of the alternative plans. At Churchill's insistence that the matter was too complicated to be settled during the conference, it was agreed that dismemberment be accepted in principle and that the matter be referred to the foreign ministers.

The question of France's participation in the occupation of Germany also was taken up. Churchill argued that the French should be granted both an occupation zone and a role in the control machinery. Stalin, who throughout the conference expressed contempt for France's part in the war, said he would not object if the United States and Britain wished to grant a zone out of their own, but that he did not think France merited a seat on the control commission. FDR agreed with Stalin, although later he would reverse himself. This matter, too, was referred to the foreign ministers.

The last issue discussed that day, reparations from Germany, proved the most divisive. A disagreement arose that would infect Soviet relations with the Western powers. Reparations had political as well as economic implications and was both a cause and a consequence of competing views on the treatment of Germany. There is ample documentation as to struggles that took place within the British and U.S. governments, and though the sources are not available, it is likely that similar arguments occurred among Soviet leaders. Everyone agreed that Germany's war-making potential, such as armament and aviation industries, should be eliminated. Beyond that, differences were vast. On the one extreme were those who agreed with Secretary of the Treasury Henry Morgenthau, Jr., who wanted to "pastoralize" Germany into a group of small states bereft of any but the lightest industry. At the other were those who wished to disarm and de-Nazify Germany but who also believed it should be permitted a modern, diversified economy without which, such people argued, European recovery would be impossible. There were variations across the spectrum.

The amount and kinds of reparations to be extracted involved more than the by-product of one's thinking about treatment of Germany. The Soviet economy had suffered great devastation during the war, and the USSR considered large-scale reparations crucial to rapid reconstruction. Had this not been so, Stalin and his subordinates might well have committed themselves to pastoralization—Germany, after all, had invaded Russia twice during the twentieth century. The problem was that although deindustrialization would benefit the Soviet Union via plant removals, nothing would be left to produce reparations in the years following. The situation, to put it mildly, was incredibly complicated.

FDR's and Churchill's flirtations with the Morgenthau plan at Quebec the previous fall had long since ended. By the time of Yalta, Churchill had taken the position that aside from the destruction of war plants, German industry should be reduced (especially in those areas that competed with British exports) but not crippled, nor should the people be impoverished by excessive extractions from current production. The experience of World War I, he believed, showed that punitive extractions failed to produce the expected benefits and would serve largely to embitter the German people.[7]

Roosevelt remained vague as to where he stood, thereby encouraging subordinate officials to compete for approval of their particular programs through endless meetings and memoranda. The State Department flatly opposed Morgenthau's plan, wanting a unified Germany with a diversified economy that would operate under Allied control. The War Department by this time tended to side with Treasury, though largely for administrative reasons. FDR seemed to agree with whomever he spoke to last, except for his determination to avoid even the appearance that U.S. taxpayers might have to support Germany because of punitive extractions.

The Soviet Union had outlined its position when Maisky met with Harriman on January 20. Germany should be broken up, Maisky told Harriman, though exactly how had not yet been decided. The country should be demilitarized industrially, with steel and other heavy industry reduced to the level necessary for German needs and a modest surplus. Because the Soviet Union placed security above all else, reparations out of current production (which Maisky estimated would be extracted over a period of ten years) would not require Germany to retain a large manufacturing capacity. Significantly, Maisky stated that "it should be recognized that she [Germany] must have an export trade in order to purchase required imports." This approach, which was called the "first charge" principle, became a matter of controversy in the months following Yalta. However reasonably Maisky stated his case, if Germany were to have the ability to provide for its own needs, reparations out of production, *and* an export trade, its industrial base would have to be far larger than advocates of pastoralization wanted.[8]

Stalin called upon Maisky to present the Soviet plan at Yalta. The latter's comments were in line with what he had told Harriman, but were more specific. In response to an earlier query by Roosevelt, Maisky said that the Soviets were not prepared to discuss the problem of German labor and that the issue was best left for the future. The Soviets wanted reparations in two forms: the removal of capital equipment within a two-year period and goods from current production for ten years. To fulfill these goals and to safeguard European security, he went on, German heavy industry should be reduced by 80 percent. The remaining 20 percent would be sufficient "to cover the economic needs of the country." The losses suffered from German aggression were beyond calculation, he said, and for this reason priorities had to be established. Those countries that had made "the highest contribution to the war and had suffered the highest material losses" should be accorded the highest priority. He proposed that the three governments set up a reparations commission to sit in Moscow and concluded that the total reparations required by the Soviet Union would amount to $10 billion.[9]

Churchill raised immediate objection and explained his position at length. Alluding to World War I, the prime minister said he believed nothing like the sum mentioned could be obtained from Germany. The attempt to do so would devastate the German economy, thereby requiring large-scale assistance from abroad, which Britain was unable and unwilling to provide. He was "haunted by the specter of a starving Germany," Churchill stated, and he ended his remarks with the comment "that if you wished a horse to pull a wagon . . . you would at least have to give it fodder." To this Stalin replied that Churchill was right, "but care should be taken to see that the horse did not turn around and kick you."

Roosevelt tried to reconcile the difference. He stated several times that he wished to see the USSR receive as much reparations as possible, but that the United States too was unwilling to underwrite aid to Germany to rectify shortages caused by excessive extractions. The United States had lost a great deal of money after the last war, he said, and "this time we would not repeat our past mistakes." He agreed with Churchill that the subject should be studied by the reparations commission the Soviets had proposed. Stalin, however, wanted decisions made before the conference ended because the reparations commission "could accomplish nothing unless it was given general directives." The foreign ministers were instructed to consult on the matter and to propose a set of "main directives" for the commission to follow.[10]

At the ministers' meeting on February 7, Molotov submitted a formal proposal on reparations. It differed from the earlier Soviet position in two respects. First, no mention was made of reducing German heavy industry by 80 percent as Maisky had suggested in the plenary session. This omission was likely because it would be more difficult to argue that Germany's economy could afford heavy reparations and provide for its own people with only 20 percent of its prewar industrial plant. Second, whereas Stalin and Molotov had previously mentioned only the figure of $10 billion the USSR sought, the new statement provided for a total of $20 billion, with half going to the Soviet Union. Molotov then called upon Maisky to explain the considerations on which the Soviets based this amount. Citing prewar figures on German national wealth and income and projecting estimates of the damages likely to have been sustained by the war's end, Maisky endeavored to show that the $20 billion could be extracted without causing Germany's living standard to go below that of its neighbors. Unaccountably, the significance of this report has been minimized or ignored—one volume devoted entirely to the reparations question omits mention of it altogether. But the report is important for two reasons. The sum the Soviets proposed would be relevant only if Maisky's speculations proved reasonably accurate. And it accepted as given the British and U.S. requirement that Germany's postwar economy be sufficient to provide a decent standard of living without outside assistance.[11]

It is interesting that no one questioned Maisky's figures then or later. Probably this was due in part to the fact that it would have been pointless to debate matters such as estimated damages when there was no way of knowing what they would be. What is surprising is that one part of Maisky's report was incorrect on its face. Everyone present knew that a portion of Germany was to be given to Poland to compensate for Soviet acquisition of Poland's eastern lands, although where the German-Polish border would be established was disputed throughout the conference. However the matter was resolved, only a truncated Germany would survive, which would have to absorb and provide for the population evicted from those areas Poland received. It is unlikely no one realized this. The most plausible explanation for the lack of any discussion is that Eden and Churchill did not raise the subject because the British refused to agree to the mention of *any* sum, regardless of the circumstances. And, as is apparent from the minutes of subsequent meeetings, Stettinius and Roosevelt probably regarded it as a matter to be adjusted within the reparations commission.[12]

Stettinius submitted a U.S. counterproposal at the ministers' meeting February 9. It resembled the Soviet paper with one exception. The USSR had asked that the $20 billion be "fixed" by the Big Three at Yalta. Stettinius proposed merely that the reparations commission "should take into consideration in its initial studies the Soviet Government's suggested total." Recognizing that such phrasing avoided making the commitment Stalin sought, Maisky objected. The statement required clarification, he said, and he suggested that the commission accept $20 billion "as a basis" for its studies. In the face of Maisky's request, Stettinius reverted to the position that no figures at all should be mentioned. The reparations commission should set the amount, he said at one point; another time he said percentages only should be cited. The U.S. strategy was clear. The Soviets could have a stated figure, but only if it were hedged. Should they push for definite wording, the United States would back away. After discussion, the Russians and Americans agreed to use the statement that the commission "should take in its initial studies as a basis for discussion the suggestion of the Soviet Government" that reparations be in the amount of $20 billion.[13]

How much of a commitment was implied by what had now become the U.S.-Soviet proposal on reparations? Had the United States been willing to bind itself to a figure of approximately $20 billion, it could have pleased the USSR enormously simply by recommending that the word "approximately" be inserted before the amount to be "fixed" by the Big Three. Instead, the United States insisted that the final figure be set by the reparations commission, which in its "initial studies" would use the Soviet "suggestion" as a "basis for discussion." If these words have any meaning at all, it is precisely to *deny* obligation rather than to incur it. The phrases were added not merely to appease the British, as some have claimed, for Churchill and Eden had made it clear all along they would agree to no figure regardless of the language used.[14]

The new proposal was taken up in plenary session the next day. As before, Churchill opposed a fixed sum and read a telegram from the war cabinet instructing him not to mention figures, which should be left to the reparations commission. FDR pointed out that mention of any numbers might be construed by the American people to mean money payments rather than payments-in-kind. This appeared to be a retreat from the proposal Stettinius had sponsored. Harry Hopkins passed Roosevelt a note that stated Andrei Gromyko had told him that Stalin "thinks you did not back up Ed [Stettinius] relative to reparations—and that you sided with the British—and he is disturbed about it."[15] Observers agree that Stalin grew agitated while arguing with Churchill, at one point saying that if the British did not want the Soviet Union to get reparations they should say so. When Roosevelt again indicated he preferred that the entire matter be turned over to the commission, Hopkins passed him another note saying that the Soviets had given in so much on other issues "that I don't think we should let them down."[16] In the end it was Stalin who relented. He offered a proposal that stated simply that the heads of government had agreed Germany must pay compensation and that the reparations commission consider the amount. Churchill agreed and asked, "What about the United States?" FDR's reply, according to Stettinius, was that "the answer is simple. Judge Roosevelt approves and the document is accepted."[17]

Stalin must have had second thoughts about his capitulation. Stettinius guessed that Molotov and Maisky had approached Stalin following the plenary session and convinced him he had conceded unnecessarily. Whatever his motivations, at a dinner that evening, he expressed dissatisfaction with the way reparations had been handled. "He said he feared to have to go back to the Soviet Union," according to the minutes, "and tell the Soviet people they were not going to get any reparation because the British were opposed to it." Churchill responded that on the contrary he hoped the USSR would get large quantities of reparations, but he again alluded to the previous war when he said the amount imposed exceeded Germany's capacity to pay. During this talk, Stalin and Roosevelt agreed to revive the Stettinius-Molotov proposal that $20 billion be taken as a basis for discussion. Churchill dissented.[18]

Why did Roosevelt acquiesce in the face of Stalin's complaint? The president went to Yalta determined to convince the Soviets of U.S. good faith to lay the basis for postwar collaboration. Repeatedly, in responding to British objections that the mere mention of a figure might be construed as a commitment, Stalin and Molotov hastened to deny the very idea. There was "no commitment involved," Stalin said on one occasion. Another time he said the reparations commission could "change figures and modify them in any way." Statements such as "our figures not sacrosanct" and "in the commission we will bring our figures, you bring yours" abound in the minutes.[19] Had FDR sided with Churchill in refusing to accept a figure even "as a basis for discussion," he would have done two things he most wished to avoid. He would have conveyed the impression that the United States was "ganging up" with Great Britain against the USSR's desire for large reparations. He also would have placed himself in the position of appearing to doubt Stalin's word. For that is precisely what the British were doing when they argued that present reassurances notwithstanding, naming a figure might later be construed as a commitment to that figure. Harry Hopkins, surely the one individual most privy to Roosevelt's thinking, raised just these considerations in the notes he handed the president.

In his account of the Yalta Conference, Stettinius reported a conversation with FDR about reparations. It would be impossible to arrive at amounts, the president told him, until the Allies determined "what was left of Germany after the destruction of war." Pending a "great engineering survey" to establish what was practical, Roosevelt said, all discussions on the subject were "purely academic."[20] It is possible that Stettinius's version of FDR's views was tailored to rationalize subsequent U.S. policies. But it is altogether consistent with what the president said before and during the conference. The previous autumn, when State and Treasury were struggling for approval of their programs, he had commented on a memorandum that the issues it discussed depended upon "what we and the Allies find when we get into Germany—and we are not there yet."[21] At Yalta, FDR urged repeatedly that the matter be turned over to the reparations commission instead of being debated before anyone had set foot on German soil. Stettinius himself had said the same thing in foreign ministers' conferences. At one point he even presumed to speak in behalf of the USSR, telling Eden that "the Soviet government was not committing itself to ten years or twenty billion dollars."[22] Clearly, both men regarded the figure as a target to be sought *after* a physical inventory could be made to determine what Germany required to maintain a Central European standard of living without outside help. That is what the Soviets throughout the conference had led them to believe.

Negotiations over Poland also revealed differences between the Western allies and the Soviet Union. Indeed, more time was spent discussing this issue than any other. There were two questions: Poland's boundaries and the postwar government. All accepted approximately the Curzon Line as Poland's eastern boundary. FDR asked that Stalin make concessions favoring the Poles, alluding to the favorable effect such generosity would have on U.S. public opinion. Stalin refused, pointing out that the line had been suggested by Lord George Curzon and Premier Georges Clemenceau. "Should we then be less Russian than Curzon and Clemenceau?" he asked.[23] More serious were differences over compensation for Poland in the west. FDR and Churchill were prepared to turn over to Poland German territory up to the Oder River. Stalin had accepted that line, but now insisted it be moved to the Oder–Western Neisse, which would cede to Poland an additional 8,100 square miles. Roosevelt and Churchill were unwilling to accept this proposal; among other things, they were afraid the threat of German revanchism would force Poland to become dependent upon the Soviet Union for protection. When no compromise could be reached, the dispute was papered over by substituting in place of a boundary the statement that Poland would receive "substantial accessions."[24]

On the problem of who would govern Poland, there were three groups to be considered: the London-based government in exile, the Polish underground (most of whose members were loyal to London), and the Lublin Committee that the Soviets had created and installed in power as Red armies moved west. FDR and Churchill wished to establish a coalition that would administer Poland provisionally until such time as free elections could be held. Stalin and Molotov disagreed. Lublin should be regarded as the legitimate provisional government, they argued, because it was functioning effectively and fully represented the Polish people. At most, they said, it might be "enlarged" by the addition of an unspecified number of representatives from Poland and from abroad.

Reconciliation would have been difficult under the best of circumstances. Relations between Moscow and the London Poles had been poisonous since the furor over the Katyn Forest massacre. The USSR correctly argued that most of the London Poles and the underground groups affiliated with them were anti-Soviet. FDR and Churchill acknowledged this fact by not insisting that the London regime be represented as such. They asked merely that individuals from a spectrum of views be invited to participate in the provisional government whether or not they had any official connection with London. As for the Lublin Committee (hereafter referred to as the Warsaw government because it had relocated there), the Americans and British regarded it as a puppet regime with little support other than that offered by the Red Army and secret police.

The situation posed a cruel dilemma for Roosevelt and for Churchill as well. FDR believed that acceptance of an "enlarged" Warsaw government would arouse protest at home and jeopardize popular support for the United Nations. Failure to reach agreement with the Soviets would have equally ominous implications. In a private message to Stalin two days after the conference began, Roosevelt posed the problem: "I have to make it clear to you that we cannot recognize the Lublin Government as now composed," he stated, "and the world would regard it as a lamentable outcome of our work here if we parted with an open and obvious divergence between us on this issue."

Assuring the Soviet leader that the United States would never support a Polish government "inimical to your interests," he submitted a list of individuals he thought might be acceptable to both sides. Stalin did not reply to this letter, but his allusion to it in the next plenary session indicated no basic disagreement with FDR's suggestions.[25]

After much debate both in plenary sessions and foreign ministers' conferences, what appeared to be a compromise was worked out whereby the Warsaw government would be "reorganized on a broader democratic basis with the inclusion of democratic leaders from Poland itself and from Poles abroad." This "new" government would be called the Provisional Government of National Unity (PGNU) and would be pledged to hold "free and unfettered elections as soon as possible." A commission consisting of Molotov and the British and U.S. ambassadors to the Soviet Union, Sir Archibald Clark Kerr and Harriman, was authorized to consult with individuals and groups. When the PGNU was set up "in conformity" with the agreement, all three powers would extend recognition.[26] FDR realized the statement was vague because it lacked a formula specifying the extent to which the Warsaw government would be altered. Replying to an adviser's complaint that the agreement could be "stretched all the way from Yalta to Washington" without violating it, he replied, "I know, Bill—I know it. But it's the best I can do for Poland at this time."[27]

What did Roosevelt think had been agreed? From statements before and during the conference, it seems clear he understood that under no circumstances would the Soviet Union permit an unfriendly government in Poland. He acknowledged that Warsaw would be the dominant faction in any reorganized structure. What he appears to have hoped for is this: If Stalin really wished to continue the wartime collaboration, he would make concessions sufficient to permit at least the semblance of an independent Poland. That is, he would allow enough non-Communists of stature to participate in the provisional government that Roosevelt and Churchill could extend recognition without incurring the criticism that they had "sold out" Poland to the Soviets. A satisfactory resolution to the problem, in final analysis, rested upon Stalin's good faith.

Even more vague was Roosevelt's proposal for what became known as the Declaration on Liberated Europe. It called upon the three leaders to commit their governments to assisting "the peoples liberated from the domination of Nazi Germany and the peoples of the former Axis satellite states of Europe to solve by democratic means their pressing political and economic problems." This was to be accomplished through relief measures and free elections. Poland would be the first test of the declaration, FDR said, and he wanted elections there to be as "pure" as Caesar's wife. "They said that about her," Stalin replied, "but in fact she had her sins."[28]

The declaration had originated in the State Department some weeks before Yalta. It had been accompanied by a proposal to create an Emergency High Commission for Liberated Europe, which would have responsibility for implementing the declaration. Apparently at the urging of James Byrnes, FDR jettisoned the idea of a commission or any other kind of machinery. What was left was a statement of good intentions that bound no one to do more than "consult." Roosevelt apparently thought that acceptance of the declaration would assure U.S. public and congressional opinion that no sphere-of-influence deals had been made and would get Stalin to acknowledge a commitment to free elections in those areas the Soviets occupied.

There was little debate over the declaration. Churchill had one reservation about a reference in the document to the principles of the Atlantic Charter. He wanted it understood, he said, that this did not apply to the British Empire, which already adhered to the charter's principles. Alluding to a speech to this effect he had made in the House of Commons, the prime minister pointed out that he had given Wendell Wilkie a copy of the speech for transmittal to the president. This afforded Roosevelt another opportunity to twit Churchill. "Was that what killed him?" he asked.[29] Accepted almost casually, the Declaration on Liberated Europe would become a source of friction in the last half of 1945.

The broad outlines of a United Nations had been drawn up the previous summer at Dumbarton Oaks. Two important questions had been left unresolved: the veto rights of a permanent member and membership in the General Assembly of Soviet "republics." On the first issue, the Soviet Union had insisted that a permanent member have the right to prevent even discussion in the Security Council of matters to which it was a party. Second, the Russians asked that all sixteen Soviet republics be granted membership in the assembly. To Roosevelt and those around him, the Soviet position on the veto was bad enough, but the very mention of additional seats in the assembly, they believed, might undermine public and congressional support for the world organization. This latter subject was considered so sensitive that it came to be referred to as "X" in internal correspondence so as to minimize the chance of leaks.[30]

At the beginning of the third plenary session held on February 6, FDR called upon Stettinius to present a detailed explanation of the U.S. position on Security Council voting. In brief, it was that any issue could be brought before the council for discussion upon the affirmative vote of seven members. A council member involved in the dispute would have no vote at this stage. Whenever any substantive decisions were contemplated, there must be unanimity, granting the right of veto to any one of them. It was of "particular importance" to the American people, Stettinius said, "that there be provision for a fair hearing for all members of the organization, large and small."

Churchill endorsed the U.S. proposal, warning that if smaller countries were prevented from expressing grievances it would look as though the Big Three were trying "to rule the world." He tried to show how a permanent member's interest would be protected by citing a hypothetical conflict between Britain and China over Hong Kong. In the last analysis, Britain would be able to invoke the veto power provided for in Stettinius's presentation. Stalin replied that Churchill was wrong if he thought other nations would be satisfied by mere discussion of issues—they would want decisions. He also asked the prime minister to clarify what he meant when he spoke of desire "to rule the world." Stalin said he was sure the United States and Britain entertained no such desire and that left only the Soviet Union. After further exchanges between Stalin and Churchill, Roosevelt ended the discussion for that day by saying that because any disputes could be raised in the General Assembly, discussing them as well in the council would not promote disunity but would show the world "the confidence which the Great Powers had in each other."[31]

Stalin's expressed doubts vanished overnight, for on the next day Molotov explained that Stettinius's report and Churchill's remarks had clarified the issue to the Soviet delegation, which now "felt that these proposals fully guaranteed the unity of the Great Powers in the preservation of peace." After several more statements along the same lines, Molotov said he did wish to raise one issue that had not been resolved at Dumbarton Oaks: admission of Soviet republics to the assembly. Instead of requesting that all sixteen be represented, Molotov now said that the Soviet Union would be "satisfied" with three, or at least two. These were the Ukraine, White Russia, and Lithuania. Citing the destruction and sacrifices these areas had endured, Molotov stated that it would be "only fair" if at least two were accorded membership.

"This is not so good," FDR told Stettinius.[32] Indeed it was not, from the standpoint of heading off criticism at home. No one could argue that the Ukraine bore the same relationship to the Soviet government as Canada did to the British. And although there was little power in the assembly as proposed, the notion that the Soviet Union would have three votes to one for the United States would provide ammunition to opponents of the organization. Roosevelt tried to push the matter offstage by emphasizing the importance of summoning a founding conference as quickly as possible, perhaps in as little as four weeks. He then went into a convoluted discussion of differences in national structures and traditions and the fact that there were large nations with small populations and small nations with large populations—the drift of which his listeners must have found difficult to follow. His point, when he got to it, was that only those nations that already had signed the Declaration of the United Nations should be permitted to attend the founding conference. Admission of other members could be taken up there—or even after the organization began functioning. FDR clearly was trying to forestall what promised to be an embarrassing situation.[33]

Roosevelt's call for an early conference reflected his concern over the willingness of the American people to remain involved in world affairs after the war ended. The Versailles treaty containing the League of Nations covenant probably would have passed the Senate had it been voted on soon after President Woodrow Wilson returned from Paris. Instead, through protracted hearings, press campaigns, and speaking tours, opponents succeeded in dissipating pro-League sentiment. The best way to ensure U.S. support for the United Nations, Roosevelt believed, was to bring the organization into existence while enthusiasm for the wartime alliance ran high. The other side of the coin, as Henry L. Stimson noted repeatedly in his diary, was that if certain outstanding issues were not resolved before the conference met, they would be raised there with possibly disastrous consequences.[34]

FDR tried to postpone a decision on the Soviet republics by suggesting that the question be referred to the foreign ministers for study. Stalin had no objection, but insisted that they report back in time for the matter to be resolved before the conference adjourned. Churchill agreed, saying he "must emphasize that this was no technical question but one of great decision." He further irritated the president by arguing against the latter's proposal that a conference be held within the next four weeks. On a note Hopkins passed to him about Churchill's wish to postpone, FDR scribbled, "All this is rot! local politics!" He then drew a line through the word "rot," but his sentiment remained clear.[35]

The foreign ministers worked out a compromise at a noon meeting on February 8; with some revision, it was accepted by the Big Three during the plenary meeting later that day. The most important points were as follows:

1. The founding conference would begin on April 25, 1945, in the United States.
2. The nations invited would be those that already had signed the United Nations declaration and those others that had declared war on the "common enemy" by March 1.

3. When the conference began, the United States and Great Britain would support a proposal to admit to original membership the Ukraine and White Russia.

Points two and three did not appear in the Yalta communiqué released on February 12 and were not made public in the United States until the story broke in the press. Roosevelt, who knew how volatile the issue was even if it did not surface until after the conference began, insured himself by asking for and receiving from Churchill and Stalin written pledges that they would support an additional two votes for the United States.[36]

The last major agreement reached at Yalta—and the one most criticized—involved the Far East. FDR's overriding concern in this regard was to ensure Soviet participation in the war against Japan. Everyone still assumed an invasion of the Japanese home islands would be necessary to compel surrender. Such an endeavor would be bloody at best, catastrophic at worst. The Soviets could provide assistance in three ways: Engage and defeat Japanese forces in Manchuria and North China, provide bases in Siberia for bombers, and interdict shipping between Japan and the mainland. It must be emphasized that the atomic bomb project could not be counted on for the Pacific task. Technical difficulties might delay construction of a deliverable weapon well beyond the month of August projected by the scientists. Wartime leaders cannot rely on "best case" assumptions, and one of FDR's most trusted advisers, Admiral William Leahy, predicted "as a munitions expert" that such a device would not explode.[37] And even if everything went as planned, the scientists could promise no more than two bombs by the end of the year, neither of which would possess greater destructive power than that of a single flight of conventional bombers. This was a gross underestimation, as it turned out, but FDR had no way of knowing. He had every reason to believe that the Soviet Union's entry into the war would greatly reduce American casualties.

The matter arose during a meeting between Roosevelt and Stalin on February 8, to which Churchill was not invited. Stalin said he wanted to discuss "the political conditions" under which the Soviet Union would join the war against Japan. These he had presented to Ambassador Harriman in Moscow two months earlier, and they had been conveyed to FDR. They were similar to what had been discussed at Teheran. The Soviets wanted the Kurile Islands and southern Sakhalin, leases on the Chinese Eastern and South Manchurian railroads as well as at Dairen and Port Arthur, and recognition of the Republic of Outer Mongolia's independence. Sakhalin and the leases had been held by Imperial Russia, but lost to the Japanese as a result of the war of 1904–1905. Unless these conditions were met, Stalin told FDR, "it would be difficult . . . to explain to the Soviet people why Russia was entering the war against Japan." He added that these conditions should be put in writing and signed by the Big Three before the Yalta meeting ended. Toward the end of the session, when talk turned to internal conditions in China, Stalin expressed his desire that the Communists and the Kuomintang "get together" to fight Japan and said that Chiang Kai-shek "should assume leadership."

Roosevelt showed his customary deference to Stalin throughout the meeting. He began by saying "there would be no difficulty whatsoever" with regard to Sakhalin and the Kuriles. Referring to leases on ports such as Dairen, FDR indicated that he preferred creating "a free port under some form of international commission." He sought this kind of arrangement, he told Stalin, because of its relation to the question of Hong Kong, which he hoped the British would give back to China. Presumably, if the Soviets agreed to make Dairen a free port, this would strengthen his position on Hong Kong, against which he "knew Mr. Churchill would have strong objections." Once again Roosevelt sought to influence Stalin by alluding to differences between himself and the prime minister. As for the railroad leases Stalin requested, FDR also suggested the alternative of forming mixed commissions.

The president said that he had not discussed these matters with Chiang—that one of the difficulties in dealing with the Chinese was that "anything said to them was known to the whole world in twenty-four hours." He showed no reluctance in agreeing to Stalin's request that a formal agreement be signed by the Big Three, nor to his suggestion that the Chinese not be informed until after conditions in the west permitted the Soviet Union to transfer twenty-five divisions to the Far East. Roosevelt told Stalin that the United States had been trying to keep China "alive" for some time and that recently some progress had been made in bringing the Communists and the Kuomintang together. The "fault," he concluded, lay more with the Kuomintang than with the "so-called Communists."[38]

Negotiations continued over the next two days based on a draft proposal Molotov handed Ambassador Harriman. The formal agreement that resulted appeared on the surface to be a compromise between Stalin's terms and Roosevelt's suggestions, but in reality it was an ambiguous hodgepodge. The Soviet Union promised to enter the war against Japan two or three months after the termination of hostilities in Europe, provided certain conditions were met. Stalin's original requests for the Kuriles, the return of southern Sakhalin, a lease on Port Arthur, and preservation of the status quo in Outer Mongolia were included without conditions. That Dairen was to be internationalized and that the railroads should be operated by a "joint Soviet-Chinese company" seemed to be concessions to Roosevelt's wishes, as did a reference to China's "full sovereignty" over Manchuria. In both cases, the insertion of a phrase that the "pre-eminent interests" of the Soviet Union should be "safeguarded" vitiated equal partnership. The matter of Chinese acquiescence to these agreements was left equally vague. One paragraph stated they would require "concurrence of Generalissimo Chiang Kai-Shek," which FDR would "take measures" to obtain when Stalin gave the go-ahead. The next paragraph said the Big Three agreed that Soviet claims "shall be unquestionably fulfilled after Japan has been defeated." These words appear to constitute a commitment whether or not Chiang concurred. Finally, the Soviet Union expressed "readiness to conclude" a pact of friendship and alliance with the Nationalist government.[39]

This Far Eastern agreement, together with the one regarding Poland, later came under scathing criticism. Right-wing critics charged that Roosevelt had "sold out" China because he had fallen under the spell of pro-Communist advisers—Alger Hiss often was cited as the villain. The fact that atomic bombs rendered Soviet assistance questionable, the subsequent course of U.S.-Soviet relations, and the "fall" of China in 1949 created a climate for this interpretation. Less ideological scholars have attributed FDR's conduct to his naive trust in Stalin, his cynicism in being willing to violate principles, or his deteriorating mental and physical condition. An otherwise judicious British scholar has written that it is necessary to go back to the days of the most cynical nineteenth century European diplomats "to find a parallel for such duplicity of conduct among allies."[40]

Consider how the situation must have appeared at Yalta. Soviet participation might shorten the war and save tens of thousands of American casualties. This aspect unquestionably weighed most heavily on FDR's mind, and whether he was morally justified in agreeing to Stalin's price, it is difficult to imagine any other leader spurning such a prospect. But what of the effect on China? There is no question that the "pre-eminent interests" clauses regarding ports and railroads undermined China's "full sovereignty" over Manchuria. Had no agreement been reached, however, the Soviet Union would have been free to bide its time until Japan was on the verge of collapse and then move into Manchuria with no restraints at all. Even more important, from Roosevelt's point of view, was the continued existence of the Nationalist government on which he pinned his hopes. Chiang's rivalry with the Communists aside, he presided over a shaky coalition that threatened to fall apart at any time. Stalin's willingness to conclude an alliance with Chiang's regime would enhance the latter's prestige and seemed to indicate the Soviet Union did not intend to destabilize the situation further by aiding the Communists.

Finally, there is the matter of informing Chiang and gaining his assent. Roosevelt considered the need for secrecy so great that only a few individuals in the U.S. delegation knew about the agreement. Had its contents been conveyed to the Chinese and leaked to the Japanese, as FDR thought likely, the results could have been devastating. Certainly Japan would not have sat idly by while the USSR transferred twenty-five divisions to the Far East. A preemptive attack against Siberia before Soviet troops were in place would have convinced Stalin at the very least that the United States could not be trusted. Besides, Chiang's government had known since Teheran approximately what the Soviets would demand. Refusing the Manchurian concessions would have been fatuous, for the Soviet Union could take what it wished as the spoils of war. Of far greater moment, opposing the agreement would have encouraged Stalin to support the Chinese Communists in order to further weaken China's ability to resist outside demands. It is fair to say, therefore, that FDR had done the best he could for the United States *and* for China.

Although other agreements were reached and many more subjects discussed at Yalta, the issues presented here comprise the major areas of concern. Reparations excepted, Stalin played from a stronger hand. The defeat of Germany was forgone, and when the fighting ended, Soviet armies would control Eastern and parts of Central Europe. Poland and other occupied nations were captive. Roosevelt and Churchill could do little more than appeal for "fair play" and the need to maintain Allied collaboration. To have refused the terms Stalin was willing to accept would have had the effect of abandoning areas the Soviets held, for no one in positions of responsibility even suggested a resort to military intervention. Roosevelt, and to a lesser extent Churchill, regarded a functioning world organization as crucial to postwar stability. But no one knew how deeply Stalin's commitment ran or at what point he might refuse to participate if his stipulations were not accepted. And he held virtually all the cards on the matter of terms under which the USSR would join the war against Japan.

Roosevelt and Churchill also suffered the weakness of constantly having to weigh decisions on the scales of public opinion. FDR was particularly vulnerable because he believed, rightly or not, that active U.S. participation in the postwar world was a fragile prospect. He was also worried about antagonizing ethnic groups, particularly Polish-Americans. A rift between the United States and the USSR on an important issue such as Poland, he feared, would be exploited by isolationists and the political right to undermine all his efforts to construct a working relationship with the Soviet Union and with the United Nations. His suggestion that the founding conference of the UN be convened within four weeks of Yalta is but one example of this attitude. His frequent references to the American people and to Congress during the negotiations were intended as bargaining tools of course, but the available documents leave no doubt that these factors permeated the thinking of FDR and those around hiim.[41] What constraints Stalin worked under remain unknown, but they did not include a critical press, an opposition party, or the need to obtain a two-thirds majority to get treaties through the Senate. Despite, or perhaps because of, such disparities in negotiating positions, FDR and his advisers had reason to be gratified with what had been achieved. "We really believed in our hearts," Harry Hopkins later recalled, "that this was the dawn of a new day we had all been praying for."[42]

NOTES

1. For the best analysis, see Russell D. Buhite, *Decisions at Yalta: An Appraisal of Summit Diplomacy* (Wilmington Del.: Scholarly Resources, 1986). Buhite describes the setting on pp. 6–7. Roosevelt had a private bathroom; 215 members of the delegation shared the other five. Churchill told Harry Hopkins they could not have found a worse place if they had done ten years of research and that he intended to bring an adequate supply of whiskey, which "is good for typhus and deadly on lice." Hopkins to Roosevelt, January 24, 1945, *Foreign Relations of the United States, The Conferences at Malta and Yalta, 1945* (Washington, D.C., 1955), pp. 39–40.

2. Four years later, Edward R. Stettinius, Jr. wrote: "The record of the Conference shows clearly that the Soviet Union made greater concessions at Yalta to the United States and Great Britain than were made to the Soviets." *Roosevelt and the Russians: The Yalta Conference* (New York: Doubleday, 1949), p. 295. The British also believed that Stalin represented the softer faction: See Hugh Thomas, *Armed Truce: The Beginnings of the Cold War* (New York: Atheneum, 1987), pp. 39–40. William O. McCagg, Jr., in *Stalin Embattled, 1943–1948* (Detroit: Wayne State University Press, 1978), shows that although Stalin did have factions to contend with, there was nothing like the simple division Western officials assumed. After August 1945, according to McCagg, p. 215, Stalin deliberately cultivated his "prisoner of the Politburo" image, unable to make concessions he would have preferred.

3. "Silly old man," wrote Sir Alexander Cadogan, permanent undersecretary of state for foreign affairs. "Without a word to Anthony [Eden] or me, he plunged into a long harangue about World Organization, knowing nothing whatever of what he was talking about and making complete nonsense of the whole thing." Diary entry, February 8, David Dilks, ed., *The Diaries of Sir Alexander Cadogan, 1938–1945* (New York: G. P. Putnam's Sons, 1972), p. 706.

4. Stettinius claimed that throughout the conference, "I always found him to be mentally alert and fully capable of dealing with each situation as it developed." *Roosevelt*, p. 73. James F. Byrnes, in *Speaking Frankly* (New York: Harper, 1947), p. 23, attributed Roosevelt's failure to consult material prepared for him by the State Department to his poor health. Cadogan found him "very woolly and wobbly." *Diaries*, p. 709.

5. In March 1942, FDR wrote Churchill that he could "personally handle Stalin better than either your Foreign Office or my State Department. Stalin hates the guts of all your top people. He thinks he likes me better, and I hope he will continue to do so." See Robert Dallek, *Franklin D. Roosevelt and American Foreign Policy, 1932–1945* (New York: Oxford, 1979), p. 338.

6. *FRUS, Yalta*, pp. 572–573.

7. *FRUS, Yalta*, pp. 167–169.

8. Copy of Harriman's memorandum of conversation is in Box 337, Isador Lubin Papers.

9. *FRUS, Yalta*, pp. 620–621.

10. *FRUS, Yalta*, pp. 621–623.

11. Maisky's presentation is in *FRUS, Yalta*, pp. 702–703. Bruce Kuklick, *American Policy and the Division of Germany: The Clash with Russia over Reparations* (Ithaca, N.Y.: Cornell University Press, 1972) does not mention it.

12. *FRUS, Yalta*, pp. 231–234, 667–671, 716–717, 792–793.

13. *FRUS, Yalta*, pp. 807–809.

14. See Robert L. Messer, *The End of an Alliance: James F. Byrnes, Roosevelt, Truman, and the Origins of the Cold War* (Chapel Hill: University of North Carolina Press, 1982), p. 49, for the view that qualifying phrases were added to satisfy the British.

15. Hopkins's note is reproduced in Stettinius, *Roosevelt*, p. 265.

16. *FRUS, Yalta*, p. 920.

17. Stettinius, *Roosevelt*, p. 266.

18. *FRUS, Yalta*, pp. 921–922.

19. *FRUS, Yalta*, pp. 902, 915, 916.

20. Stettinius, *Roosevelt*, pp. 230–231.

21. *FRUS, Yalta*, p. 159.

22. *FRUS, Yalta*, p. 875.

23. *FRUS, Yalta*, p. 669.

24. *FRUS, Yalta*, pp. 231–234, 667–671, 716–717, 792–794.

25. *FRUS, Yalta*, pp. 711, 728–729.

26. *FRUS, Yalta*, pp. 803–807, 846–848, 867–868, 870–873, 973–974.

27. William D. Leahy, *I Was There* (New York: Whittlesey House, 1950), pp. 315–316.

28. The declaration is in *FRUS, Yalta*, pp. 971–973; the Roosevelt-Stalin exchange, p. 854.

29. *FRUS, Yalta*, p. 856.

30. See report of telephone conversation with Stettinius, March 22, 1945, Vol. 6, Grew Papers. Stettinius called to request that FDR brief the U.S.

delegation to the San Francisco conference on "Subject X," because several reporters had the story and it was bound to break in the near future.

31. Stettinius's presentation is in *FRUS, Yalta,* pp. 661–666; Churchill-Stalin exchange, pp. 664–665; FDR's remark, p. 667.

32. Stettinius, *Roosevelt,* p. 174.

33. *FRUS, Yalta,* pp. 712–713.

34. "I had never felt that it was a wise thing to go ahead with the San Francisco conference without having first adjusted all the problems that might come up between us and Russia and Great Britain first," he wrote. "Now we are reaping the penalty for that piece of heedlessness." Stimson Diary, April 23, 1945. He had expressed his reservations even before the Yalta Conference: See his memorandum to Stettinius, January 23, 1945, *FRUS, Yalta,* pp. 78–81.

35. *FRUS, Yalta,* p. 729.

36. *FRUS, Yalta,* pp. 966–968.

37. As late as August 1945, Leahy referred to the bomb as "a professor's dream." Leahy, *I Was There,* p. 269.

38. *FRUS, Yalta,* pp. 766–771.

39. *FRUS, Yalta,* p. 984.

40. John Wheeler-Bennett and Anthony Nichols, *The Semblance of Peace: The Political Settlement After the Second World War* (London: Macmillan Ltd., 1972), p. 352.

41. Record of conversation among FDR, Stettinius, and other State Department officials, January 8, 1945, *FRUS, Yalta,* p. 66–68. Unless compromise on the voting formula could be reached at Yalta, FDR stated, a UN conference might be "delayed for a long time to come, with resultant slackening of interest and possible growth of opposition." See also Stettinius, Calendar Notes, January 28, Stettinius Papers; and Byrnes, *Speaking Frankly,* p. 40.

42. Robert Sherwood, *Roosevelt and Hopkins: An Intimate History* (New York: Harper, 1950), pp. 869–870.

CHAPTER THREE

After Yalta: The Rifts Begin

President Roosevelt reported on the Yalta Conference before a joint session of Congress on March 1, 1945. That day, the *New York Times* reported that all those who had accompanied him to the Crimea "say he is in great health and never looked better." The facts were otherwise. He apologized for giving his speech while sitting, alluding to the "ten pounds of steel" on his legs and the lengthy journey he had completed. His hands shook, and at times his speech was slurred. His message was optimistic. He described in general terms the agreements reached— omitting the Far East accord—and said they provided a foundation for lasting peace. Instead of the older systems of power balances and spheres of influence that had always failed, he offered the United Nations, in which all "peace loving" nations could participate. What he needed now was domestic support to carry through the work done at Yalta. "I am confident that the Congress and the American people," he concluded, "will accept the results of this Conference as the beginnings of a permanent structure of peace." The onus for failure, in other words, lay on those who would undermine the results of Yalta and oppose joining the UN.[1]

FDR's attempt to "sell" Yalta had been preceded by a vigorous campaign on the part of James Byrnes. Byrnes had attended the plenary sessions and the formal dinners and had taken part in shaping some agreements, such as the Declaration on Liberated Europe. He had not been present at the foreign ministers' meetings where many of the agreements were drawn up, however, and had left the conference before some crucial decisions were made. He nonetheless presented himself as the president's "expert" on Yalta. In the weeks before FDR's speech,

Byrnes lobbied congressmen of both parties, journalists, and everyone else who might be helpful. Often hazy on details, he depicted Yalta as an unalloyed triumph for American principles and for Roosevelt personally. Byrnes prepared the ground so well that one reporter, in an article entitled "Yalta Legman," wrote that FDR's March 1 speech was significant only "in adding personal touches."[2]

There are indications that Roosevelt was less confident than he appeared. Unfortunately, his habit of telling different things to different people makes it difficult to determine his state of mind at the time.[3] If he was apprehensive, he was justified—a few days after his speech, Ambassador Harriman reported that a deadlock had developed within the tripartite commission formed to help create a provisional government in Poland. The issue involved poisoned U.S.-British relations with the Soviet Union in the months following and caused both sides to question the other's good faith.

The Yalta agreement on Poland had stated that the Warsaw regime would be "reorganized on a broader democratic basis with the inclusion of democratic leaders from Poland itself and from Poles abroad." Roosevelt and Churchill regarded this as a compromise between Stalin's position that the Warsaw group merely be "enlarged" and their own desire to create a genuine coalition. Roosevelt was disappointed that no formula for reorganization had been specified, but thought he had done his best. His hope was that Stalin would permit the inclusion of enough prominent non-Communists to give the appearance of a representative government. On the day FDR appeared before Congress, however, Molotov in the commission introduced a new element by claiming that only those individuals approved by Warsaw could be invited to Moscow for consultation. When an astonished Harriman pointed out that nothing in the accord nor in any of the discussions at Yalta suggested that the participants intended to grant Warsaw this right, Molotov replied that it was the "sense" of the agreement. If this procedure were not followed, "we might make a mistake and find a fascist in our midst." Molotov further disappointed his counterparts when he retracted an earlier suggestion that Western observers be sent to Poland.[4]

Citing FDR's acknowledgment at Yalta that the accord could be "stretched" from there to Washington, some scholars have presented the dispute merely as a matter of differing interpretations. The United States and Britain acted provocatively, therefore, by insisting that the Soviet Union accept their view. That is mistaken. Harriman was correct in insisting that no one at Yalta had even hinted Warsaw should have the right to decide which Poles could be consulted. Both sides had suggested candidates without reference to securing Warsaw's approval.

When Harriman in the commission mentioned inviting two individuals Stalin specifically had approved at Yalta, Molotov countered that nothing said there mattered except the wording of the accord, which was the "anchor" they had to work with.[5] Interpreting the "sense" of the agreement, apparently, was an ability only the Soviets possessed.

The situation was potentially disastrous. To many, Poland already had become a test case as to whether the wartime collaboration would continue. Failure to resolve this issue would jeopardize other agreements and undermine FDR's reputation as well. He had referred to the Polish accord as a "compromise," but Byrnes had depicted it as *the* symbol of Roosevelt's success in persuading Stalin to follow democratic principles in all of Eastern Europe. In the press, it often was referred to as "the President's plan."[6] For Roosevelt to accept a provisional government consisting only of Warsaw and its handpicked allies was out of the question. A domestic furor would have erupted, which he feared would destroy prospects of joining the UN. An open break with the Soviets would have equally devastating consequences.

Churchill soon began importuning Roosevelt to join him in confronting Stalin directly to break the impasse. Because the British had gone to war over Poland in 1939, it was an even more sensitive issue to them. Through most of March, the president spurned Churchill's pleas because he hoped Stalin would come around and because he was afraid of causing a rupture over a situation he was powerless to alter. Evaluating one message Churchill proposed they send, Roosevelt warned that "it might produce a reaction contrary to your intent."[7]

Soviet actions during these weeks raised further doubts about Stalin's desire to reach accommodation. Reports from inside Poland indicated that the Communists, aided by the Red Army and the NKVD, were systematically crushing political competition by closing newspapers, breaking up organizations, and arresting individuals in large numbers. The Soviets denied any repression was taking place, but barred Westerners from Poland on the ground their presence would be insulting to the Warsaw regime. The conviction grew in Washington that the stalemate in the commission had less to do with conflicting interpretations than with sealing off Poland until Warsaw had eliminated all potential challenges to its domination.[8]

Moscow's efforts to compel recognition of Warsaw before *any* reorganization also seemed ominous. In addition to demanding Polish representation in other organizations, the Soviets let it be known that their interest in the UN depended upon whether a delegation from Warsaw was invited to the founding conference at San Francisco in late April 1945. The announcement that Molotov would not attend was perceived as a signal to that effect. So long as Warsaw was excluded, the Soviet Union did not regard the organization sufficiently important to send its foreign minister. Some hints were dropped that Russia might not participate at all if its demands were refused.[9]

The Soviets resorted to even cruder tactics. As their armies moved into Poland, they came across prisoner-of-war camps the Germans had abandoned, some of which contained Americans. The USSR obstructed efforts by the United States to treat and repatriate these men, many of whom were sick or wounded. The matter appeared settled at Yalta by an agreement providing for prompt repatriation, exchange of information, and the right to send in medical teams. When Soviet behavior did not change after the conference, FDR repeatedly appealed to Stalin on humanitarian grounds and because of the effect news of such obstructionism would have on U.S. public opinion. Stalin responded by claiming that Russian prisoners of war were being treated more harshly by the United States. Molotov revealed Soviet motives in telling Harriman that repatriation would proceed more smoothly if the United States negotiated directly with Warsaw. Harriman angrily referred to this tactic as a "club." Secretary Stettinius informed Roosevelt: "It would appear that the Soviet authorities may be endeavoring to use our desire to assist our prisoners as a means of obliging us to deal with the Warsaw government." As one scholar has written, such conduct helped convince U.S. policymakers "of the extent to which the Soviet Union would stoop in pursuance of its aims."[10]

The contrast between Stalin's demeanor at Yalta and subsequent Soviet actions must have puzzled Roosevelt. All along he had conceded that Warsaw would be the dominant faction in a reorganized government. What he and Churchill needed was the inclusion of enough members of other parties to counter allegations that they had abandoned Poland to the Communists. As the prime minister put it, "If we do not get things right now, it will soon be seen by the world that you and I by putting our signatures to the Crimea settlement have underwritten a false prospectus." Since Stalin had seemed sympathetic to their plight, why did he not permit some of those who had been discussed at the conference to participate? FDR's advisers suggested two possibilities. One was that a militant faction in the Kremlin, believing Stalin had conceded too much at Yalta, had forced him to take an uncompromising stand. The other was that Stalin himself had come to realize how unpopular the Warsaw regime really was and feared that even a few representative non-Communists would serve as rallying points for the opposition.[11] What Roosevelt thought Stalin's motives were is unknown; in any case, he was concerned more about consequences.

The most charitable view of Stalin's conduct is that he believed the October 1944 percentages deal with Churchill acknowledged—with FDR's tacit consent—Soviet domination of Eastern Europe. At Yalta, Stalin agreed to the Polish accord and the Declaration on Liberated Europe merely as a gesture to British and U.S. public opinion; he assumed Churchill and Roosevelt understood this. He thus had cause to feel aggrieved when the two Western leaders began insisting these agreements be implemented even to a modest degree.[12] But Poland had not been included in the percentages arrangement. More to the point, if Stalin had any concern about American and British domestic opinion, why did he refuse to accept even token progress on the Yalta agreements so soon after Churchill and Roosevelt had publicly defended them?

At Yalta, Roosevelt had emphasized his belief in the necessity of large-power cooperation to maintain world peace. He made clear he regarded Soviet participation in the UN and in the Pacific war as of the utmost importance. His earnestness may have persuaded Stalin that the Soviet Union could act with impunity in Eastern Europe without danger of a break. Time worked in Stalin's favor. The longer settlements were delayed, the more securely the USSR could fasten its grip on the region. When it appeared desirable, Stalin could always offer a concession or back away from an extreme position, thereby showing how reasonable he was. Churchill was less placatory than FDR, but Great Britain could exert little influence without U.S. support.

Whatever Stalin's motives, Roosevelt's unwillingness to confront him ended in late March. The founding conference of the UN was scheduled to convene in less than a month. Roosevelt feared the consequences if the USSR boycotted it over seating a delegation from Warsaw or precipitated an open fight. Equally important, Churchill began threatening to discuss the Polish question "openly" in the House of Commons. FDR thought such a step would be fatal to reconciliation and would place him in an awkward position. If he supported Churchill's version of events, he would alienate Stalin; if he waffled, he would expose himself to charges that he did not care about Polish independence.

An apparently unrelated matter stiffened FDR's resolve. In February, the Office of Strategic Services in Switzerland had learned that a German SS officer, Major General Karl Wolff, wished to meet with Allied authorities. Wolff believed he could persuade the German commander in Italy, Field Marshall Albert Kesselring, to surrender the troops under his jurisdiction. Before sending agents to meet with Wolff in Bern, the British and Americans notified Soviet officials without inviting their participation. The Soviets demanded representation. They were told it was purely a local military matter, but that they would be invited to attend if negotiations progressed to a formal stage—that is, if someone authorized to treat in Kesselring's behalf appeared at Allied headquarters in Caserta, Italy. On March 22, Molotov handed Harriman a note stating that the Soviet government considered what was being done "not a misunderstanding but something worse." When Roosevelt tried to assure Stalin that the Western Allies were acting in good faith, he received an even ruder reply. The Germans were using the talks as a cover, Stalin charged, and already had transferred three divisions from Italy to the Eastern front. The situation "creates grounds for distrust." Such language goaded Roosevelt into action.[13]

The president cabled Churchill on March 29 that "the time had come" to bring the matter to a head. "I am acutely aware of the dangers inherent in the present course of events," he said, "not only for the immediate issues involved and our decisions at the Crimea but also for the San Francisco Conference and future world cooperation." He included a message he proposed to send Stalin. In it Roosevelt bluntly informed him that the United States would not accept Warsaw's right to determine which Poles could participate in reorganizing the government, nor would he recognize a "thinly disguised continuance" of that regime as the provisional government provided for at Yalta. He reminded Stalin that the accord had been a compromise between the Soviet desire merely to "enlarge" the Warsaw group and the Western position that a new government be formed. In obvious reference to the repression then taking place in Poland, FDR asked that "political tranquility" be restored and that U.S. and British representatives be permitted to observe. He closed by warning Stalin that unless the matter was settled "fairly and speedily," the threat to Allied unity they had tried to deal with at Yalta "will face us in an even more acute form."[14] The message was sent to Moscow on April 1.

This cable demonstrates that Roosevelt had abandoned his policy of drift in favor of the firm representation Churchill had been advocating. Stettinius described it as "powerful," Stimson called it "pretty strong," and Secretary of the Navy James V. Forrestal said it was "strong." A few days later, FDR commended Churchill for the "very clear strong message" the latter had sent Stalin. "We must not permit anybody to entertain a false impression that we are afraid," he said. "Our armies will in a very few days be in a position that will permit us to become 'tougher' than has heretofore appeared advantageous to the war effort."[15]

Meanwhile, Soviet behavior continued to reveal disregard for Western sensibilities. On April 4, the State Department informed Harriman of reports that the Soviet Union had begun turning over to Poland former German territories about which no agreement had been reached at

Yalta. That same day, the ambassador of the London Poles informed the department that a group of underground leaders who had entered into negotiations with Soviet military authorities had disappeared. It was later revealed they had been arrested as saboteurs and taken to Moscow.[16]

The Bern incident grew even more vitriolic. In response to Stalin's complaint that the situation "creates grounds for distrust," FDR denied wrongdoing by the United States and Great Britain and suggested the entire affair might be a German trick to sow discord among the Allies. Stalin replied on April 3 with even more insulting allegations. He said he had learned that agreement with the Germans already had been reached to open the Italian front in return for favorable peace terms. He went on to say that knowledge of the arrangement had caused the Germans to stop fighting in the west, while they continued to resist the Soviets. Stung by these charges, Roosevelt directed subordinates to draft a harsh reply that not only rejected the Soviet version of events but expressed his "bitter resentment" at Stalin's informants for their "vile misrepresentations."[17]

The adament messages FDR and Churchill sent about Poland and the Bern incident appeared to produce some results. Stalin's April 7 reply to Roosevelt concerning Poland offered little. He made some proposals, but did not retreat on the matter of Warsaw's right of veto, and he insisted that Great Britain and the United States were digressing from Yalta. But in his reply to Churchill, a copy of which he sent Roosevelt, he stated he "would be ready to influence" the Warsaw regime to withdraw its objection to inviting Stanislaw Mikolajczyk, former prime minister of the London government, provided he made a public statement supporting the Yalta decisions and favoring friendly relations with the Soviet Union. Everyone understood that Stalin's use of the word "influence" was a bow to the fiction of Warsaw's independence. Both the British and Americans regarded Mikolajczyk as the most widely admired figure in Polish politics. As Molotov only four days earlier had said he was unacceptable, Stalin's proposal appeared to open the door "a crack," in Harriman's words.

That same day Stalin replied to Roosevelt's biting cable about the Bern incident. Without retracting his complaints, he insisted he had never doubted the trustworthiness of either FDR or Churchill. He professed to see the matter as a case of differing views toward procedures to be followed among the Allies during surrender talks, although that is not what he had implied previously. "I have a feeling that this is about the best we are going to get out of them," Churchill informed Roosevelt, "and certainly it is as near as they can get to an apology." FDR's answer to Stalin was courteous but cool. He had no wish to collide with the Soviet Union over such a matter, yet he reaffirmed his claim that the fault lay with Stalin's misunderstanding, not with U.S. and British conduct.[18]

Stalin's retreat on the Bern issue and his willingness to have Mikolajczyk participate in reorganizing the Warsaw government suggested that firmness was the wisest policy. Yet Roosevelt had no wish to back Stalin into a corner and began to fear that was what Churchill might do. The prime minister for some time had been warning that he might have to discuss the Polish matter "openly." In his April 1 cable to Stalin he made his threat explicit: "If our efforts to reach an agreement about Poland are to be doomed to failure I shall be bound to confess the fact to Parliament when they return from Easter recess."[19] Announcing that negotiations had broken down was a step FDR did not want to take. By the time Stalin replied to their April 1 cables, Churchill's deadline was less than two weeks away.

On April 10, FDR approved a message to Churchill about Poland: "I shall, of course, take no action of any kind, nor make any statement without consulting you," he said, "*and I know you will do the same.*" In a note to the president accompanying this draft, Stettinius spelled out its purpose:

> In view of the statement in the Prime Minister's message to Stalin that he might have to make a public announcement in the House of Commons on a breakdown in the Polish negotiations, we feel it would be wise for you to send, if you approve, the following cautionary message to the Prime Minister to make sure that he does nothing along those lines without consultation.

A memorandum attached to the file copy was even more explicit: The message's purpose was "to discourage him [Churchill] from making a hasty speech in Parliament on breakdown of Polish negotiations."[20]

Churchill replied the next day. He said that Stalin's proposal about Mikolajczyk "if seriously intended, would be important." "I have to make a statement in the House of Commons next Thursday," he continued, "and of course I shall like to know your views about how we should answer Stalin as soon as possible." He had a feeling that the Soviets "do not want to quarrel with us" and pointed out that FDR's strongly worded defense of the Bern talks "may have seriously and deservedly perturbed them. Our angle of approach and momentum remain exactly what they have been in both matters under dispute as set forth in our telegrams."

What did Churchill mean? Did his reference to Stalin's proposal and his remark that the Soviets "do not want to quarrel" signify that he believed a breakthrough over Poland lay at hand? If so, perhaps he would refrain from making any drastic statements in Parliament. Or did Stalin's concession confirm his belief that the Soviets would respond only to bold measures? Even the possibility that Churchill meant to carry out his threat could not be ignored. Later that day Roosevelt sent his last—and most persistently misunderstood—message to Churchill: "I would minimize the general Soviet problem as much as possible because these problems, in one form or another, seem to arise every day and most of them straighten out as in the case of the Bern meeting. . . . We must be firm, however, and our course thus far is correct."

Scholars of all persuasions have treated this cable as though it constituted FDR's last considered judgment on relations with the Soviet Union. If it did, his words might bespeak what one writer has referred to as "cautious optimism." But Roosevelt did not know he was going to suffer a fatal stroke the following day. His message was a reply to "Your 944," which was Churchill's cable saying he had to speak in the House "next Thursday" about Poland, and it was written specifically to dissuade him from making any rash announcements. Roosevelt's concluding sentence about being firm and correct did not refer to the general policy of trying to get along with the Soviet Union, as might be inferred if read without regard for context. "Our course thus far" consisted of the April 1 cables about Poland and vigorous defenses of the Bern negotiations, both of which were "firm." Although FDR wanted to restrain Churchill from going too far, he had revised his assumptions about the best way to deal with Stalin.[21]

Early in the afternoon of April 12, while sitting for a portrait in Warm Springs, Roosevelt complained of a "terrific headache" and collapsed. He died two hours later at the age of sixty-three. The effect of his death is difficult to recapture. He had been a towering figure through two great traumas—the depression and the war. Whether or not one agreed with his policies, the very length of his tenure made him seem almost a permanent fixture. Now, when victory over the Axis powers was only a matter of time, he was gone. His domination of national politics and his international stature would have made anyone who took his place appear inadequate.

The contrasts between Harry S. Truman and his predecessor made the transition seem even more shocking. Roosevelt's patrician bearing, his easy confidence, and his eloquence gave him a presence Truman utterly lacked. FDR had been on the national scene for decades. Before becoming president, he had been assistant secretary of the Navy during World War I, vice presidential candidate in 1920, and after his struggle with polio, governor of the State of New York. Truman swam in smaller pools. He had commanded an artillery battery in France during the war, started and lost a men's shop in Kansas City, and served three terms as a county judge before becoming senator in 1935. Despite the favorable attention he had received for his committee work on war profiteering, his achievements were diminished by references to him as a "failed haberdasher" and to his association with the Pendergast machine. His stiff public demeaner and a slightly owlish appearance caused by thick, round eyeglasses did not inspire confidence.

Truman was born in Lamar, Missouri, in 1884. His father was a prosperous farmer and livestock dealer. After several moves, the family settled in Independence when Harry was six because his mother wanted him to attend better schools than those available in rural areas. Though a bookish, unathletic boy, Truman seems to have gotten along well with his classmates through the years. The family fortunes having sagged by the time he graduated high school, he had to forgo college in order to help make ends meet. He worked for a construction company and a bank, among other places, and for several years managed one of the family farms. His intelligence and industry impressed those who knew him. As had his father, Truman dabbled in local politics and obtained several part-time political appointments to augment his income. Clearly an ambitious young man, he also enlarged his circles by joining organizations such as the Masons and the National Guard.

Truman signed up for active duty in the guard a few months after the United States entered the war in April 1917. First elected lieutenant by the other men, he made captain and was placed in charge of a battery during the last months of fighting. Like many Americans, he saw just enough combat to regard the experience as a great adventure, a testing of his manhood he had passed. He was fond of recounting his wartime experiences in later life and always retained a soft spot for the "boys" with whom he had served.

He made two important commitments soon after his discharge in May 1919. He married Bess Wallace, whom he had courted for years, and in partnership with a friend raised enough capital to open a men's store in downtown Kansas City. Only the marriage lasted. The shop failed after two years, not because of his ineptitude as later critics suggested, but because a postwar depression caught the partners with inventory acquired at high prices in the face of drastically declining sales. To his credit, Truman refused to file for bankruptcy even though it took him fifteen years to pay off creditors.

For the next decade, Truman mixed in both business and local politics. The most important position he held was as presiding judge of Jackson County, which included Kansas City, Independence, and surrounding communities, from 1927 to 1935. This was an administrative rather than a judicial position, in effect making him chief executive of the county. During his tenure, Truman initiated a broad range of structural and financial reforms. He won support for and administered an ambitious highway program that was a model of its kind, and he greatly extended the county's social services. Though not without detractors, he became prominent enough to be seriously considered as gubernatorial candidate in 1932. Then, with Tom Pendergast's blessing, he ran for and won a U.S. Senate seat in 1934.

Truman's relationship with the Pendergast machine has been controversial ever since. The Pendergasts led a powerful faction of the Democratic party that at times dominated Missouri politics. The organization, to which Truman's father had belonged, was especially strong in Jackson County. Truman's rise could not have occurred without Pendergast support, but he was no lackey. As a man with roots in the farming community, a war veteran, and later a proven administrator with contacts throughout the state, he was a figure in his own right and an effective campaigner. The truth appears to be that Truman accepted machine politics as a way of life, and though he did not accept graft himself, he witnessed and participated in practices he knew were questionable if not illegal. Despite the embarrassment this association subsequently caused him, he never repudiated "Boss Tom"— even when the latter was indicted for tax fraud.

As senator, Truman concentrated on domestic issues, but of course voted on and spoke about matters pertaining to foreign policy. If he possessed a coherent world view, it is not apparent in what he wrote or said. He almost always supported the administration and was particularly outspoken about the need to create an effective world organization. He expressed the popular belief that the United States had "missed the bus" in failing to join the League of Nations and must not repeat that error. Whatever his predilections, his freedom of action during the early months of his presidency was circumscribed by the numerous commitments FDR had made. These he was determined to carry out despite any personal reservations he may have had about their wisdom.

Truman's experience and his view of history predisposed him to personalize foreign relations. In both Missouri politics and in the Senate, a man's word was capital on which he traded. One who failed to make good on agreements could scarcely expect cooperation from others in making new ones. Trumen applied the same standard in dealing with foreign leaders, often reducing complex issues to simple matters of whether or not an individual was being "honest." He also used familiar criteria in sizing up his counterparts after personal encounters: He was impressed by firm handshakes and steady gazes, put off by those who used flowery language.

He considered himself a student of history, which superficially he was. He became enamored of the subject as a youth and remained an avid reader most of his life. Always self-conscious about his lack of higher education, he delighted in impressing others with his knowledge of the past. But his reading was neither systematic nor critical. He regarded the study of history less as a tool of analysis than as a means of discovering "lessons," particularly those drawn from actions of great men, which he indiscriminately applied to current situations. There are frequent references in his letters and diaries to what anyone from Alexander the Great to "Old Andy" Jackson would have done in a given circumstance. Whether these analogies actually informed his judgment in particular cases, or served merely as props to justify his opinions to himself and others, can only be surmised. In any event, they reinforced his tendency to emphasize individual conduct rather than historical or cultural factors.[22]

In his memoirs, Truman recalled that although he had been concerned about the president's health for some time, "now that the worst had happened I was unprepared for it."[23] Never a secure individual, his shock at being catapulted into the presidency so suddenly can only be imagined. Ordinarily he placed great store on giving the appearance of confidence and decisiveness, but during the first few days, he was clearly awed by his new responsibilities. He soon recovered, at least outwardly, and concealed from subordinates whatever doubts he may have had about his capacity for the job. Some have emphasized FDR's failure to keep him apprised of developments in foreign affairs, but his lack of knowledge should not be exaggerated. Only solitary confinement could have kept him unaware of the drift of Soviet-U.S. relations, which were widely discussed in the press and in Congress. And James Byrnes, firsthand witness to Roosevelt's deteriorating condition, had taken it upon himself to keep Truman advised, especially after Yalta. Truman showed his reliance upon Byrnes by ordering a plane sent to fetch him back to Washington only hours after Roosevelt died.[24]

Stettinius regarded problems with the Soviet Union of such immediacy that he spoke of them to Truman while they awaited arrival of the chief justice of the Supreme Court for the swearing-in ceremony on the evening of April 12. They talked at greater length next morning. During both conversations, Truman said "we must stand up to the Russians at this point," or words to that effect. These statements have been cited as evidence that he meant to change Roosevelt's policies even before he assumed office—a time when observers agree he was still badly shaken. Such an interpretation, unlikely on its face, ignores the context of Truman's remarks. FDR already had "stood up" over Poland and the Bern talks. His and Churchill's cables, it appeared, had moved Stalin to offer the concession about Mikolajczyk. Stettinius approached Truman so quickly because he wanted to make sure the latter would adhere to the position Roosevelt had moved to during the last two weeks of his life: Stand firm while trying to convince Stalin that failure to resolve the Polish question would jeopardize other issues. More specifically, he sought Truman's endorsement of a reply along these lines, which the State Department already had prepared for transmittal to Warm Springs. It was intended as a joint communiqué from Truman and Churchill that would be delivered to Stalin personally by the U.S. and British ambassadors. During a meeting that afternoon, Truman approved the message—redrafted to fit the new situation— and it was cabled to Churchill at 4:30. The new president's statements about standing up to the Soviets therefore meant that he intended to continue FDR's most recent approach, not deviate from it.[25]

In view of Roosevelt's death, Stalin would have had no cause to be offended if the United States had taken a few more days to respond. Stettinius moved so quickly because he wanted to dissuade Churchill from announcing to Parliament that differences over Poland were irreconcilable. The suggested communiqué would make it more difficult for him to do so, as it would place him in the position of defying America's wish to continue negotiations. The accompanying cable written for Truman reflected this concern. Acknowledging past difficulties, it said, "I feel very strongly that we should have another go at him [Stalin]." It recognized the "compulsion" Churchill was under to go before Parliament, but urged forbearance. "Once public announcement is made of a breakdown in the Polish negotiations, it will carry with it the hopes of the Polish people for a just solution of the Polish problem to say nothing of the effect it will have on our political and military collaboration with the Soviet Union."[26]

Help arrived from an unexpected source. When informed by Harriman of FDR's death, Stalin asked if there were anything he could do. Harriman replied that he should send Molotov to the San Francisco Conference after paying his respects to the new president. Stalin also agreed to have Molotov continue negotiations over Poland during his stay in Washington. Stettinius took advantage of this development. On the morning of April 14, he met with Anthony Eden, who had just arrived in Washington. Eden gave the commitment that in view of Molotov's trip, "the PM won't speak. All he will say is that he is still hopeful and that the three foreign secretaries will discuss the matter in Washington." Whether Churchill otherwise would have carried out his threat is unknown, but from the U.S. standpoint, a dangerous crisis had passed.[27]

The joint communiqué, with one minor alteration Churchill suggested, was delivered to Stalin on April 18. The first part denied, as Roosevelt had, Stalin's claim that the Anglo-American position digressed from Yalta and that anything said or written there implied that Warsaw should be able to determine which Poles should participate in the new government. The second part sought to convert one of Stalin's complaints into a means of breaking the impasse. In his April 7 cable, Stalin had charged that Clark Kerr and Harriman wanted to invite an unlimited number of Poles to Moscow, whereas at Yalta "all three of us agreed that not more than five persons from Poland and three persons from London should be called for consultation." Following up on this point, the communiqué put forward a list of names broken down by groups: three Warsaw officials; two individuals from within Poland not connected with that regime (one of whom Stalin would select from a list of four); and from London, Mikolajczyk and two others who were not members of the government in exile. The communiqué asked that the April 1 cables from Roosevelt and Churchill be reconsidered "since they set forth the larger considerations which we still have very much in mind and to which we must adhere." There was nothing in this message that can be considered "tougher" than the stand FDR had taken. Indeed, at Yalta he had proposed that only two, rather than three, officials from Warsaw be invited.[28]

Hopes that Molotov's trip might result in a breakthrough were vitiated by the announcement, on the eve of his arrival, that the Soviets had signed a mutual assistance pact with Warsaw over Anglo-American protests. The Soviet claim that "there had been a great public demand" in Poland for the treaty was given no credence. This move provided further evidence that Moscow intended to legitimize the Warsaw regime in violation of Yalta. The only consolation U.S. policymakers could take was that the process leading up to the pact had been set in motion before Molotov's visit had been agreed upon and before the April 18 communiqué had been delivered.[29]

On April 20, Truman talked with Harriman, who had preceded Molotov to Washington. Harriman painted a bleak picture of Soviet behavior, saying that the West faced a "barbarian invasion of Europe." He added that the situation was not hopeless, provided the United States stood up to the Soviets on important issues. As that is what appeared to have produced Stalin's retreat on Mikolajczyk, Harriman's advice reinforced what Truman had been hearing from others. The president said he intended to be "firm but fair," later stating that he "would make no concessions from American principles or traditions for the fact of winning their favor." When Harriman asked how important Poland was to the forthcoming UN conference, Truman "immediately and decisively" replied that the treaty of adherence would not pass unless the matter was decided in conformance with Yalta. He said he intended to tell Molotov "just this in words of one syllable." A few minutes later, in response to Harriman's question whether the United States would go ahead with the UN if the Soviets abstained, Truman admitted that without Russia "there would not be much of a world organization."[30]

The Truman-Harriman conversation is significant for two reasons. It shows the dilemma Truman genuinely believed he faced: If he gave in to the Soviets over Poland, the UN treaty would be rejected by the Senate; if he stood firm, the USSR might abandon the organization. Second, it demonstrates that his subsequent warning to Molotov that U.S. participation in the UN depended upon resolving the Polish question represented his assessment of domestic political realities rather than a mere threat.

Truman met with Molotov early in the evening of April 22. After exchanging pleasantries, each stressed his commitment to settling the Polish issue and establishing the United Nations. Truman stated repeatedly that he stood by the Yalta decisions and intended to carry them out faithfully. He then advised Molotov that the "proper solution of the Polish question was of great importance because of its effect on American public opinion and that in his opinion it was the most important that faced us." Later he added that it "had become for our people a symbol of future development of our international relations."[31] The session ended amicably with toasts to Churchill, Truman, and Stalin. This was the only scheduled meeting between them, and Truman considered his temperate language as speaking "plainly to the Soviets."

Later that evening, Molotov met with Stettinius and Eden. Their discussions were little more than a reprise of what had taken place in the tripartite commission. Both Eden and Stettinius expressed displeasure over the mutual assistance pact with Poland because it signified that Moscow was "satisfied" with Warsaw's legitimacy without reorganization. Molotov defended the act, claiming it fulfilled the desires of Polish and Soviet peoples to "assist each other." When asked about the Anglo-American communiqué of April 18, he replied that he had not had time to study it carefully before the next session. Stettinius stressed the need to move quickly: "If we can't make some concrete progress before the San Francisco Conference it will have a very adverse effect on American public opinion and we, therefore, might find it difficult to gain the consent of the American people to join the world organization."[32]

When the foreign ministers convened next morning, Molotov injected a new element. At the end of Stalin's reply to Roosevelt's last message, he had suggested that the ratio of old and new members in a reorganized Polish government approximate that established in Yugoslavia between Tito adherents and other groups. This appeared almost as an after-thought—he had not mentioned it in his reply to Churchill—and in any case seemed to be applicable only *after* the dispute over who could be invited was resolved and consultations were under way. Now Molotov offered what he called the Yugoslav "precedent" as an alternative means of solving the problem at one stroke. If the Americans and British accepted the Yugoslav formula, there need be no consultations at all, not even with Warsaw, and the Provisional Government of National Unity provided for at Yalta could be organized without delay. To Eden's complaint that he could not understand how Molotov could present the Yugoslav formula without securing Warsaw's consent, while insisting he would have to do so before accepting any other proposals, the foreign minister replied merely that it was "a concrete example of how we could arrive at a solution without calling in Poles." Stettinius and Eden rejected this offer (the Yugoslav ratio gave Tito's followers twenty-one of twenty-seven positions in the government), arguing that it meant abandoning the Yalta agreement. Molotov in turn said that no progress could be made on the Truman-Churchill communiqué without Warsaw's approval.

Toward the end of the meeting, when it became obvious there would be no compromise, a revealing exchange between Stettinius and Molotov took place. Concerned, as ever, about the domestic impact an open rift might produce, Stettinius asked whether they could at least announce that the Yalta accord was still in effect, that various groups would be invited to Moscow, and that negotiations would continue. Molotov refused. Stettinius then inquired whether they could agree to say that the names of Poles to be invited would be decided before Molotov left for San Francisco. The foreign minister again refused. In short, Molotov was unwilling to agree even to Stettinius's desire to issue a reassuring statement for public consumption. To no avail, the latter explained that "he was most anxious to indicate to the world that we are working in collaboration and unity, particularly prior to the solemn task just facing us of setting up a world organization."[33]

Molotov obviously meant to exploit that anxiety by offering what amounted to an ultimatum. If the United States wished to avoid an open fight over seating a delegation from Poland at the conference, it could do so by accepting either the Yugoslav formula or Warsaw's right of veto. Anything short of that, Molotov had made clear, would provoke a struggle because of the time necessary to "consult" with the Warsaw Poles. The Soviet Union meanwhile would be free to determine the intensity of the dispute, including the threat to walk out. Truman could acquiesce or face the consequences.

During his first days in office, Truman stated repeatedly that he intended to carry out FDR's agreements to the letter. He had little choice regarding Poland. Thanks in part to Byrnes's efforts, the Yalta accord on Poland had been presented to the public as an equitable and democratic solution. Under these circumstances, it would have been difficult for Roosevelt himself to have recognized Warsaw, or Warsaw with a few additions, as the PGNU. Had Truman done so, he would have been accused of having betrayed Poland by failing to uphold the agreement his predecessor had negotiated.

It is within this context that Truman's second, previously unscheduled, meeting must be viewed. Eden had persuaded Stettinius to "mobilize the President to talk like a Dutch Uncle to Molotov" if the foreign ministers could not agree. When their session on the morning of April 23 ended in deadlock, Stettinius prevailed upon Truman to see Molotov that evening to explain to him "in blunt terms the effect of his attitude on future co-operation between the great powers." Eden and Stettinius believed, incorrectly, that the only hope of resolving the Polish question prior to San Francisco lay in Truman's ability to convince Molotov how crucial the issue was to the Americans and British.[34]

That afternoon Truman called an impromptu meeting with his advisers to assess the risks involved. Stettinius led off with a report on what had happened thus far. The gist of his presentation was that Warsaw did not represent the Polish people and "that it is now clear that the Soviet Government intended to try to enforce upon the United States and British governments this puppet government." Truman spoke next, saying he had told Molotov the previous evening that he intended to carry out all the Yalta agreements. Then he added the frequently quoted remarks "that he felt our agreements with the Soviets so far had been a one way street and that could not continue; it was now or never. He intended to go on with the plans for San Francisco and if the Russians did not wish to join us they could go to hell."

His comments, or merely the more colorful phrases, have been cited as proof of Truman's eagerness to launch the Cold War only eleven days after taking office. They were nothing of the sort. The Russians had offered an ultimatum without specifying what they would do were it rejected. Would Molotov return home instead of proceeding to San Francisco? If he did attend the conference, would the Soviet delegation walk out if Warsaw were refused admittance? Truman had no way of knowing, but thought these were real possibilities. What he was saying, albeit in characteristically earthy terms, was that he was prepared to run the risks rather than capitulate over Poland.

Truman solicited the others' views. Forrestal, Harriman, and Leahy advised standing firm. Although admitting the problem was "new to him," Stimson recommended caution because "we might be headed into very dangerous water." Marshall agreed, pointing out that the Soviets could delay entering the war against Japan until "we had done all the dirty work." In response, Harriman asked Major General John R. Deane, who commanded the United States Military Mission in the Soviet Union, to give his opinion. Deane said he believed the Soviets would enter the Pacific war as soon as they were able, regardless of what happened on other issues, because "they could not afford too long a period of let down for their people were tired" and because there was only a short season in which offensive action in Manchuria was possible. Truman closed the meeting by saying he was "satisfied that from a military point of view there was no reason why we should fail to stand up to our understanding of the Crimean agreements." He asked Stettinius to prepare a message he would hand Molotov for Stalin, a list of points he would make orally, and a press release.[35]

When he saw Molotov that evening, Truman expressed regret that no progress had been made on Poland. He said the United States could not be a party to the formation of an unrepresentative government and that he was disappointed by the Soviet refusal to consult with independent Poles. He then raised the topics suggested by State: The United States intended to proceed on the UN, but that failure to settle the Polish question would cast "serious doubts" on the prospects of postwar collaboration. Further, as FDR had pointed out in his last message to Stalin, congressional approval of economic as well as political measures depended on public support. This was an obvious reference to a postwar loan for the USSR. Molotov accused the United States and Great Britain of reneging on Yalta and said he could not understand why they refused to accept the Yugoslav formula. An angered Truman countered that a settlement had been reached over Poland and all that was necessary was for the Soviet Union to carry it out. The exchange grew heated as both men defended their positions. Truman abruptly terminated the meeting. "That will be all, Mr. Molotov," he said. "I would appreciate it if you would transmit my view to Marshal Stalin."[36]

Truman's behavior was unfortunate. Trying to persuade Molotov to make concessions was one thing, accusing the Soviet Union of breaking a signed agreement quite another. Harriman, who attended this session, later wrote that he regretted Truman "went at it so hard" because that gave Molotov "an excuse to tell Stalin that the Roosevelt policy was being abandoned." The president himself expressed doubts a few days later. He had given Molotov "the one-two to the jaw," he told Joseph E. Davies, but then he asked plaintively, "Did I do right?" Still, the meeting ended less dramatically than presented in most accounts, including Truman's. He had the last words, which his memoirs quote as follows:

> Molotov: "I have never been talked to like that in my life."
> Truman: "Carry out your agreements and you won't get talked to like that."

No such remarks appear in the notes that interpreter Charles E. Bohlen made, and he later told an interviewer they were never uttered.[37] But focusing exclusively on Truman's demeanor misses several key facts. His bluntness could have had no effect on the immediate issues; there was insufficient time for that. Second, the message to Stalin he handed Molotov asked that negotiations continue though the Soviet Union insisted that settlement was impossible before San Francisco unless the United States and Great Britain conceded Warsaw's right of veto or accepted the Yugoslav formula.

Most analyses of these events fail to mention that the foreign ministers met again later that evening. Molotov took a harder line than before. He had refused comment on the Truman-Churchill communiqué, saying it was for Stalin to answer and that Warsaw had to be consulted first. The Americans and British hoped Stalin would respond favorably—whether or not he actually conferred with the Poles—or at least suggest alternatives to pursue at San Francisco. If that possibility had emboldened them to reject the choices offered, Molotov tried to set them straight. He said it was not enough that the Soviet Union negotiate with Warsaw—the tripartite commission had to do so as well. Because Harriman and Clark Kerr were among Molotov's listeners and all three were going to San Francisco, not to Moscow, the commission could not meet with the Warsaw Poles before the conference began. Two options now were reduced to one: Accept the Yugoslav formula or face at San Francisco a disruptive struggle, the consequences of which were left in doubt but which might include the USSR's departure from the UN conference.[38]

Stalin's eagerly awaited reply conceded nothing. He not only rejected the U.S. and British proposals, but professed to see them as evidence that the Western powers meant to undermine the decisions made at Yalta. Accusing them of conspiring against the Soviet Union, he said he wanted to reach a harmonious solution, but to accept their terms he would have to "renounce" Soviet security interests. This he would not do because "I cannot turn against my country." He ended by confirming Molotov's position: "There is one way out of this situation; to adopt the Yugoslav example as a pattern for Poland."[39]

No progress was made at San Francisco. Molotov sponsored admittance of the Warsaw delegation in a way calculated to embarrass the United States. At Yalta, FDR had agreed to Stalin's request that the Soviet Union receive two additional votes in the UN by offering membership to White Russia and the Ukraine. He had also expressed opposition to inviting Argentina because of its fascist government and its failure to join the war. Desirous of gaining Argentina's admittance for hemispheric reasons, Latin American states seized the initiative by linking the two issues. They made their votes on admission of the Soviet republics contingent on U.S. support for Argentina. Truman reluctantly acquiesced in order to redeem Roosevelt's pledge on additional votes for the Soviet Union. Undoubtedly aware of the reason for this shift, which the administration could not justify publicly, Molotov used it to advantage. He coupled his demand for seating Warsaw with vivid denunciations of those who would admit a pro-Nazi government such as Argentina while spurning poor, war-torn Poland. This from the man who had signed the Nazi-Soviet pact, speaking in behalf of a regime headed by one whose previous employment had been in the Polish section of the notorious Lubyanka prison in Moscow.[40]

The irony went unappreciated, especially in liberal quarters. U.S. support for Argentina "put our delegation in the wrong," editorialized the *Nation,* and gave the Soviets "moral leadership at the conference." Walter Lippmann and the editors of the *Washington Post* condemned the Truman administration for what the *New Republic* referred to as "coddling the fascists." The Soviet Union did not walk out when the effort to seat Warsaw failed—it probably never intended to—but it had achieved a propaganda victory.[41]

During Truman's first weeks in office, a myth developed that, in various guises, persists. Put simply, it is that Roosevelt throughout the war had sought to establish a sound working relationship with the Soviet Union. There were disagreements, but these were to be expected in the course of a protracted struggle. He steadfastly rejected the advice of those who wanted to "get tough," believing differences were negotiable provided both sides acted in good faith. To the end of his life, according to this view, he was optimistic that collaboration would continue in the postwar world. His dream died with him. When Harry Truman assumed office, he fell under the influence of hard-liners Roosevelt had ignored. This, coupled with his natural pugnacity, resulted in a "sudden reversal" of Rooseveltian policies and began the descent into what became known as the Cold War.[42]

Contemporary journalists and political commentators had reason to believe this version of events. Roosevelt publicly exuded confidence regarding Soviet-U.S. relations and creation of the UN. There was speculation in the press over failure to resolve the Polish question, but the administration periodically issued statements that prospects were good for a compromise settlement. FDR's own "reversal" on Poland of April 1 went unreported, as did the bitter exchange of cables over the Bern incident. When open struggles over Poland, Argentina, and other matters erupted at San Francisco, therefore, some people understandably concluded that Harry Truman was responsible. But the airing of these disputes was inevitable in any case. Stimson in his diaries had predicted this would happen well before FDR's death. That Roosevelt would have instructed the U.S. delegation to vote to seat Warsaw (thereby causing a mutiny led by Republican member Arthur Vandenberg) or to bar Argentina (thereby losing Latin American support for seating the two Soviet republics) is difficult to imagine.

Perpetuation of the reversal myth in works written by scholars having access to the documents is harder to explain. Such accounts minimize or ignore the fact that FDR himself had decided the time had come to bring the Polish issue "to a head," in his words. They also fail to point out that the cables Truman subsequently approved in no way stiffened the U.S. bargaining position. Instead, they confuse style with substance by concentrating on the peppery language he used with his advisers and in his clash with Molotov. A 1985 statement of the reversal theme provides an example. By omitting mention of FDR's strong cable to Stalin on April 1, the author is able to characterize Roosevelt's message five days later to Churchill about getting "tougher" as an aberration, when it was perfectly consistent. Roosevelt's approval of the message is explained away by the simple allegation that ill health may have prevented him from giving it "any consideration at all."[43] Had he lived, there would have been no confrontation with Molotov, who was not even scheduled to visit Washington. His legacy to Truman, however, was unequivocal: Warsaw must not be permitted the right to veto other Poles, nor could the United States recognize a "thinly disguised continuance" of that regime.

NOTES

1. *New York Times,* March 1, 1945, p. 1; Samuel I. Rosenman, *The Public Papers and Addresses of Franklin D. Roosevelt* (New York: Harper, 1950), Vol. XIII, pp. 570–586.

2. "Yalta Legman," *Newsweek,* March 19, 1945, p. 52.

3. Adolph A. Berle, Jr., who saw FDR just after his return from Yalta, reported him saying: "Adolph, I didn't say the result was good. I said it was the best I could do." As quoted in Robert Dallek, *Franklin D. Roosevelt and American Foreign Policy, 1932–1945* (New York: Oxford, 1979), p. 521. About the same time, FDR said to Leon Henderson regarding the treatment of Germany: "The British, French and ourselves would abide by agreement but the Russians would do to suit themselves." Arthur Schlesinger, Jr., "West European Scholars Absolve Yalta," *Wall Street Journal,* June 16, 1987, p. 30.

4. Molotov at first tried to justify his position by claiming the communiqué stated that the commission should hold discussions with the Warsaw group "in Moscow in the first instance." After pointing out to him that the phrase actually read "in the first instance in Moscow" (meaning *where* the initial talks should be held), Harriman and Clark Kerr argued that even the mistranslation scarcely sustained the notion of a veto power. The Soviets later abandoned this point. *Foreign Relations of the United States, 1945* (Washington, D.C., 1967), V, pp. 129–130, 134–138, 140–144. See also Laurance J. Orzell, "A Painful Problem: Poland in Allied Diplomacy, February-July, 1945," *Mid-America* 59 (October 1977), pp. 147–169.

5. *FRUS, 1945,* V, pp. 142–144.

6. *New York Times,* February 14, 1945, p. 1.

7. *FRUS, 1945,* V, p. 157.

8. *FRUS, 1945,* V, pp. 145–147; and Robert J. Maddox, "Roosevelt and Stalin: The Final Days," *Continuity: A Journal of History* 6 (Spring 1983), p. 118.

9. Maddox, "Roosevelt and Stalin," p. 118; and Orzell, "A Painful Problem," pp. 160–161.

10. Russell D. Buhite, "Soviet-American Relations and the Repatriation of Prisoners of War, 1945," *The Historian* XXXV (May 1973), pp. 384–397. The quotation is from p. 396.

11. Charles E. Bohlen later told President Truman that "we all had felt that the Soviet failure to carry out the agreement reached there [Yalta] had been due in large part to opposition inside the Soviet Government which Stalin encountered on his return." See Memorandum of Conversation, May 15, Vol. 7, Grew Papers. On March 7, Harriman cabled his view that the Soviets (and Warsaw) refused to permit "strong opposition leaders" from participating because "they would become the champions of Polish independence from Russian domination." *FRUS, 1945,* V, pp. 145–146.

12. For a discussion of this thesis, see Russell D. Buhite, *Decisions at Yalta: An Appraisal of Summit Diplomacy* (Wilmington, Del.: Scholarly Resources, 1986), pp. 130–131. Another explanation is that because the Soviets were excluded from effective participation in administering Italy, Stalin was simply following the "Italian precedent" in Eastern Europe. To equate the governing of Italy with the brutal repressions in Poland and elsewhere is farfetched. The Americans and British would have been pleased if the Soviets followed the Italian model in Eastern Europe.

13. *FRUS, 1945,* III, pp. 736–740.

14. Roosevelt to Churchill, March 29, *FRUS, 1945,* V, pp. 189–190; Roosevelt to Stalin, April 1, pp. 194–196.

15. The phrases cited are from Stettinius "Memorandum to the President," April 20, President's Secretary's File, Truman Papers; Stimson Diaries, April 2; and Forrestal Diaries, April 2, Vol. II, p. 240. Roosevelt's message to Churchill, April 6, Map Room File, Roosevelt Papers.

16. *FRUS, 1945,* V, pp. 189–190.

17. *FRUS, 1945,* III, pp. 740–745.

18. Exchange of cables about Poland is in *FRUS, 1945,* V, pp. 196–198, 201–205, 213–216; about Bern, *FRUS, 1945,* III, pp. 749–751, 756.

19. Winston S. Churchill, *Triumph and Tragedy* (Boston: Houghton Mifflin, 1953), p. 437.

20. *FRUS, 1945,* V, p. 209 (emphasis added). Memorandum attached to file copy is in Map Room Files, Roosevelt Papers.

21. Churchill's cable is in *FRUS, 1945,* V, p. 209; FDR's, p. 210. Herbert Feis used the term "cautious optimism" in *Churchill-Roosevelt-Stalin: The War They Waged and the Peace They Sought* (Princeton, N.J.: Princeton University Press, 1957), p. 596.

22. For Truman's early years, see Jonathan Daniels, *The Man of Independence* (Philadelphia: Lippincott, 1950); Cabell Phillips, *The Truman Presidency: The History of a Triumphant Succession* (New York: Macmillan, 1966); and Richard Lawrence Miller, *Truman: The Rise to Power* (New York: McGraw-Hill, 1986). Thomas Heed analyzes Truman's accomplishments as county judge in "The Birthing of a Progressive Reformer: Harry S. Truman as Presiding Judge," in William F. Levantrosser, ed., *Harry S. Truman: The Man From Independence* (New York: Greenwood Press, 1986). Deborah Welch Larson's *Origins of Containment: A Psychological Explanation* (Princeton, N.J.: Princeton University Press, 1985), as the title states, attempts to analyze Truman and those around him in psychological terms. Chapter 3 of her book is on his formative years.

23. Harry S. Truman, *Year of Decisions* (Garden City, N.Y.: Doubleday, 1955), p. 5.

24. Robert L. Messer, *The End of an Alliance: James F. Byrnes, Roosevelt, Truman, and the Origins of the Cold War* (Chapel Hill: University of North Carolina Press, 1982), p. 68; and Truman, *Year of Decisions,* p. 22.

25. "He [Truman] then stated, as he had yesterday, that we must stand up to the Russians at this point and that we must not be easy with them." April 13, Calendar Notes, Stettinius Papers.

26. *FRUS, 1945,* V, pp. 211–212.

27. Memorandum of Stettinius telephone conversation with James Dunn, April 14, Calendar Notes, Stettinius Papers.

28. *FRUS, 1945,* V, pp. 219–221.

29. On April 21, the Soviets notified the American chargé in Moscow that the pact "corresponds in full to the aspirations and vital interests of the Soviet and Polish peoples." *FRUS, 1945,* V, p. 234. Two days later, it was reported

from Paris that a disillusioned French delegate to the Warsaw government described the situation as "appalling." The regime would be "non-existent if it were not for the Red Army's support, as the greater part of the population appears to be anti-Russian." Cable Summaries, January-April 1945, Stettinius Papers.

30. *FRUS, 1945,* V, pp. 231–234.

31. *FRUS, 1945,* V, pp. 235–236. Truman based his remarks on a memorandum prepared by James C. Dunn and Charles E. Bohlen, which Stettinius forwarded to him without change. Stettinius's copy is in Box 735 of his papers, Truman's in President's Secretary's File, Truman Papers.

32. *FRUS, 1945,* V, pp. 237–241.

33. *FRUS, 1945,* V, pp. 241–251.

34. Wilson D. Miscamble, "Anthony Eden and the Truman-Molotov Conversations, April 1945," *Diplomatic History* 2 (Spring 1978), pp. 167–180.

35. See "Bohlen Memorandum of White House Meeting," April 23, *FRUS, 1945,* V, pp. 252–255.

36. *FRUS, 1945,* V, pp. 256–258; and Charles E. Bohlen (with Robert Phelps), *Witness to History, 1929–1969* (New York: Norton, 1973), p. 209. The press release issued after the meeting stated merely that because of the limited time available prior to the opening of the UN conference and because Molotov had to consult with his government, "discussions in regard to the Polish situation will be continued by the three foreign ministers at San Francisco." *Department of State Bulletin,* 1945, Vol. 12, p. 802.

37. Harriman remark from W. Averell Harriman and Elie Abel, *Special Envoy to Churchill and Stalin, 1941–1946* (New York: Random House, 1975), p. 454; Truman statement to Davies in the latter's journal, Joseph E. Davies Papers; Truman account of meeting with Molotov is in *Year of Decisions,* p. 79–82; Bohlen's denial in Robert J. Donovan, *Conflict and Crisis: The Presidency of Harry S Truman, 1945–1948* (New York: Norton, 1977), Note 33 for Chapter 4, p. 445. Scholars tend to ignore the fact that Truman, Byrnes, and others wrote (or had written for them) their memoirs during the 1950s when their conduct in office was under attack for their having been "soft" on communism. At pains to deny such notion, Truman in particular was prone to exaggerating his "toughness" in dealing with the Soviets.

38. *FRUS, 1945,* V, pp. 259–262.

39. Stalin to Truman, April 24, *FRUS, 1945,* V, pp. 263–264.

40. Robert James Maddox, *The New Left and the Origins of the Cold War* (Princeton, N.J.: Princeton University Press, 1973), pp. 88–90. For the fullest discussion, see Randall B. Woods, "Conflict or Community? The United States and Argentina's Admission to the United Nations," *Pacific Historical Review* XLVI (August 1977), pp. 361–386.

41. "Spain and Argentina," *New Republic* CXII (April 30, 1945), p. 573; and Woods, "Conflict," pp. 363–364. See John Lukacs, *1945: Year Zero* (Garden City, N.Y.: Doubleday, 1978), Chapter 7, for a survey of reportage from San Francisco. Liberal journals tended to praise everything about the Soviets, as exemplified by the following description of the wooden Molotov in *The Atlantic*

Monthly: "Short, compact, massive-browed, as trim and collected as a tailor's model, he radiates force. . . . He moves easily on his feet, yet one feels watching him, that some strange force anchors him to earth." Lukacs suggests the "strange force" was gravity.

42. Two of the more strident examples of this thesis are David Horowitz, *Free World Colossus,* rev. ed. 1971 (New York: Hill and Wang, 1965) and Gar Alperovitz, *Atomic Diplomacy: Hiroshima and Potsdam, The Use of the Atomic Bomb & the American Confrontation with Soviet Power* (New York: Simon & Schuster, 1965, updated and expanded version by Elisabeth Sifton Books, 1985).

43. Warren F. Kimball, "Naked Reverse Right: Roosevelt, Churchill, and Eastern Europe from Tolstoy to Yalta—and a Little Beyond," *Diplomatic History* 9 (Winter 1985), pp. 22–23.

CHAPTER FOUR

From V-E Day to Potsdam

The German military threat held the Grand Alliance together. As that threat waned, relations between the Soviet Union and its Western allies deteriorated. Truman inherited a cluster of issues over which his predecessor had temporized or, as in the case of Poland, faced only during the last days of his life. Truman was not allowed the luxury of time. Disputes FDR had concealed burst into the open when the founding conference of the United Nations met in San Francisco. Then, less than a month after Truman assumed office, the war in Europe ended. Matters such as the treatment of Germany had to be confronted in an atmosphere of suspicion. The new president was in an awkward situation: Successes would be attributed to Roosevelt's wise statesmanship, failures to Truman's bungling or his innate hostility toward the Soviet Union.

The men from whom Truman sought advice ranged the political spectrum. Some, such as Leahy and Forrestal, were hard-liners who doubted whether wartime collaboration could continue. Harriman and others were more optimistic, provided the United States and Britain stood firm on larger issues. What Westerners viewed as gestures of good faith, these men argued, Stalin saw as weaknesses to be exploited. They believed that firmness without bluster was the best way to establish a working relationship. Stettinius, having witnessed FDR's shift on Poland, shared Harriman's views. But he was far more inclined to compromise in order to preserve the United Nations, which by this time had become a consuming goal for him. As secretary of state and head of the U.S. delegation, he had a personal interest in the organization's success. At the far end of the spectrum were Joseph Davies and Harry Hopkins. Davies, an ardent admirer of Stalin, justified almost everything the latter did. Hopkins was more realistic, but he too believed Stalin was a reasonable man who could be trusted. Truman not only consulted Davies and Hopkins, but sent the former to Churchill and the latter to Stalin as his personal representatives—scarcely the conduct of a man bent upon reversing Roosevelt's policies.

Amidst the welter of advice, Truman relied most heavily on that of James F. Byrnes. Their friendship had continued despite what had happened at the 1944 convention, and Truman undoubtedly appreciated the solicitude Byrnes had shown before FDR's death. He admired Byrnes's intellectual capacity and his ability to get things done. As "practical politicians," which to Truman was a calling of the highest order, they spoke the same language. Having sent a plane to Spartanburg for Byrnes the evening Roosevelt died, Truman invited him to the White House the next day. They discussed "everything from Teheran to Yalta." Truman later wrote that he told Byrnes he intended to make him secretary of state after the San Francisco Conference. Byrnes asked for and received assurance that he would play a far greater role in shaping policy than had secretaries under FDR. Truman's respect for him was, however, tempered by doubts about his personal loyalty, as shown by a later diary entry referring to "my able and conniving Secretary of State."[1]

Byrnes's relationship with Roosevelt and the fact that he had attended the Yalta Conference enhanced his value to Truman. Byrnes had kept a shorthand record of the plenary sessions, which he had discussed with Truman before FDR's death. He presented a translation of them to the new president in an ostentatiously bound volume classified "Top Secret." He warned Truman that the document should be kept "under lock and key" because revelation of its contents "could cause a war on several fronts." Truman assured him "no other person than he himself will see the notes."[2]

Byrnes's most important contribution was his firsthand assessment of Stalin. At Yalta, the dictator had used neither Communist slogans nor Marxist jargon. He was arguably more hardheaded and practical than either Roosevelt or Churchill. Byrnes's evaluation was congenial to Truman: The man they were dealing with was no different from the mayors, bosses, and senators they had dealt with all their political lives. Those who interpret Truman's conduct as reflecting some sort of visceral anticommunism have been misled by after-the-fact statements in his memoirs and elsewhere. At the time, his references to Stalin were personal, likening him to any "smart political boss." Byrnes shared this view. Months after he became secretary of state, he claimed that negotiations with the Soviets were the same as those in the Senate:

"You build a post office in their state and they'll build a post office in your state."[3] Truman held no illusions about building a relationship with Stalin through personal charm, of which he had little. He hoped to accomplish it through plain talk.

Truman's decision to send Hopkins to Moscow best illustrates this approach. The day after FDR's death, Stettinius told the new president that Hopkins was "the one person who really thoroughly understood" Roosevelt's relations with Stalin and Churchill, and he hoped this knowledge would be used. "I have the greatest regard for Hopkins," Truman replied. "He is a grand friend, and I plan to use Hopkins to the limit of his strength." Next morning he met Hopkins and, as noted in his diary, "We discussed Stalin, Churchill, de Gaulle, Cairo, Casablanca, Teheran and Yalta." Hopkins's evaluation of Stalin coincided with that of Byrnes. "Stalin is a forthright, rough, tough Russian," he told Truman, "but he can be talked to frankly." In his memoirs, Truman wrote that he discussed with Hopkins the possibility of sending him to Moscow on the trip to Hyde Park for Roosevelt's funeral. Other evidence indicates that Harriman and Charles Bohlen, a Soviet expert who had served as Roosevelt's interpreter at Yalta, made the suggestion to Hopkins later, in mid-May, and then secured Truman's assent. It was at this time that Truman began sounding out others on the idea. Of those he talked with, including the ailing Cordell Hull whom he visited at the Bethesda Naval Hospital, only Byrnes opposed it for reasons that are not clear. On May 19, the president cabled Stalin requesting that he meet with Hopkins as soon as the latter could get to Moscow.[4]

Truman's instructions to Hopkins are revealing. He said he wanted to have a "fair understanding" with the Soviets and that Hopkins "could use diplomatic language, or he could use a baseball bat if he thought that was proper approach to Mr. Stalin." This was a typical bit of Trumanesque bluster, for he must have known Hopkins would be more likely to use a catcher's mitt than a bat. That was why he was appointed. More to the point, Truman told him to make clear to Stalin that what happened in Eastern Europe and the Baltic states "made no difference to U.S. interests only so far as World Peace is concerned." Poland ought to have elections at least as free as political bosses such as Tom Pendergast would allow "in their respective bailiwicks." Finally, Stalin should make some gesture "whether he means it or not to keep it before our public that he intends to keep his word." That was what "any smart political boss" would do. In short, the president wanted Stalin to know he would accept virtually any settlement in Poland if it appeared to be in conformity with Yalta.

In his memoirs, Truman included the part about the baseball bat, but omitted his willingness to accept gestures in lieu of substance.[5]

Truman believed that differences with the Soviet Union were reconcilable, provided there was a frank exchange with Stalin. He was encouraged by reports that at least some of the disagreements were caused by Stalin's ignorance as to what the United States was after. The idea that Stalin represented the "soft" faction in Moscow and Molotov the "hard" had been held for months. Shortly before Hopkins left, Harriman told Truman that "Stalin was not getting accurate reports from Molotov or any of his people and as a result had grown deeply and unjustifiably suspicious as to our motives." Bohlen corroborated this observation. Truman said he agreed and later, while Hopkins was in Moscow, told a Treasury Department official that "Stalin didn't know half the things that were going on" because the "Molotov clique" was keeping things from him.[6] This interpretation apparently explained the contrast between Stalin's reasonable conduct at Yalta and what had happened since.

Only a week before Truman asked Stalin to receive Hopkins, an incident involving Lend-Lease augured badly for the mission. On May 11, three days after Germany's surrender, Undersecretary of State Joseph C. Grew and Foreign Economic Administrator Leo T. Crowley met with Truman. They carried a memorandum, endorsed by the War and Navy departments and by Harriman, recommending that the Lend-Lease programs for the Soviet Union be "adjusted immediately" in view of cessation of hostilities in Europe. On the assumption that the Soviet Union would enter the war against Japan, the memorandum proposed that shipments of military and other supplies destined for use in the Pacific be continued, along with materials needed to complete industrial plants already under construction. All other shipments "should be cut off immediately as far as physically practical," and goods diverted to meet programs for Western Europe. The president approved the proposal and gave Grew and Crowley his own memorandum stating that "you should, until further notice, proceed on the assumption that the U.S.S.R. will enter into the War against Japan."

The following day subordinate officials, interpreting literally the phrase "cut off immediately as far as physically practical," issued instructions to unload ships destined for the Soviet Union and to reroute those at sea. A furor erupted that caused the instructions to be rescinded within hours. In a telephone conversation with Grew that afternoon, Crowley blamed a member of the Soviet Protocol Committee who, he said, had "got a little bit off the track."[7] The situation was embarrassing regardless of personal responsibility, for everyone understood Stalin would interpret what had happened as a heavy-handed attempt to apply economic coercion.

Whether Crowley's explanation to Grew was correct or represented an effort to cover himself is unimportant. What is important is that those responsible for the memorandum to Truman never intended it to be interpreted so zealously. Assistant Secretary of State William L. Clayton, who had shepherded drafts of the document through committees, countermanded the stop orders as soon as he learned of them. Two days later, he referred to the action as "some strange misconstruction of the new policy." Harriman, whose advice had been solicited through the drafting stages, later wrote that he was "taken aback." No wonder. He had warned specifically against implementing the cutback in such a way as to convey "any implication of a threat or any indication of political bargaining." Grew, acting secretary while Stettinius was at San Francisco, believed there "was absolutely no truth in the rumor" that the loading of ships had been stopped until he found out otherwise. As he had gone with Crowley to obtain Truman's approval of curtailment, he would have known if such a drastic policy had been discussed.[8]

Disagreement among historians over what almost certainly was a bureaucratic foul-up has tended to obscure the more basic consideration. Lend-Lease to the USSR was curtailed, after all, and the Soviets were sure to be displeased however it was carried out. But the intent was not to bludgeon the Soviet Union as some have claimed, nor was it solely to keep faith with congressional sentiment that Lend-Lease be restricted to uses directly related to the war effort. The officials involved expected to exercise considerable latitude in dispensing supplies in the future, especially after the existing protocol expired on June 30. The message they intended to convey was that henceforth the aid provided would be at the administration's discretion and that it could be further reduced or cut off without violating agreements. They wanted Lend-Lease as "leverage," in Grew's phrase, to influence Soviet behavior without overt threats.[9]

In a garbled account, Truman later claimed he had not read the memorandum before signing it. While this may be true, it is inconceivable that Grew and Crowley did not brief him. As Crowley told Grew, "He wanted to be sure that the President thoroughly understands the situation and that he will back us up and keep everyone else out of it." Both men knew the Soviets would protest, and they did not want them "running all over town looking for help." Truman was surprised by the way curtailment was handled, not because he had failed to read the memorandum, but because those who explained it to him did not know it would be construed so harshly. This blunder aside, Truman knew perfectly well what was intended. Several hours before Grew and Crowley presented the memorandum, Stimson (who already had a copy) urged Lend-Lease reduction. "I found him vigorously enthusiastic for my view," Stimson wrote in his diary. "He said it was right down his alley." Truman had been convinced that "the Soviet Union needed us more than we needed them," and regulating the Lend-Lease faucet was one way of emphasizing this point.[10]

By the time the Hopkins-Stalin talks began on May 26, Lend-Lease had become a lever in Soviet hands. Stalin excoriated the cutback as "unfortunate and even brutal." If it was intended to "soften up" the Soviets, he said, it was a "fundamental mistake" and would have "the exact opposite effect." In response to Hopkins's explanation that the immediate curtailment was "a technical misunderstanding" that had been countermanded within twenty-four hours and had no "fundamental policy significance," Stalin still referred to it as a "scornful" act. The Soviets had intended to make a "suitable expression of gratitude" for Lend-Lease, but U.S. actions made that impossible. In the face of Hopkins's repeated assurances that there was no intent to use reduction as a "pressure weapon" because the United States "does not go in for those methods," he finally said he believed Hopkins and was "fully satisfied."[11]

Hopkins and Stalin discussed other issues during the course of their talks, but Poland was the main reason for Hopkins's trip. This matter was discussed in five of the six sessions between May 26 and June 6. Hopkins tried to convince Stalin that the United States had no ulterior motives with regard to Poland and no wish to establish a government unfriendly to the Soviet Union. The problem was that Poland had become a symbol of whether the Allies could continue working together now that the war in Europe had ended. Failure would be damaging. Stalin emphasized British culpability, claiming they wished to establish a new buffer state against the Soviet Union, and repeated his earlier assertions about Poland's importance to Soviet security. To Hopkins's relief, he indicated during their second meeting that he was willing to discuss names of those who could be invited for consultation. At the same time, he warned that Warsaw would "not accept" having more than four of the eighteen or twenty positions in the new government go to other Poles.[12]

Stalin and Hopkins on May 31 agreed to a list of names. Although Mikolajczyk was included, the list represented a retreat from the Truman-Churchill proposal of April 18, to which Truman had said "we must adhere." Of the three Poles to be invited from London, Hopkins agreed to substitute for one a man Stalin admitted was a "communist sympathizer." There were similar substitutions for those to be invited from within Poland. Truman gave "wholehearted approval" to the list and tried to convince Churchill "this is the best solution we can hope for under the circumstances." The president also backed off on another issue. He had instructed Hopkins to make a strong plea for release of the sixteen arrested underground leaders because of the "unfavorable reaction of American public opinion." When Stalin insisted they be brought to trial, Hopkins was instructed not to push the matter.[13]

Meanwhile, disageement over voting in the UN Security Council had developed at San Francisco. At Yalta, it was agreed that a permanent member would have the right to veto measures in a dispute to which it was a party, but would have no vote on the question of whether to bring the dispute before the council. It was of "particular importance" to Americans, Stettinius had argued, that all members have the right to a "fair hearing." This was not enough for smaller nations, who feared the veto still ensured large-power domination. On May 22, a subcommittee forwarded a list of questions to the sponsoring nations.

Up to this point, there appeared to be unanimity among the Big Five (the Big Four plus France) over the veto. In meetings held to formulate a response to the questionnaire, Soviet representative Andrei Gromyko reverted to the position that had produced a deadlock at Dumbarton Oaks: The veto power should extend even to whether a dispute could be placed on the council agenda. The British and Americans were astonished by this and by Gromyko's claim that it was consistent with Yalta. Discussion of an issue, he argued, might be "the first step of the chain of events leading to enforcement measures" and that first step "might ultimately lead to war." Stettinius was certain that neither the smaller nations nor the U.S. Senate would accept an absolute veto, and he feared Republican members of the delegation might defect if he gave in. The crisis intensified when *New York Times* reporter James Reston published accounts of the controversy on June 2 and 3 that blamed the Soviets. The articles made it more difficult for Stettinius to work behind the scenes, and speculation grew as to whether the conference might have to be adjourned.[14]

Stettinius already had decided that the most promising way to resolve the situation lay in an appeal to Stalin. Hopkins's presence in Moscow was a fortunate coincidence. After securing Truman's approval, the secretary on June 2 sent a strongly worded cable asking that Harriman and Hopkins bring the matter to Stalin's attention. "I know that in the past Marshal Stalin did not know himself of some of the decisions that were being taken and communicated to us," Stettinius said. He told them to ask Stalin whether "he realized fully" what effects Gromyko's instructions would have on the world organization. "Please tell

him in no uncertain words that this country could not possibly join"
the UN if the permanent members were to have an unrestricted veto,
he continued, and he referred to such a stipulation as "a wholly new
and impossible interpretation." Stettinius ended on an ominous note.
He asked Harriman to let him know how long it would take to get
Stalin's response, "since we will have to take the necessary steps to
wind up the conference here if we have nothing favorable from you
in this regard."[15]

Hopkins raised the subject during the final meeting on June 6. He
tried to impress upon Stalin how serious it was and emphasized that
the Yalta formula "safeguarded the freedom of discussion and the right
of any member to bring before the council any situation for discussion."
Molotov replied that the Soviet position "rested squarely" on the
Crimea decision. According to Bohlen's notes, there followed a discussion between Stalin and Molotov in Russian during which it became
clear that Stalin "had not understood the issues involved and had not
had them explained to him." Stalin finally said he thought the matter
insignificant and they should accept the U.S. position. He expressed
his approval to Hopkins and blamed the smaller nations for the controversy, saying they had a tendency to "exploit and even create differences" among the great powers A jubilant Hopkins cabled Truman:
"Marshal Stalin agrees to accept the United States position regarding
voting procedure in the Council."[16]

The Hopkins mission confirmed Truman's assumption about the
Soviet government and the proper way to deal with it. Stalin's accusations about Lend-Lease showed how blunt and undiplomatic he could
be. His concessions on Poland seemed to indicate he did seek accommodation, just as Hopkins, Davies, and Byrnes had predicted. The
manner in which the veto had been resolved appeared to validate the
idea that difficulties had been caused by the Molotov faction, which
misled or kept Stalin ignorant. The lesson was clear: Deal with Stalin
as much as possible, negotiate in plain language, and make clear that
it was in Soviet interests to cooperate. "I'm not afraid of Russia,"
Truman wrote in his diary the day Hopkins left Moscow. "They've
always been our friends and I can't see any reason why they shouldn't
always be." He expressed his optimism publicly a week later: "The
Russians are just as anxious to get along with us as we are with
them," he told a press conference, "and I think they have showed it
very conclusively in these last negotiations."[17]

The decision to send Hopkins to deal with Stalin had the added
significance of marking a reversion to Roosevelt's policy of disasso-
ciating the United States from Britain. Truman had dispatched Davies
to meet with Churchill while Hopkins was in Moscow, but the difference

was obvious: Hopkins was instructed to negotiate, Davies to "exchange views." Sending a holder of the Order of Lenin as the president's personal representative must have been galling to Churchill, who for months had been growing more belligerent toward the Soviet Union. Churchill vehemently denounced Soviet actions while Davies as vehemently defended them. One issue provoked an emotional exchange. The prime minister had been urging another meeting of the Big Three. Truman was amenable, but had Davies inform Churchill he preferred to meet Stalin alone before the conference. Churchill grew so agitated over the prospect that only Davies's threat to get up and leave calmed him down.[18]

Truman gave further evidence that he intended to pursue an independent course. He spurned the prime minister's repeated pleas to delay pulling back U.S. troops into assigned zones of occupation as a bargaining counter on other matters. When it became clear Truman would not budge, Churchill responded sarcastically: "Obviously we are obliged to conform to your decision. . . . I sincerely hope that your action will in the long run make for a lasting peace in Europe."[19]

The British were obliged to conform to the U.S. decision on Poland as well, and it became clear that Truman was eager to dispose of the issue. The tripartite commission reconvened in Moscow on June 11, less than a week after the last Hopkins-Stalin session. The trials of the underground leaders began as the consultations got under way. After several days of discussions among the Poles, an agreement was reached whereby Warsaw received fourteen of the twenty positions in the new government. Harriman's opinion was that "this settlement has been reached because all the non-Lublin [Warsaw] Poles are so concerned over the present situation in Poland that they are ready to accept any compromise which gives some hope for Polish independence and individual freedom." When Clark Kerr asked for a "definite pledge" on holding free elections, moreover, Molotov and the Warsaw officials would do no more than indicate general acceptance of the Yalta decisions.[20]

Despite these ominous signals, Truman believed it was the best arrangement they could get and asked Churchill to join in extending recognition to the Provisional Government of National Unity, which came into being on June 28. He told the prime minister that delay would serve no purpose and "might even prove embarrassing to both of us." A reluctant Churchill asked for a few more days to settle affairs with the government in exile, and he suggested they extend recognition on July 4. Whether this constituted an example of Churchillian humor is unknown, but extending recognition on U.S. Independence Day was a bit much for Truman, so it was put off until July 5.[21] Free elections were never held, and non-Communist members eventually were forced out. Stalin had obtained the friendly Poland he sought.

Recognition of the Polish PGNU defused the situation in Eastern Europe. But some differences remained. The Western allies clashed with Tito over the city of Trieste, and Stalin refused Truman's appeal to use his influence in restraining the Yugoslav. Reports from Bulgaria and Romania indicated the Soviets were solidifying power and excluding British and Americans from participating in the control commissions. Truman had no wish to cause a breach over any of these matters. An arrangement was worked out with Tito that provided for withdrawal into zones so as to eliminate the possibility of armed clashes. With regard to Bulgaria and Romania, the dominating interest over which Churchill had ceded to the Soviets in the percentages deal, Truman contented himself with reminding Stalin of the Declaration on Liberated Europe and asking that travel restrictions on U.S. members of the control commissions be lifted. He hoped to resolve these problems when the Big Three met.[22]

Reparations from Germany had yet to be settled. The State and Treasury departments continued to jockey for acceptance of their respective plans after Roosevelt's return from Yalta. Stettinius had the advantage of possessing notes taken there. To Morgenthau's great indignation, he refused to make them available even though on one occasion their contents were revealed to an individual who held no government position. Morgenthau's leverage had come from his personal relationship with FDR. During one meeting with his staff, he called Stettinius "my white-haired hope," while he was referred to in State Department memoranda as "our boyfriend." Roosevelt vacillated, usually agreeing with whoever saw him last, and in late March ordered the departments to compromise. The result was an ambiguous document weighted toward Treasury's views.[23]

Shortly after Yalta, Roosevelt had appointed Isador Lubin to head the U.S. delegation on the Reparations Commission. An academic man, Lubin nominally worked for the Bureau of Labor Statistics, but his primary function has been as aide to Harry Hopkins. The appointment probably signified that FDR intended to keep negotiations in his own hands via Hopkins. Lubin was dedicated to pastoralization: A draft he submitted on the instructions he wanted was referred to by a State Department official as "the most extreme statement regarding the economic treatment of Germany." Lubin told a friend he intended "to battle the matter out with State" and would refuse to serve if he did not get "95%" of what he wanted. Unfortunately, he did not enjoy the confidence of Treasury officials. His appointment was referred to as a "farce," a "joke," and Morgenthau thought it was a mistake. He patronizingly spoke of Lubin as a "good" statistician, not a "great" one, and thought he lacked the stature to head the delegation.[24] With Roosevelt dead and Hopkins incapacitated by illness, Lubin's role lost its purpose, and he was one of the first officials Truman replaced.

The president's choice was Edwin W. Pauley, a friend, millionaire oilman, and former treasurer of the Democratic National Committee. Pauley was Truman's kind of man: bluff, outspoken, and a success in the business world. Truman later wrote that "I felt that the position required a tough bargainer, someone who could be as tough as Molotov." Pauley explained the situation during his first meeting with a Treasury representative. He said Truman placed highest importance upon the mission because he believed its work would have "a great influence on the fate of humanity." He had been selected, Pauley went on, because he enjoyed the president's "utmost confidence." Because Truman wanted to "handle this matter himself," Pauley was to report "directly and personally." "It is no longer a State Department mission," he concluded, "but it is a Presidential mission."[25] Whereas Lubin had been designated minister, Pauley had been given the rank of ambassador. Lubin agreed to stay on in second place.

Pauley's appointment has been interpreted as evidence that Truman meant to use reparations to coerce the Soviets. His remark about wanting someone who could be "tough as Molotov" lends apparent support. The evidence suggests otherwise. Truman's concerns were three: to destroy Germany's war-making capacity, to avoid becoming involved in forced labor, and above all, to make sure the United States would not have to prop the German economy because of excessive reparations. During a conversation before negotiations began, he told one individual that the United States "held all the cards and that the Russians had to come to us." When asked whether he meant industrial equipment, Truman said "he thought they would take all of that out of Germany." The cards were "credits and technical assistance." Preparations were being made to secure legislative approval for a $1-billion credit for the Soviet Union.[26]

Nor did Pauley interpret his role as being "tough" with the Soviets over reparations so as to make them more amenable on other issues. After a tour of Germany, he told a Treasury official that the damage to German industry had been far less than he had been led to believe. There was a "much more reasonable chance" the United States would agree with the Soviet Union on a reparations program than with Britain or France. "He also said that he felt Russia had suffered so much in this war that they were entitled to most anything they might want out of Germany."[27]

Reparations negotiations were doomed because of differences over procedure. At Yalta, an agreement had been reached whereby the commission should consider in its "initial studies" the Soviet suggestion that reparations be set at $20 billion. U.S. policymakers assumed that "initial studies" meant on-site inspections of German industry after the war ended. After his return from Yalta, Stettinius explained to Morgenthau and Stimson how the figure had appeared. The United States had agreed with the Soviet Union that the amount could serve as a basis for discussion. It was, however, a "nominal figure," and the "exact sum of reparations will have to be determined after the Allies are in Germany and can make an estimate of the German capacity to make reparation."[28]

Following Roosevelt's death, the assumption that inventory would precede the setting of reparations was passed along. In a telephone conversation with Pauley, Stettinius put it this way:

> There isn't much to talk about. When we were in the Crimea, the thing was so general and it was left wide open. The Russians said they would like to get to grips with this thing. We agreed to having a commission established and appointed a member. Then they came up with the fact that they thought 20 would be an appropriate starting figure. We couldn't take a position until we found out what the condition of German industry was. It might be 20, 30, 40 or even 10, but we were willing to start with that figure.

Truman thought the inventory procedure had been agreed upon at Yalta. In a diary entry on the eve of Pauley's departure for Germany and the Soviet Union, he wrote that Pauley was "ordered to assemble a bunch of experts, and he did assemble a bunch of real experts, to go to Russia and Germany and work out a reparations program." Indeed, at this stage Truman believed that "the main stumbling block" would be the question of forced labor rather than the procedures followed by the commission.[29]

The Soviets gave notice even before negotiations began that they intended to follow a different course. They declined an invitation to accompany the U.S. delegation on a preliminary tour of Germany, insisting that reparations figures must be set in Moscow before on-site examinations were conducted. This, they said, was in conformity with the principles established at Yalta. They argued that the $20-billion figure, or something approximating it, was a commitment rather than a goal to be sought. Previous assurances about establishing a Central European standard of living were ignored.

When the announcement was made that Pauley and a delegation of experts would proceed to Moscow after a tour of Germany, U.S. chargé d'affaires George F. Kennan expressed misgivings in a cable to Harriman, who was still in Washington. The idea that reparations would be negotiated on the basis of economic conditions in Germany and its capacity to pay, he said, was mistaken. The Soviets would base their demands on political rather than economic considerations. "In the end, it will come down to a simple horse trade," he predicted. "How much are we going to make available to the Russians from our zone, and what price are we going to demand for it?" Harriman had discussed the matter with both Truman and Pauley and knew they were determined not to accept a settlement that would require the United States to support Germany because of reparations. "Mr. Pauley's instructions are very firm," he replied, "and while we may not reach any agreement I have no fears about us giving in."[30]

Kennan's analysis proved accurate. When the Reparations Commission met in Moscow on June 21, Maisky presented without supporting data a proposal based on the $20-billion figure. Pauley, having no counterproposal pending determination of Germany's capacity to pay, asked Maisky to provide estimates upon which the Soviet proposal was based. Maisky failed to do so then and for three weeks. Pauley wrote him complaining that "we have not received a single figure" and that the Soviet Union had made no effort to "enlighten" either the U.S. or British members as to the basis of the proposal. He pointed out that no one had access to Germany at the time of Yalta, and any figures discussed could have been based only on prewar data "of a very general character." Now that a physical inventory could be made of German assets, the commission was in a position to make "reasonably accurate estimates" of future German needs. "Only by deducting permitted German minimum requirements from the sum of actual present assets and estimated future production, can realistic net reparations figures be reached." Amounts fixed before making an inventory, he concluded, almost certainly would be too high or too low.[31]

To make matters worse from the U.S. standpoint, the USSR by its own action had drastically reduced the reparations base. Well before the commission first met, reports began reaching Washington that the Soviets were systematically dismantling and shipping eastward everything they could lay their hands on in the areas they occupied. Such extractions, furthermore, were labeled "war booty" and would not be counted as reparations. Second, the territory turned over to Poland contained 12 percent of Germany's movable capital assets and "a large part of the food surpluses of Germany." Just ten days before the Potsdam Conference met, Marshal G. K. Zhukov informed the United

States that these resources would not be "available in the joint administration of Germany." The millions of Germans evicted from this region emigrated west, "bringing their mouths with them" as Churchill put it.[32]

The commission adjourned without accomplishing anything other than agreement that each delegation would recommend the adoption of a "statement of principles" as suggested by Pauley. These principles had more to do with the way reparations would be collected than with amounts available. The exception, a statement of the "first charge" principle, was not recognized by the Soviets, contrary to what Maisky had told Harriman. Truman approved Pauley's refusal to discuss sums before an investigation of German industry. In a diary entry made aboard ship while en route to the Potsdam Conference, he wrote: "Byrnes and I discussed Pauley's plans on reparations. The smart boys in the State Department, as usual, are against the best interests of the U.S. if they can circumvent a straightforward hard hitting trader for the home front. But they are stymied this time. Byrnes and I shall expect our interests to come first. Pauley is doing a job for the United States." As this notation indicates, Truman wanted Pauley to be tough in protecting "our interests," which were to avoid having to augment the German economy because of reparations. There is no suggestion in Pauley's instructions or in the negotiations that he was to convey the impression that concessions on other issues would influence the U.S. position.[33]

Two days before Germany surrendered, Churchill had proposed a Big Three meeting. In the weeks following, he sought to impress Truman with the need for such a conference, which he thought must be held as quickly as possible. Stalin was reneging on his pledges everywhere except Greece, he warned, and an "iron curtain" was advancing across Europe. He emphasized the importance of Anglo-American unity to stem the tide.

Truman had other ideas. He was becoming suspicious of Churchill's motives at the time the latter was appealing for action. Regarding the German surrender, Truman wrote in his diary that "Churchill was trying to force me to break faith with the Russians" by issuing a bilateral announcement of the capitulation rather than waiting for simultaneous news releases by all three powers. At the same time, Churchill began pleading in behalf of a proposal Truman had rejected: that they delay their withdrawal of troops into the previously determined zones of occupation. Truman regarded such a course as a violation of Roosevelt's word and would have no part of it. He noted in his diary on May 19 that he had told Davies "I was having as much difficulty with Prime Minister Churchill as I was having with

Stalin—that it was my opinion that each of them was THE PAW OF THE CAT to pull the chestnuts out of the fire and if there were going to be any cat's paw I was going to be the paw and not the cat."[34]

The president demonstrated his unwillingness to make common cause with Britain by refusing Churchill's request that they meet before a conference with Stalin. He wanted to avoid the appearance that they were "ganging up." He wished to meet with Stalin instead, and he had in mind not discussions a day or two before the conference but separate talks "in Alaska or Siberia or on a warship somewhere in the neighborhood." Little wonder that Churchill, when informed by Davies, burst out that "such a meeting would be tantamount to a deal." He scotched the idea on May 31 by notifying Truman that "I should not be prepared to attend a meeting which was a continuation of a conference between you and Marshal Stalin."[35]

The timing of the Big Three meeting at Potsdam has been a subject of scholarly interest. The extreme view is that Truman, beginning in late April or early 1945, developed a sophisticated "strategy of a delayed showdown" pending the test of a nuclear device that he hoped to use as a diplomatic weapon.[36] His refusal to schedule the meeting before July 15 is cited as evidence. But there was no strategy, sophisticated or otherwise—only a series of decisions made as events developed. The last thing Truman wanted was a showdown at Potsdam.

When Churchill began importuning him about scheduling a conference quickly, Truman replied that "it will be extremely difficult" to get away from Washington before the end of the fiscal year (June 30), but he probably would be able to leave after that. In a meeting with Eden and other officials on May 14, Truman elaborated: "He would have to be in touch with Congress with regard to the budget." That is what he had been telling his advisers, several of whom agreed with Churchill that the meeting should be held as soon as possible. Truman suggested to Eden that the conference be held in "early July," *before* an atomic device would be tested.[37]

Truman changed his mind during the following week. On May 21, he informed Churchill that "I may, within the next two weeks, have more information bearing on a date and location for the proposed tripartite meeting if Stalin agrees to participate." What he did not tell the prime minister was that Hopkins would be conferring with Stalin during "the next two weeks" or that he already had been instructed to propose that the conference began on July 15, one day after the atomic test. Truman continued to use his preoccupation with the budget as the reason for delay, but this now was a convenient fiction. "The budget," he told Davies, really meant "atomic bomb experiments."[38]

The significance of postponing the conference until after the atomic test has been widely misunderstood. Truman did not plan to use it as a bargaining device and did not decide whether to inform Stalin about it until after the conference began. Stalin could hardly have been expected to make concessions over something he knew nothing about. Indeed, a concern among U.S. officials was how Truman should respond if "the Russians bring up the subject and ask us to take them in as partners." This question has enormous implications. It assumes Stalin knew about the atomic project, for otherwise there would be no subject for him to bring up. What is more, the United States assumed the Soviets had an atomic program. That explains the advice Stimson gave Truman in case the matter arose: Tell him "that we were very busy on this thing and working like the dickens and we knew he was busy with this thing and working like the dickens, and that we were pretty nearly ready and we intended to use it against the enemy, Japan."[39]

Had Truman meant to employ atomic diplomacy at Potsdam, his actions in the weeks before are inexplicable. Poland is a case in point. Hopkins was instructed to impress upon Stalin the importance of resolving the issue before the Big Three meeting. And Truman, instead of waiting until he could play the atomic card, hastened to recognize the Polish government eleven days before the conference. He hoped to have German reparations out of the way as well, but balked at Soviet insistence that sums be set in Moscow before analysis of Germany's capacity to pay.

The importance of having a successful test lay in its ramifications for the war against Japan. Because of Soviet actions in Eastern Europe, U.S. officials were increasingly wary about the USSR's intentions in the Far East. Roosevelt had agreed to the price Stalin demanded for entry because he thought he had no choice in view of the projected casualties. Truman still sought Soviet participation, but a successful test would place him in a better position to judge how far he would have to go. To use the analogy Truman and Stimson employed so often, the atomic card was not to be thrown down to impress the USSR. It was to be kept in hand to determine when the United States could refuse to bid any higher.

In his diary and in letters to his family, Truman expressed his displeasure at having to attend the Potsdam meeting. His comments have been interpreted as everything from a wish that the conference be held later than mid-July to his lack of confidence in facing the wartime leaders. More likely they reflected his loathing for the formalities he would have to endure. As he put it in one letter, "I have to take my tuxedo, tails . . . preacher coat, high hat, low hat and hard hat as well as sundry other things."[40] No doubt Truman preferred playing poker and "striking blows for freedom" with the boys, but this should not be permitted to obscure his confidence that the meeting could help "overcome the misunderstanding and difficulties which have arisen since the Germans folded up."[41] His desire to talk with Stalin before the conference undermines the notion either that he wanted to procrastinate or that he was bothered by a sense of inadequacy. The Hopkins mission appeared to affirm what his advisers had been telling him: Stalin could be "talked to," and accommodation was far more likely when the issues were put directly rather than filtered through the Molotov faction. With Byrnes at his side, Truman hoped to deal with Stalin in straightforward language.

NOTES

1. Harry S. Truman, *Year of Decisions* (Garden City, N.Y.: Doubleday, 1955), p. 22. Diary entry, July 7, is in Robert H. Ferrell, ed., *Off the Record: The Private Papers of Harry S. Truman* (New York: Harper, 1980), p. 49.

2. As quoted in Robert L. Messer, *The End of an Alliance: James F. Byrnes, Roosevelt, Truman, and the Origins of the Cold War* (Chapel Hill: University of North Carolina Press, 1982), pp. 68–69.

3. Entry for May 22, Truman Diary, President's Secretary's File, Truman Papers. Byrnes's remark is quoted in Messer, *Alliance,* p. 92.

4. Truman's remark to Stettinius is in Calendar Notes, April 13, Stettinius Papers; Hopkins's reference to Stalin is in Truman, *Year of Decisions,* p. 31; see page 257 for Truman's claim to have suggested the mission on the trip to Hyde Park. In a diary entry for May 19, however, Truman wrote: "After some discussion with Mr. Harriman, Ambassador to Russia, Harry Hopkins' name came up as a possible messenger to Stalin for me personally." Ferrell, *Off the Record,* p. 31.

5. Diary entries, May 19 and 22; and *Year of Decisions,* p. 258.

6. Harriman and Bohlen statements are in Memorandum of Conversation, May 15, Vol. 7, Grew Papers. Truman remark is from Report by [Lt.] Col. [Bernard] Bernstein, June 5, Book 852, pp. 53–62, Morgenthau Diaries. Truman told Bernstein that "if you could sit down with Stalin and get him to focus on the problem, Stalin would take a reasonable attitude."

7. Grew-Crowley memorandum and Truman's in President's Secretary's File, Truman Papers; Grew-Crowley telephone conversation, May 12, in Vol. 7, Grew Papers.

8. Crowley quotation in Minutes of Secretary's Staff Committee, May 14, Notter File, Box 304; Harriman's advice, *Foreign Relations of the United States, 1945* (Washington, D.C., 1967), V, p. 998; Grew's remark, May 12, Vol. 7, Grew Papers.

9. Minutes of Secretary's Staff Committee, May 18, Notter File, Box 304.

10. Truman's version in *Year of Decisions,* pp. 227–228; Crowley quotation, *FRUS, 1945,* p. 999; Stimson Diary, May 11, Stimson Papers.

11. *FRUS, The Conference of Berlin (The Potsdam Conference), 1945,* (Washington, D.C., 1960), I, pp. 32–33.

12. Hopkins-Stalin talks on Poland are in *FRUS, 1945,* V, pp. 299–314.

13. "Memorandum of the Fifth Hopkins-Stalin Conversation at the Kremlin, May 31"; Truman to Churchill, June 1; Truman to Hopkins, June 5; Truman to Churchill, June 7; all in *FRUS, 1945,* V, pp. 309–313, 314–315, 326–327, 331–332.

14. Stettinius Diary, entries May 26, June 1, June 2; *New York Times,* June 2 and 3.

15. Stettinius to Harriman, June 2, *FRUS, 1945,* III, pp. 117–118.

16. *FRUS, 1945,* I, p. 1171.

17. Truman Diary, June 7; *Public Papers of the Presidents: Harry S. Truman, 1945* (Washington, D.C., 1961), p. 123.

18. *FRUS, Potsdam,* I, pp. 64–78.

19. *FRUS, 1945,* III, pp. 133–135.

20. Harriman to Secretary of State, June 21, 23, *FRUS, 1945,* V, pp. 352–360.

21. *FRUS, Potsdam,* I, pp. 733–734.

22. Lynn Etheridge Davis, *The Cold War Begins: Soviet-American Conflict over Eastern Europe* (Princeton, N.J.: Princeton University Press, 1974), Chapter 8.

23. See Memorandum of Conversation, Morgenthau and his staff, March 19, 1945, Morgenthau Diary, Book 829 (II). The individual was Samuel Lubell, then associated with Bernard Baruch. See Lubell memorandum to Baruch, Baruch Papers, "Selected Correspondence," March 1945. "White-haired hope" is from Morgenthau memorandum cited above; "boyfriend" is from *FRUS, 1945,* III, pp. 469–470.

24. For Lubin's "extreme statement" and intention to fight for "95%," see memorandum by Joseph E. DuBois on conversation with Lubin, March 27, Book 833, Morgenthau Diaries. For Morgenthau's evaluation of Lubin, March 13, Book 827 (II), p. 159.

25. Truman, *Year of Decisions,* p. 308; for Pauley's statements, see DuBois memorandum of meeting with Pauley and Lubin, April 28, Book 842, pp. 8–9, Morgenthau Diaries.

26. Bernstein report of conversation with Truman, June 5, Book 852, pp. 53–62, Morgenthau Diaries.

27. Joseph E. DuBois to Harry Dexter White, June 14, Book 857, pp. 221–223, Morgenthau Diaries.

28. *FRUS, 1945,* III, p. 435.

29. Memorandum of telephone conversation between Stettinius and Pauley, April 29, Calendar Notes, Stettinius Papers; entry for May 19, Truman Diary.

30. *FRUS, 1945,* III, pp. 1211–1221.

31. Pauley to I. Maisky, July 3, Clark Clifford Papers.

32. Harriman to Secretary of State, April 6, in Forrestal Diary, Vol. II; *FRUS, Potsdam,* I, pp. 756, 783; II, p. 842. Churchill quotation is from John L. Snell, *Wartime Origins of the East-West Dilemma over Germany* (New Orleans: Houser, 1959), p. 204.

33. Truman Diary entry for July 7. A British review of the negotiations belies the notion that Pauley sought to use reparations as a bargaining counter or that he wished to stall until the atomic bomb put the United States in a stronger position. "Mr. Pauley did not hide the fact that his desire was to leave Moscow for Terminal [code name for the Potsdam Conference], carrying with him as much as he could by way of results. His desire to score a quick personal success made him an obvious victim for delaying tactics, and Mr. Maisky did not hurry." See memorandum by a British treasury official, July 16, *Documents on British Policy Overseas,* Series I, Vol. I (London: Her Majesty's Stationery Office, 1984), pp. 327–328.

34. Truman Diary entries, May 10, 19.

35. Davies talks with Churchill, *FRUS, Potsdam,* I, pp. 64–78, Churchill cable, p. 89.

36. Gar Alperovitz, *Atomic Diplomacy, Hiroshima and Potsdam: The Use of the Atomic Bomb & the American Confrontation with Soviet Power* (New York: Simon & Shuster, 1965, updated and expanded version by Elisabeth Sifton Books, 1985), Chapter 3, "The Strategy of a Delayed Showdown."

37. *FRUS, Potsdam,* I, pp. 3–11.

38. *FRUS, Potsdam,* I, p. 19; Davies Diary entry, May 21. See also Stimson Diary, June 6.

39. Stimson Diary entries, June 6 and July 3.

40. Truman, *Year of Decisions,* p. 331.

41. Appointment Sheet, May 21, in Ferrell, *Off the Record,* p. 33.

CHAPTER FIVE

The Potsdam Conference

President Truman and Secretary of State Byrnes departed for Europe aboard the cruiser USS *Augusta* on July 7, 1945. During the voyage, Truman enjoyed himself by taking brisk walks on deck, chatting with crew members, playing poker, and watching evening movies in Byrnes's cabin. He conferred daily with the secretary and various advisers and studied the position papers prepared on issues to be discussed at the forthcoming conference. At the bottom of one list of recommendations he brought with him, someone had added the comment, "In other words, we think that as a well known Missouri horse trader, the American people expect you to bring something home to them."[1] The statement was appropriate, for Truman by this time regarded Stalin as a horse trader. The *Augusta* docked at Antwerp on July 15. The presidential party motored to Brussels, where it boarded a plane for Berlin, then drove the last few miles to Babelsberg, a residential area near Potsdam. All three delegations were quartered in Babelsberg; the Little White House was a three-story edifice that formerly belonged to a German publisher. Conference sessions would be held in Potsdam at the Cecilienhof Palace, once owned by a German crown prince.

The conference was scheduled to open July 16, but Stalin, who apparently had suffered a mild heart attack, did not arrive until the following day. Churchill paid Truman an informal visit that first morning. The president's reaction is illuminating. Referring to the prime minister as a "most charming and a very clever person," Truman afterward wrote that "He gave me a lot of hooey about how great my country is and how he loved Roosevelt and how he intended to love me etc. etc." Churchill's flowery language left Truman unmoved. "I am sure we can get along," he noted, "if he doesn't try to give me too much soft soap" because that kind of soap "burns to beat hell when it gets in the eyes."[2] Later that day, Truman toured the ruins of Berlin and, as he had been on the flight from Brussels, was impressed with the devastation. These experiences may have confirmed his belief that Germany could not pay the reparations the Soviets were asking for.

The next day, shortly before noon, Stalin arrived at the Little White House for a meeting arranged by Joseph Davies. The conversation between Truman and Stalin touched a number of issues, from Franco's Spain to the USSR's entry into the Far Eastern war. What stands out was Truman's determination to ingratiate himself with the Soviet leader. Consider the following exchange from Bohlen's sketchy notes:

> T[ruman]: . . . I am here to—be yr friend—deal directly yes or no [I am] no diplomat.
> S[talin]: good—[frankness] help—work—USSR—always go along with US.
> T: friends—all subject differences. settle frankly.[3]

That is what Truman thought Stalin wanted to hear—that the two could negotiate on a frank and friendly basis. His statement about being no diplomat, Truman noted in his diary, pleased Stalin. What the latter thought is unknown, but the president was optimistic. "I can deal with Stalin," he wrote. "He is honest—but smart as hell."[4]

"I can deal with Stalin"—not as fatuous as Roosevelt's boast that through his charm he and Stalin talked like "men and brothers," but close. Just as FDR thought he could win the Soviet over with warmth and wit, Truman thought he could do the same with frank talk. He later noted that throughout their conversation Stalin "looked me in the eye when he spoke," which made him "hopeful." Truman's confidence that he had sized up his man correctly must have increased when Stalin scornfully said of the Chinese that "they don't understand horse trading." Whereas Churchill had given him "a lot of hooey" and had to be watched for "soft soap," Stalin was an "honest" horse trader who looked a man straight in the eye.

The evening before, Stimson had brought the first report that an atomic device had been detonated. The message lacked detail, but indicated that the test exceeded expectations. Succeeding cables described more graphically the explosion's effects. In recording Truman's responses to the information as it came in, Stimson used phrases such as "highly delighted," "greatly reinforced," "tremendously pepped up," and "he said it gave him an entirely new feeling of confidence." Placing such remarks entirely within the context of Truman's attitude toward the Soviet Union, some historians have used them as evidence that he was emboldened to get "tough." This was true only in the limited sense that the bomb influenced his thinking about how far the United States should go to ensure Soviet participation in the Far Eastern war. As Byrnes later wrote in a private report, the need for Soviet assistance could not be dismissed even after the news from Alamogordo because "the experts advised us that the experiment did not offer conclusive proof that a bomb would of certainty explode when dropped from a plane."[5] The fact is that Truman would have been "tremendously pepped up" regardless of the state of U.S.-Soviet relations by a development that made it likely the war could be ended without an invasion of Japan.

The first plenary session met at 5:00 P.M. on July 17. Stalin proposed that Truman preside, which Churchill seconded. Truman immediately began submitting documents on what he said were the "most important" items the United States wanted on the agenda. These involved a Council of Foreign Ministers (consisting of the five permanent members of the UN Security Council), administration of Germany, carrying out of the Declaration on Liberated Europe, and admission of Italy to the United Nations. Being thrust to the fore so quickly must have rattled Truman, for only then did he pause to express his appreciation for having been named chairman and then go on to say that he hoped he would merit the same friendship as had been shown his predecessor. After an exchange of amenities, Churchill proposed that Poland be placed on the agenda, and Stalin submitted a shopping list that included disposition of Germany's merchant fleet and navy, reparations from Italy, trusteeships, and relations with Germany's former allies.[6]

The only subject discussed at length that first day was the U.S. proposal Truman read for a Council of Foreign Ministers. The council would be charged with drawing up peace treaties for nations such as Bulgaria and Romania, as well as for Germany when a government was set up there, and proposing settlement of territorial questions. The rationale was that the experience at Paris after the last war had demonstrated that a general peace conference without adequate preparation produced a chaos of claims. Both Stalin and Churchill argued against China's right to participate in European questions, whereupon Truman agreed. There were questions as to how formation of the council would affect existing organizations such as the European Advisory Council. They were referred to the foreign ministers.

Actually, the U.S. proposal as originally stated was misleading. Truman and his advisers already had decided that they wanted no full-dress peace conference. They wished to have the council hold several meetings on the outstanding issues, to which only those nations with direct interests would be invited. Some writers have seen duplicity in the way this matter was handled, though to what end is not clear, for when Byrnes explained the U.S. position to Molotov privately, the latter concurred. Agreement was reached to establish the council, with restrictions placed on the participation of both China and France.[7]

The two plenary sessions that followed on the eighteenth and nineteenth produced neither agreements nor discord. Stalin emphasized his interest in a share of the German merchant and naval fleets and his desire to take steps against Franco, who he said was a "danger" to Europe. Churchill and Truman avowed their dislike of Franco, but expressed reluctance to interfere in Spain's domestic affairs—especially to do anything that might ignite another civil war. The prime minister, even more garrulous than at Yalta, spoke at length about the difficulties Britain was having in settling affairs with the London Poles. Almost as if the three were feeling one another out, potentially divisive issues were referred to the foreign ministers for "further study."

One item, settled after only a brief discussion on the eighteenth, would have important bearing on the vexatious matter of reparations. Referring to a document on the administration of Germany, Churchill asked what territorial entity was meant. He said if it were prewar Germany, he agreed. Stalin replied vaguely that "Germany is what she has become after the war." When Truman proposed they should consider Germany as it existed in 1937, Stalin suggested adding "minus what Germany had lost in 1945." Truman insisted that the 1937 boundaries be used for negotiation. Stalin assented. There was no hint of acrimony in this or any other exchange that day, and Truman's diary account is revealing. "There were three proposals," he noted, "and I banged them through in short order, much to the surprise of Mr. Churchill." Then, almost proudly, "Stalin was very much pleased."[8]

The first real differences began to emerge during the fifth session on July 21. In discussing a document on the Declaration on Liberated Europe, Stalin proposed an amendment for recognition of Romania, Bulgaria, Hungary, and Finland. Truman replied that he could not accept the amendment. In that case, Stalin said, consideration of the U.S. proposal on Italy would have to be postponed because the two issues could not be considered separately. Truman responded sharply. "When these countries were established on a proper basis, the United States would recognize them and not before." He stated that "the meeting would proceed and that this question would be passed over." It should be stated that he was taking no new ground, as the United States had notified the Soviets on June 18 that while it had no objections to recognizing Finland, it would not do so for the other three nations.[9]

The president displayed equal firmness about Poland's western boundary. At Yalta, no agreement had been reached because Roosevelt and Churchill had refused to accept the Oder–Western Neisse line Stalin proposed. As early as May it was reported to Washington that the Soviets were turning over control of the disputed territory to Warsaw. Then, just ten days before the Potsdam Conference began, Marshal Zhukov had informed the United States that no reparations would be available from the region east of the Oder-Neisse.[10] Such action not only violated the Yalta accord, it meant that reparations would have to be obtained from a truncated Germany. As Truman put it to Stalin, he "was unable to see how reparations or other questions could be decided if Germany was carved up."

The president undoubtedly had been thinking of this several days earlier when he insisted that the Germany of 1937 be used as the basis for negotiations. Stalin attempted to justify what had been done as dictated by the necessities of war. The German population in the disputed areas, he claimed, had fled, leaving only Poles to administer the region. He could not see the harm done by establishing "a Polish administration where only Poles remained." When Truman repeated his remark about carving up Germany, Stalin refused to back off. "The Soviet Union was not afraid of the reparations question," he said, "and would if necessary renounce them."[11]

Realizing that a confrontation lay at hand, both men grew more placatory. Stalin took the lead. Alluding to Truman's point that a Polish-German boundary had not been specified at Yalta, he said that the "frontier question is still open and the Soviet Union is not bound." "You are not?" asked Truman. Stalin replied "No" and launched into another explanation of Soviet behavior. He asked Truman to appreciate the reasons for not setting up a German administration "which would stab one in the back" while friendly Poles were there. The president expressed "his agreement and sympathy for this situation" and soothingly pointed out that "each was stating in a friendly way his own point of view." Churchill detailed the hardships if a greatly reduced Germany had to provide for the millions of refugees fleeing from lands turned over to the Poles. A discussion of this and related matters followed, but Truman returned to his original point before closing. Making "a frank statement of what he thought," he said he "could not agree to the separation of the eastern part of Germany under these circumstances" because the issue had to be considered with regard to reparations and supply problems—to which Stalin replied, "Are we through today?" Truman said they were.[12]

Meetings held during the next few days produced little. The matter of recognition and concluding peace treaties with the former German satellites, particularly Bulgaria and Romania, remained deadlocked. Truman and Byrnes emphasized their wish that governments of these nations be "friendly" to the Soviet Union, but complained that U.S. representatives in the control councils not only were excluded from active participation, but often were not even informed of decisions. Indeed, stringent restrictions on travel made it difficult for them to find out what was going on. Stalin and Molotov responded in several ways. Shortly before the Potsdam Conference, Soviet members of the councils had informed their counterparts that reforms in the ways the councils were operated would be instituted. Alluding to these reforms, Stalin and Molotov said they would reduce or eliminate Western complaints. At other times, they simply denied U.S. and British allegations—"all fairy tales," Stalin said at one point—or countered with protests about Italy or Greece.[13]

Truman and Byrnes must have been mystified by Soviet recalcitrance. U.S. and British recognition of the Polish Provisional Government of National Unity must have indicated to Stalin that token reorganizations of the governments of Bulgaria and Romania would be satisfactory. The United States pointed out repeatedly that it had no wish to become involved in elections: It merely wanted the right to have correspondents and officials present to report on them. As the historian Lisle Rose put it, the implication was obvious: "As long as American observers were present, Washington would not significantly object to rigged elections in Eastern Europe."[14]

Negotiation over German reparations proved equally inconclusive, although Byrnes introduced a plan later adopted. The Americans continued to oppose setting sums before a physical inventory and were determined that the United States would not have to keep Germans from starving. Their concerns were magnified by several considerations. Handing over to Poland German territories east of the Oder–Western Neisse would simultaneously reduce the base for reparations and place a further burden on what remained of Germany to provide for millions of evicted people. Also, early Soviet plant and equipment removals under the guise of "war booty" and "restitution" were unacceptable to U.S. and British officials, who wanted them counted as reparations.[15]

For all these reasons, the United States and Britain refused to agree on a figure even though Molotov offered to reduce Soviet claims by $2 billion. Byrnes began to push the idea that each nation should take what it desired from its own zone but in other matters, such as transportation and communication, Germany would be treated as a whole. The Soviet zone contained almost half of Germany's assets, he said, and differences could be made up by exchange of goods between zones. For a time, the Soviets rejected this proposal as contrary to the Yalta accord.

While issues continued to pass between the three leaders and the foreign ministers, new items were introduced. On July 22, while discussing revision of the 1936 Montreux Convention that gave Turkey the right to close the Turkish Straits to armed ships in time of war, the Soviets expressed interest not only in free passage for their ships, which Britain and the United States supported, but in naval bases and modifications of Soviet-Turkish boundaries. They also talked about acquiring trusteeships over Italian colonies in Africa and the Mediterranean and over Korea. Ambassador Harriman expressed alarm: "They are throwing aside all their previous restraint as to being only a Continental power and not interested in any further acquisitions," he said to Stimson, "and are now apparently seeking to branch out in all directions." The next morning Stimson went to see Truman, who confirmed what Harriman said. The president assured him that the United States was "standing firm" and went on to say that he thought a good deal of what the Soviets were asking was "bluff, and told me what he thought the real claims were confined to." Stalin was doing what any good horse trader would do.[16]

Truman threw down his own challenge that afternoon, July 23. The first item was resumption of talk about the Montreux Convention. Stalin argued that because Turkey was too weak to guarantee free passage of ships "in case complications arose," the Soviet Union must have bases where "in cooperation with its allies the Russian fleet could protect the Straits." Truman agreed that the convention should be revised, but proceeded far beyond what the Soviets were talking about. "He had come to the conclusion after a long study of history," he said, "that all the wars of the last two hundred years had originated in the area from the Black Sea to the Baltic and from the eastern frontier of France to the western frontier of Russia." Because he did not want to "engage in another war twenty-five years from now over the Straits or the Danube," he proposed internationalization of all inland waterways bordering on two or more states, as well as those passages generally referred to as "straits." The Soviet Union, Great Britain, the United States, and those nations directly involved should guarantee free navigation. Agencies should be set up for the Danube and Rhine and, later, for the Kiel Canal and the Turkish Straits. Stalin understandably replied that he would have to read Truman's paper "attentively" before he could discuss it.[17]

At the eighth plenary session on July 24, Truman asked whether his proposal on waterways had been considered. Stalin pointed out that the paper mentioned only the Danube and Rhine, whereas Truman had spoken of the Turkish Straits. The president wished the two questions to be considered together. Stalin was curt. Their views differed, he said, so they should postpone the issue and move on to the next question. When Churchill supported Truman, Molotov sarcastically asked why the British did not advocate such an arrangement for the Suez Canal. To the prime minister's sputtering replies that the "question had not been raised" and that there had been "no complaints," Molotov countered that he was raising it and that they should ask Egypt about complaints. Stalin plainly wanted no part of Truman's scheme. After repeating his remark that they should move on to the next question, he closed the discussion by proposing "that each of them work on the matter." He wanted naval bases, not international agencies.[18]

At the end of this session, Truman took a step that has remained controversial to this day. Purposely leaving his own interpreter, he walked around the conference table to where Stalin was standing with the Soviet interpreter, V. N. Pavlov. With deliberate casualness, he told Stalin that the United States had developed a "weapon" or "bomb" (it is unclear which word he used, much less how it came out in translation) of tremendous destructive force. Showing no surprise or interest in pursuing the matter, the Soviet leader replied that he was glad to hear it and hoped it would be used to good effect against the Japanese. Later, while waiting for their cars to be brought around, Churchill—who knew what the president intended to do—asked, "How did it go?" Truman replied, "He never asked a question."[19]

What has puzzled scholars is what Truman intended to convey to Stalin and for what purpose. The most common view is that by his casual approach and failure to mention an atomic bomb, he wished to mislead Stalin into thinking he was referring only to some powerful conventional weapon. That way the Soviets could be kept in the dark until after the bombs had been dropped, while permitting Truman to claim later that he had been a good ally by informing them. Such a thesis neglects one crucial fact. Truman could not have known that Stalin would refrain from asking about the nature of the weapon. If he had inquired, it is difficult to imagine Truman replying "I don't know" or "I won't tell you." Informing Stalin about *atomic* bombs, after all, was what he, Byrnes, Stimson, and Churchill had been talking about. That he changed his mind without informing the others seems unlikely. Had Truman pursued the conversation in the face of Stalin's indifference, it would have placed him in the position of appearing to encourage questions he did not wish to answer.

Stalin's failure to press for details did not preclude the possibility that the Soviets would do so in the days following. Byrnes expected they would: "Byrnes said that everything is fine tonight," his aide noted, "but by tomorrow he thinks the importance of what Truman told Stalin will sink in and well may it."[20] This raises a question. If the United States assumed Stalin had no knowledge of the atomic program and believed Truman was referring merely to a conventional weapon, what did Byrnes think would "sink in"? During the weeks before Potsdam, there had been discussion over how to respond should the Soviets raise the nuclear issue "and ask us to take them in as partners." Stimson's advice was to tell Stalin that the United States was working on it and knew the Soviets were, but to withhold details. Stimson had told FDR months earlier that he believed Soviet espionage had penetrated the atomic project, and it is unlikely that he failed so to inform Truman. And when Harriman reported three days after Hiroshima that Stalin had told him the Soviets had an atomic program, no one in Washington evinced surprise or requested any follow-up.[21] All this suggests that when the president told Stalin about the new weapon, he assumed the latter would know what he was talking about— if not at the moment then after the information had time to "sink in." Truman and Byrnes naturally were delighted that Stalin chose not to pursue the matter then or later in the conference because it meant there would be no embarrassing requests to send technical observers or to be taken in as partners.

On the morning of July 23, the day before Truman spoke to Stalin, the president had asked Stimson to confer with General Marshall about whether "we needed the Russians in the war or whether we could get along without them." In a meeting that afternoon, the general gave a noncommittal reply. Pinning down the Japanese army in Manchuria already had been achieved, he said, because the Japanese were moving into defensive positions near the border in response to Soviet troop buildups. Even if the Japanese were forced to surrender without the USSR's assistance, nothing could prevent the Soviets from invading Manchuria, "thus permitting them to get virtually what they wanted in the surrender terms."

Truman's query might have represented a cynical effort to exclude the Soviets, now that the bomb promised to bring an early end to the war. The USSR's pledge as to when it would enter the conflict, however, was contingent. At Yalta, Stalin had said two to three months after defeat of Germany. In his talk with Hopkins and during the conference, he spoke of mid-August, but he pointed out repeatedly that a declaration would occur only after negotiations with China over the Yalta Far Eastern accord had been concluded. As these negotiations had bogged down a few weeks before Potsdam, Truman and Byrnes regarded this condition as an unsubtle effort to force the United States into pressing

China for concessions in return for the USSR's early entry. Possession of the bomb made this objective still desirable but not crucial.[22]

That same day Truman had requested that Stimson obtain more information as to when the first bomb would be ready. The president had brought with him the draft of a message calling upon the Japanese to surrender unconditionally. This draft, with a few modifications made during the conference, became known as the Potsdam Declaration. Truman told Stimson that he proposed to "shoot it out [to Chiang Kai-shek, for his approval] as soon as he heard the definite day of the operation." Timing was important. The president wanted the Japanese to consider and respond to the declaration. If they accepted, of course the war was over. If they did not, he wanted the first bomb dropped as soon as possible, to drive home the declaration's warning that the alternative was "prompt and utter destruction."[23]

The secretary received a reply from Washington that evening, which he conveyed to Truman next morning: The first bomb would be ready within two weeks. Orders were immediately issued to General Carl Spaatz that the first bomb should be dropped as soon after August 3 as weather permitted. Truman told Stimson that these orders would stand unless he, the president, determined that Japan's reply to the declaration was acceptable. After securing Churchill's approval, Truman had the declaration sent to Chiang, who also approved but with the request that his name appear before Churchill's for prestige purposes. Truman accepted this alteration and issued the declaration on July 26. Molotov complained about not being consulted. He was told that because the Soviets were not at war with Japan, the United States feared they would be embarrassed if word leaked that they had participated in composing it.[24]

Possession of the bomb may have influenced one other decision at Potsdam regarding the USSR and the Far East. On July 29, as the conference neared its end, Molotov suggested to Byrnes that after Soviet-Chinese negotiations, the United States and its allies address a formal request to the Soviet Union asking that it join the war against Japan. This disturbed Byrnes and Truman. Truman saw in it "a cynical diplomatic move to make Russia's entry at this time appear to be the decisive factor to bring about victory." After almost four years of war against the Japanese, he had no wish to have the United States act as a supplicant for what was expected to be a brief contribution. Also, the Soviet-Japanese nonaggression pact at that time had almost a year to run. Because the Soviet Union was expected to publish the request, the United States would be placed in the position of publicly asking another nation to violate a treaty. After consulting the British, Truman and Byrnes escaped the dilemma by sending a note to Stalin suggesting that he base Soviet entry upon the Moscow Declaration of October 30, 1943, and upon the as yet unratified United Nations Charter. Truman might have manifested less concern for appearances had there been no atomic bombs in the offing.[25]

Meanwhile, there was only one plenary meeting between July 25 and 31. After a morning session on July 25, Churchill, Eden, and Labour leader Clement Attlee, who was a member of the delegation, left for London to await the results of national elections. The elections had been held earlier, but tallies could not be completed until votes from the military services were received. To the great surprise of Truman and Byrnes, and likely Stalin, the Labour party won. The new prime minister, Attlee, and Foreign Minister Ernest Bevin arrived in Potsdam on July 28. An unprepossessing man in appearance and manner, Attlee permitted Bevin to take the lead in discussions. The change brought about no discernible differences in negotiating, although Churchill later said he would have seen the conference break up before agreeing to some of the compromises Attlee accepted. In all probability, he would have done nothing of the sort.

After a meeting on the evening Attlee returned, proceedings again were interrupted because Stalin reportedly had developed a cold. Truman wrote to his mother and sister that "I really think he's not so sick but disappointed over the English elections." Perhaps he was. Stalin may have hoped that representatives of Labour would be more sympathetic to Soviet goals than were Churchill and Eden. If so, he was mistaken. Bevin's first words upon arriving reportedly were "I will not have Britain barged about."[26] He acted that way at his first session. While Attlee puffed on his pipe, Bevin repeatedly called into question Stalin's remarks in a less than cordial manner. Stalin may have concluded that a "cold" would be a convenient way to postpone sessions while compromises were worked out with the Americans.

Molotov visited the Little White House at noon July 29 to talk with Truman and Byrnes. Whereas other disputed issues had been put aside for resolution by the Council of Foreign Ministers, everyone agreed on the importance of settling reparations and Poland's western boundary before the conference ended. Byrnes handed Molotov a paper providing that the Big Three, pending the final settlement, agree that territories east of the Oder–Eastern Neisse be under the administration of the Polish government. Molotov said that Stalin probably would not accept this proposal because land between the Eastern and Western Neisse also should be administered by Poland. Truman replied that he thought the U.S. paper would be acceptable because it represented "a very large concession on our part."[27]

Byrnes next brought up the matter of reparations, asking whether the Soviets had considered his suggestion that each country extract what it chose from its own zone, with discrepancies being made up by exchange of goods. Molotov said they had and did not object "in principle." When he asked how much capital equipment the Soviet Union could expect to get from the industrial Ruhr, Byrnes said one-quarter of what was available. Molotov complained that percentages of unstated amounts were insubstantial—the Soviets wanted specific figures. He suggested either $2 billion or 6 billion tons of capital equipment. The secretary hewed to the position the United States had established earlier: Amounts could not be determined pending physical inspection of Germany's capacity to pay. This part of the conversation ended inconclusively, but Molotov's acceptance in principle of Byrnes's plan was a step toward resolving the problem.[28]

Byrnes met with Molotov the next day before the scheduled meeting of the foreign ministers. The secretary offered three proposals that, he stressed, the United States regarded as a package—acceptance of any one was contingent upon acceptance of all. The first gave the Soviets all they had asked for with regard to Poland: The territories east of the Oder–Western Neisse rivers would be placed under Polish administration pending a final settlement. The last clause was a fig leaf for what everyone knew amounted to alienation of this region from Germany for the foreseeable future.

Byrnes handed the foreign minister a document that was a mini-package regarding Italy and the former German satellite states in Eastern Europe. It was a masterpiece of ambiguity. Its substance was that the Council of Foreign Ministers be instructed to begin preparing at its first meeting a peace treaty for Italy and a plan for its admission into the UN. Truman had proposed this at the opening session. The council also was instructed to draw up treaties for Bulgaria, Romania, and Hungary, but the treaties would not be concluded until those nations had "recognized democratic governments." This gave quasi-legitimacy to the Soviet-sponsored regimes in these countries, without committing the United States and Britain to recognize them in their present forms.

Byrnes's final proposal dealt with reparations. He offered the Soviet Union 15 percent of the Ruhr's industrial equipment found to be surplus and another 25 percent to be exchanged for food and raw material from the eastern zones. When Molotov asked who would determine what was surplus in the Ruhr, which lay in the British zone, Byrnes said the zone commander. The foreign minister demurred, saying that such determination should be made by either the control council or the Reparations Commission. He said the equipment turned over without exchange should be 25 percent rather than 15 percent. To Byrnes's reply that the British probably would not accept this figure, he countered that if that were true, the Soviet Union should receive percentages of equipment from all the western zones rather than just the Ruhr. He suggested 10 percent outright and 15 percent in exchange. Agreement was not reached at this meeting, although Molotov said he was satisfied that progress was being made.[29]

It should be obvious that at this stage the United States was negotiating on its own with the Soviet Union. The British fumed on the sidelines. As one member of their delegation complained, "Jimmy B. is a bit too active and has already gone and submitted various proposals to Molotov which go a bit beyond what we want at the moment."[30] Truman and Byrnes were anxious for results and willing to make concessions, and they treated Britain as a balky junior partner. Nowhere was this more evident than in their actions at the foreign ministers' meeting immediately after Byrnes's talk with Molotov. Although they continued to haggle over details, they spent most of the time trying to dragoon a reluctant Bevin into accepting what they had decided.

Stalin recovered from his "cold" sufficiently for a plenary session the afternoon of July 31. That morning, Byrnes met again with Molotov to talk over the U.S. "package." The secretary all along had said that the United States insisted the USSR approve all three proposals. This time he was more blunt. The United States had gone as far as it could. Unless the package was accepted in its entirety, "the President and I would leave for the United States the next day."[31]

President Truman called upon Byrnes to present his proposals as soon as the plenary session got under way. The secretary did so, emphasizing that the United States regarded them as inseparable. Stalin and Molotov objected, saying each issue should be considered apart. "Mr. Byrnes can use such tactics as these if he wishes," Stalin said sharply, "but the Russian delegation will vote on each issue separately." Actually, only the proposal on reparations produced much debate. Stalin accepted the idea of each nation taking reparations from its own zone, but wanted the Soviet Union to receive more generous shares of assets from the western areas. Whereas Byrnes had proposed that 7.5 percent of surplus industrial equipment be turned over free and 12.5 percent in exchange for raw materials, he now adopted the 10 percent and 15 percent Molotov had mentioned. In addition, Stalin asked that the Soviet Union receive $500 million of shares in industrial and transportation enterprises in the western zones, 30 percent of German overseas investments, and 30 percent of the German gold captured by the Western Allies. Over Bevin's protest that the American proposal was "liberal" as it stood, a compromise was worked out whereby the

Soviets would get the higher percentages of industrial equipment in return for dropping their claims to shares, investments, and gold.[32]

The remainder of this session and the final meetings on August 1 were devoted to discussions on noncontroversial issues and preparation of the conference protocol and communiqué. Only one other exchange bears mention. Three times Truman had brought up his scheme for internationalization of waterways, only to have Stalin refuse to discuss it because of "differences." All the president could get was agreement that it be taken up at a future meeting of the Council of Foreign Ministers. Toward the end of the first meeting on August 1, Truman asked that mention be made in both the protocol and communiqué that the matter had been considered. Stalin argued that it had not been dealt with and ought to be excluded. He was particularly adamant about keeping it out of the communiqué. Truman, who had become enamored of the plan, appealed to him: "Marshal Stalin, I have accepted a number of compromises during this conference to conform with your views, and I make a personal request now that you yield on this point." Without waiting for the interpretation, Stalin burst out heatedly, "Nyet!" And, in English, "No, I say no!" Truman, flushing in anger, turned to his aides and said, "I cannot understand that man."[33]

The final meeting began a little before 11:00 that evening. After several minor amendments were discussed, Truman, Stalin, and Attlee signed the protocol. The atmosphere was outwardly cordial, despite the earlier Truman-Stalin fracas, and they engaged in a good deal of banter throughout the meeting. They complimented one another as well as the foreign ministers and proclaimed the conference a success. At last, at about 12:30 A.M., Truman spoke the final words: "I declare the Berlin Conference closed."

Byrnes later referred to Potsdam as "the success that failed."[34] By that he meant that the agreements were sound enough, but Soviet behavior in the months following undermined them. At the time, Truman also believed the conference was a success—and with good reason. Above all, he had secured Stalin's confirmation that the Soviet Union was preparing to join the war against Japan. The reservation that this would not occur until the conclusion of negotiations with China was not critical, because the atomic bomb might render it nonessential and because the invasion was months away. Byrnes's "package" conceded more territory to Poland than the United States wished, but it had secured an agreement on reparations that promised to spare the United States from having to sustain Germany because of excessive payments—a potentially explosive issue at home. Relations with the East European nations remained moot: The United States had refused to recognize their governments, but had signaled the Soviet Union that cosmetic changes would be sufficient. Finally, Truman had informed Stalin of the "weapon," whether or not he thought the Soviets knew what he was referring to, without incurring requests for information or participation he was not prepared to grant.

Historians have treated the conference with more skepticism. There have been three criticisms. First, failure to inform Stalin fully and frankly about the bomb must have aroused his already formidable suspicions about the good faith of his allies and contributed to, if it did not cause, the subsequent arms race. Second, reports on the success of the nuclear device emboldened Truman and Byrnes to shun compromises they otherwise might have made, because they assumed the newly acquired power would enable them to get their way later. Finally, Byrnes's reparations plan led to the permanent division of Germany, as they should have known it would.[35]

Such criticisms necessarily are speculative, as are efforts to deal with them—history cannot be rerun to see how events would have developed had individuals acted differently. Truman's handling of the bomb with Stalin may well have increased the latter's doubts, but one must consider the alternative. If the president had made clear he was talking about atomic weapons and even if he had made some allusion to a partnership, would Stalin have refrained from developing his own program? The idea that he would have been content to follow the U.S. lead at a time when the Soviets were years away from building a bomb is tantalizing, but it does not comport with anything we know about the way his mind worked. More probably he would have considered any such suggestion as a device to guarantee America's continued technological superiority in this area. Even if he "trusted" Truman, which is unlikely, he would have had to consider the president's mortality and the possibility that a successor might renege on any agreements.

The thesis that Truman and Byrnes grew "tougher" after the reports from Alamogordo is easier to handle—it is contradicted by the facts. The United States made concessions from its stated position on practically every issue of importance. The briefing book paper on Poland's western boundary stated that the United States "with reluctance" would accept the Oder–Eastern Neisse.[36] Byrnes not only offered that line, but when the Soviets balked, he agreed to the Oder–Western Neisse— an additional area of 8,100 square miles and a prewar German population of 2.7 million. At Yalta, FDR had refused to recognize such a westerly boundary. Truman and Byrnes agreed to Soviet acquisition of Königsberg in response to Stalin's request for "one ice-free port" on the Baltic, even though Königsberg is not ice-free and the Soviets already had several more-accessible ports.[37] Against the advice of the

British, the United States consented to raise the percentages of industrial equipment the Soviets would receive from the western zones to what Molotov originally had proposed. As for the former German satellites, the United States retreated from insisting on "supervision" of elections to the more or less harmless "observation" of them. Far from retrenching until their newly acquired power was demonstrated over Hiroshima, Truman and Byrnes eagerly sought all the agreements they could get.

The charge that Byrnes's reparations plan led directly to the division of Germany at first seems obvious. That he and Truman should have known this would happen is less clear. And that they intended it all along, as some have alleged, is simply not true.[38] As Byrnes repeatedly pointed out to Molotov, "under his scheme nothing was changed in regard to overall treatment of German finance, transport, foreign trade, etc." When subordinate officials in Washington raised the question of whether joint administration of Germany was being abandoned, a long cable came from Potsdam explaining how the new arrangement would be worked out within the framework of "common policies."[39] Reparations was one of the few issues for which the failure to gain agreement would have worked to the advantage of the United States—the bulk of German industry lay in the western zones. Yet Truman and Byrnes were willing to trade Poland's western boundary to secure Soviet acceptance of the U.S. plan. The division of Germany may be seen as an outcome of the Cold War rather than of reparations policy, for it is as difficult to imagine the Soviets accepting a unified non-Communist Germany as it is the United States accepting a unified Communist one.

The Machiavellian view of Truman's and Byrnes's conduct at Potsdam omits a key consideration. Both knew their performance would be appraised by the American public. Even if they had been inclined to wait until the bomb was dropped, the need to demonstrate tangible accomplishments was evident. Truman had been in office a few months, Byrnes a few weeks, and both wanted a successful conference. Consider Truman's appeal to have his plan for waterways mentioned in the communiqué. When Stalin refused, the president plaintively asked whether he would be free to speak of it to the Senate. That is not the behavior of a global strategist but of "a well known Missouri horse trader."

NOTES

1. Memorandum for the President, July 6, Samuel I. Rosenman Papers, Truman Library.

2. Diary entry July 16, Robert H. Ferrell, *Off the Record: The Private Papers of Harry S. Truman* (New York: Harper, 1980), pp. 50–53.

3. Truman-Stalin meeting in *Foreign Relations of the United States, The Conference of Berlin (The Potsdam Conference), 1945* (Washington, D.C., 1960), II, pp. 52–54.

4. Ferrell, *Off the Record,* p. 53.

5. Stimson phrases are from entries July 18, 21, 23, Stimson Diary; Byrnes remark from memorandum headed "White House 1943 Atomic," Folder 596(2), Byrnes Papers. The paper obviously is misdated because it refers to events in 1945.

6. *FRUS, Potsdam,* II, pp. 52–54.

7. Byrnes-Molotov meeting, July 24, *FRUS, Potsdam,* II, pp. 354–355.

8. Truman-Stalin exchange about German boundaries, *FRUS, Potsdam,* II, pp. 89–90; Truman Diary entry, July 18, in Ferrell, *Off the Record,* pp. 53–54.

9. *FRUS, Potsdam,* II, p. 207.

10. *FRUS, Potsdam,* I, p. 756.

11. *FRUS, Potsdam,* II, p. 208–209.

12. *FRUS, Potsdam,* II, p. 209–210.

13. Stalin remark, *FRUS, Potsdam,* II, p. 362.

14. Lisle A. Rose, *After Yalta* (New York: Charles Scribner's Sons, 1973), p. 48.

15. *FRUS, Potsdam,* II, pp. 808–809, 850–852, 889.

16. Entry for July 23, Stimson Diary.

17. *FRUS, Potsdam,* II, pp. 303–305.

18. *FRUS, Potsdam,* II, pp. 365–367.

19. Winston S. Churchill, *Triumph and Tragedy* (Boston: Houghton Mifflin, 1953), pp. 669–670.

20. Walter Brown's notes, July 24, Folder 54(1), Byrnes Papers.

21. Harriman to President and Secretary of State, August 9, Map Room Files, Truman Papers.

22. Marshall's evaluation in entry July 23, Stimson Diary; for statements that Soviets would be ready to join the war by mid-August, but would not do so until Sino-Soviet negotiations were completed, see *FRUS, Potsdam,* II, pp. 476, 1585.

23. Truman quotation in entry for July 23, Stimson Diary; Potsdam Declaration is reprinted in Truman, *Year of Decisions,* pp. 390–392.

24. Walter Brown's notes, July 27, Folder 54(1), Byrnes Papers.

25. Molotov request, *FRUS, Potsdam,* II, p. 476; Truman statement in *Year of Decisions,* p. 402; note to Soviets about entering war in Folder 602, Byrnes Papers.

26. Hastings Ismay, *The Memoirs of General Lord Ismay* (New York: Vikings, 1960), p. 403.

27. Truman-Molotov-Byrnes meeting, *FRUS, Potsdam,* II, pp. 471–476.

28. *FRUS, Potsdam,* II, pp. 473–476.

29. *FRUS, Potsdam,* II, pp. 480–483.

30. David Dilks, ed., *The Diaries of Sir Alexander Cadogan, 1938–1945* (New York: G. P. Putnam's Sons, 1972), p. 777.

31. James F. Byrnes, *Speaking Frankly* (New York: Harper, 1947), p. 85.

32. Stalin's remark, *FRUS, Potsdam,* II, p. 530; Bevin's, p. 532.

33. Robert Murphy, *Diplomat Among Warriors* (New York: Pyramid Books, 1964), p. 312.

34. Byrnes, *Speaking Frankly,* Chapter 4, "Potsdam—The Success That Failed."

35. All three theses are put forward in Charles L. Mee, Jr., *Meeting at Potsdam* (New York: M. Evans, 1975). With regard to the arms race, Mee writes on pp. 222–223 that although few turning points in history can be specified accurately, one "can be dated with extraordinary precision: the twentieth century's nuclear arms race began at the Cecilienhof Palace at 7:30 P.M., on July 24, 1945."

36. See Briefing Book Paper, "Suggested United States Policy Regarding Poland, *FRUS, Potsdam,* I, pp. 743–747.

37. *FRUS, Potsdam,* II, p. 305. For a delightful discussion of this issue, see George F. Kennan, *Memoirs: 1925–1950* (Boston: Little, Brown, 1967), pp. 263–265. Kennan points out that the postwar edition of *Soviet Encyclopedia* specifically designated Königsberg as "ice free," although an earlier edition had not. "If anyone thought, after 1945, that he saw ice in the canal at Königsberg," Kennan writes, "he didn't."

38. For the strongest statement of this theme, see William Appleman Williams, *The Tragedy of American Diplomacy,* rev. and enl. ed. (New York: Dell, 1962), pp. 250–252. Original ed. 1959.

39. *FRUS, Potsdam,* II, pp. 938–940.

CHAPTER SIX

The Far East

Open disagreement between the United States and the Soviet Union about the Far East emerged only after Japan's surrender. But the seeds of contention had been planted earlier. At Yalta, Roosevelt had secured Stalin's pledge to enter the Asian conflict at a price FDR thought justified given the prospects of materially shortening the war and reducing heavy U.S. casualties. He also believed that he had helped strengthen Chiang Kai-shek's beleaguered regime by a Soviet promise to recognize and deal with it as the legitimate government of China. During the following months, however, disputes over Poland and other issues began to raise suspicion about how the Soviets would carry out the Yalta accord. Some officials thought the question ought to be reexamined to protect U.S. interests. Complications arose when it became likely that atomic bombs might bring Japan to an early surrender, with little or no help from the USSR.

The agreement Roosevelt had negotiated with the Soviets involved disposition of the Kuriles, Sakhalin, and Outer Mongolia, but Manchuria was by far the most important territory. Manchuria had long been a source of contention between Russia and Japan and was a cause of the Russo-Japanese war of 1904–1905. The United States had developed modest economic interests there, which it tried to protect by encouraging other powers to follow Open Door principles. Japan's occupation during the early 1930s had produced the first challenge to the League of Nations and eventually led to Tokyo's withdrawal from the organization. The U.S. response was the Stimson Doctrine, which held that the United States would not recognize territorial changes brought about by force of arms. Japan's rejection of Open Door principles, first in Manchuria, then in China proper, helped exacerbate the estrangement with the United States that culminated in Pearl Harbor.

As time wore on, ambiguities in the Yalta Far Eastern accord caused increasing apprehension among those who were aware of its existence. Stalin at first had requested outright leases in Manchuria, not only for a naval base at Port Arthur, but for the commercial port of Dairen and several key railroads giving the Soviet Union outlets to warm water. Roosevelt had not opposed leasing Port Arthur, but had urged that Dairen and the railroads be administered by mixed commissions. In final form, the agreement provided that Dairen would be "internationalized" and that the railroads would be "jointly operated" by a mixed Soviet-Chinese company. In both cases, the "preeminent interests of the Soviet Union shall be safeguarded," while at the same time "China shall retain full sovereignty in Manchuria."[1]

What did this mean? At best, from the U.S. standpoint, it meant that although neither the Chinese nor anyone else could interfere with Soviet use of the railroads and ports, the USSR's influence in Manchuria would be limited to what was necessary to protect these interests. Beyond that, China would exercise "full sovereignty." And Dairen as a free port rather than a leasehold appeared to constitute a victory for the Open Door policy. But just as the Soviet interpretation of "friendly" governments in Eastern Europe went far beyond anything the United States had contemplated, what was to prevent Stalin from reducing Manchuria to a protectorate under the guise of safeguarding the Soviet Union's "preeminent interests"?

The importance of the Manchurian agreement to the Truman administration can scarcely be exaggerated. The Yalta accord on the Far East had been kept secret from Congress and the press, but its existence would have to be revealed sometime. If the Soviet Union sealed off Manchuria with Washington's acquiescence, charges would be raised that FDR had closed the Open Door to appease Stalin. This would be damaging to Byrnes because of his self-proclaimed status as the "Yalta expert" and by extension to Truman, who had appointed him secretary of state. If the administration attempted to thwart such a move, Stalin could pursue it by working with the Chinese Communists. Either way, U.S. interests would be jeopardized.

When he returned to Washington following FDR's death, Ambassador Harriman conveyed to Truman and other officials his fears about Stalin's intentions regarding China. He thought it imperative that Chiang's government unite with the Chinese Communists to present a front against Soviet encroachment. At the same time, George F. Kennan filed a gloomy report from Moscow. He believed that Stalin meant to regain all the rights and privileges Russia had held in the Far East, and more. Just as the Soviet Union was creating a glacis of "friendly" states on its western borders, Kennan predicted that it would try to dominate contiguous regions in the east. In short, Kennan argued, if desire to achieve Soviet participation in the war against Japan caused the United States to place "undue reliance" upon Stalin's willingness to support U.S. objectives in China, the result would be "tragic." The warnings caused Secretary of State Stettinius on April 23, 1945, to cable the ambassador in Chungking, Patrick J. Hurley, to impress upon Chiang the necessity of military and political unification so that relations with the Soviet Union "may eventually become one of mutual regard and permanent friendship."[2]

A few weeks later, Joseph C. Grew, acting secretary while Stettinius was at the San Francisco Conference, initiated a review of the situation. Grew, who had been ambassador to Japan during the prewar years, had become alarmed at the drift of relations with the Soviets. On May 12, he sent a memorandum to the Departments of War and Navy, asking their opinion on several matters relating to the Yalta Far Eastern accord. His first question was whether Soviet entry into the war against Japan was militarily so crucial as to preclude reopening negotiations to secure U.S. objectives in China and Korea. Second, he asked if the United States should reconsider Yalta in light of developments or feel obligated to carry it out. Specifically, Grew wanted to ensure that the Soviet Union would help bring about unification of China under Chiang, reaffirm Chinese sovereignty over Manchuria, and agree to a four-power trusteeship for Korea.[3]

Stimson, who knew that work on the atomic bomb was proceeding on schedule, could not comment on its significance to Grew's first question, which of course had bearing upon the second. He had favored a policy of delay on these issues until the bomb could be used. Unable to discuss this except with his aides and Truman, he responded with a presentation of items to be considered rather than a series of recommendations. He pointed out that although the USSR's entry probably would shorten the war considerably, the decisions as to whether to go in, and at what stage, would be made independently of the United States. Further, Stimson said, the Soviet Union unilaterally could acquire the rights set down in the Yalta agreement. After further exchanges, all three cabinet heads agreed that the United States should adhere to Yalta while seeking assurance that Stalin would respect the rights of China. Truman carried out the latter recommendation by instructing Harry Hopkins to review the Far Eastern situation when he talked with the Soviet leader in Moscow. The president's largest concern, however, was "getting as early a date as possible on Russia's entry into the war against Japan."[4]

Hopkins raised the subject of the Far East during his third session with Stalin on May 28. He began by saying that General George C.

Marshall and Fleet Admiral Ernest J. King were anxious to learn when the Soviet Union would enter the war. Stalin replied that his armies would be ready by August 8 (three months after V-E Day), but the date operations would begin hinged upon agreement with China confirming Soviet rights in the Yalta accord. This was necessary to justify the move "in the eyes of the Soviet people." Both were agreed that for security reasons the Chinese should not be informed of the Yalta agreement until Foreign Minister T. V. Soong visited Moscow in early July. By that time, Stalin said, Soviet troop movements would have become obvious to the Japanese.

Stalin discussed the problem of how to deal with Japan. Presumably referring to the forthcoming meeting of the Big Three at Potsdam, he said that talks would have to be held about zones of operations for the armies, zones of occupation, and the question of unconditional surrender. When Hopkins asked about the latter, Stalin replied that although one could argue in favor of conditional surrender out of expediency, in the long run "unconditional surrender which would destroy the military potential of Japan would be better." He advocated abolishing the imperial office as a means of ensuring lasting peace. The emperor was little more than a figure head, but might be succeeded "by an energetic and vigorous figure who could cause trouble." Stalin stressed the need to crush Japan's military potential; for that reason, overtures for peace with conditions should be spurned. He did suggest the possibility that the Allies could pretend to accept a conditional surrender but then impose "successively harsher terms" when they were in a position to do so. This he described as "unconditional surrender by stages."[5]

When conversation shifted to China, Ambassador Harriman, who accompanied Hopkins to the sessions, took the lead. He had attended the Roosevelt-Stalin meeting at Yalta about the Far East and had helped draft what became the accord. Harriman reminded Stalin of Truman's statement to Molotov in Washington that he intended to carry out all of FDR's commitments. The marshal replied that he appreciated this, but the Chinese were involved. Harriman then stated that "it was obvious that the Soviet Union would re-assume Russia's historic position in the Far East"—for that reason, both nations should settle political and economic matters by "mutual agreement." As an example, he cited America's policy of the Open Door.

Stalin's responses to Harriman and to a few comments Hopkins made could have come straight from a U.S. position paper. He said the United States must play "the largest part" in helping China get back on its feet because only the United States had the capital to be of assistance. He emphasized that the Soviet Union had no territorial designs on Manchuria, Outer Mongolia, or anywhere else. He was committed to unification of China and thought Chiang, as "the best of the lot," was the only one who could bring it. He was prepared to allow Chiang to set up an administration as quickly as possible in Manchuria or anyplace else Soviet armies entered. Harriman thanked him for answering "so clearly and frankly" and assured him that "there was no intention on our part as far as he knew" to alter FDR's policy of unconditional surrender. Before the discussion turned to other matters, Hopkins brought up Korea, which he said the United States believed should be under a trusteeship consisting of the Soviet Union, the United States, Great Britain, and China. Stalin said he "fully agreed."[6]

In reporting what had taken place during the discussion, Hopkins ended a cable with the remark "We were very encouraged by the conference on the Far East." So was President Truman. A few days later, in the middle of one of Henry Stimson's lectures on the significance of the atomic bomb in relations with the USSR, Truman asked whether the secretary had heard what Hopkins had accomplished. Stimson said he had not, and Truman explained that according to Hopkins, "there was a promise in writing by Stalin that Manchuria would remain fully Chinese except for a ninety-nine-year lease of Port Arthur and the settlement of Dairen which we had hold of." Whether Truman spoke in error or Stimson got it wrong in his diary is unclear, for there was nothing "in writing" except Bohlen's notes of the conversation. Truman's enthusiasm, however, is unmistakable. To Stimson's warning that "fifty-fifty control" of the railways would make the USSR the dominant power, the president replied "he realized that but the promise was perfectly clear and distinct."[7]

Hopkins's talks must have encouraged Truman to believe that dealing with Stalin was the best approach. In response to Hopkins's cables about Asian matters, the president said he would inform Foreign Minister Soong, then at San Francisco, that Stalin wanted to see him not later than July 1 and that the United States would provide air transportation. When Soong arrived in Moscow, Truman added, the Yalta accord would be revealed to Chiang. Unless this cable and his subsequent actions constituted a charade (for which no evidence has yet been found), Truman wanted Sino-Soviet agreement before the Potsdam Conference in order to get the Soviet Union into the Pacific war at the earliest possible date. In short, he sought Sino-Soviet accord before atomic diplomacy in any form could be used to influence the settlement in behalf of U.S. interests.[8]

Stettinius in San Francisco was to tell Soong that Stalin wanted him to go to Moscow for discussion of important matters and that the president wanted to see him first. How much Soong knew about the Yalta accord is uncertain, but Ambassador Hurley already had informed Chiang in fairly specific terms about Soviet desires in the Far East. Soong was aware that Hopkins had raised the subject in his talks with Stalin. He tried to pry more information out of Stettinius. The secretary asked Truman for permission to speak freely so as to avoid later charges of deception, but was turned down. If Soong was apprehensive as he flew to Washington, he had good reason.[9]

Apparently Truman did not decide how much to tell the foreign minister until the last minute. While Soong was en route, the president had Grew ask Stettinius's advice, which was the same as before: full disclosure. Truman may have been influenced by word from Hurley that a Soviet official had discussed Chinese affairs with Chiang a few days earlier. In any event, when Soong met the president and others on June 9, Truman informed him fully as to Soviet-U.S. agreements, although in a peculiar way. He confined his remarks to optimistic generalities about Soviet intentions. Then he showed the foreign minister a message that Hurley was to reveal to Chiang on June 15. It listed seven points constituting the "understanding" Hopkins had reached with Stalin, and it repeated verbatim Soviet demands set down in the Yalta accord. Truman also instructed Hurley: "Inform Chiang Kai-shek that President Roosevelt at Yalta agreed to support these Soviet claims upon the entry of Russia in the war against Japan. I [Truman] am also in agreement."[10] Soong did not receive a copy of the agreement reached at Yalta, but Grew later gave him a paraphrased version. Probably Truman followed this procedure in order to give Soong the facts without formally revealing the Yalta accord before June 15.

Some of the points, such as the lease on Port Arthur, Soong found objectionable on their face. The word "lease" was anathema to the Chinese because it recalled territorial impositions inflicted on them by other powers in the past. Equally disconcerting was his inability to extract from the Americans their interpretation of vague but ominous phrases. What was meant by Soviet "preeminent interests" with regard to Dairen and the connecting railroads? As Soong had told Stettinius, without U.S. support China was helpless in dealing with the Soviet Union. He believed it essential, for the purpose of negotiating with Stalin, to have some sense of what the United States considered reasonable constructions of Soviet claims. An American president had signed the Yalta accord, after all without China's participation. Now the Chinese had to know the limits of what they were expected to concede.[11]

Soong failed to get commitments of any kind. He talked with Grew several times and had another meeting with Truman on June 14, but both officials refused to say more than that the United States adhered to the Yalta accord and details would have to be worked out with the Soviet Union. They were telling him he would have to do the best he could, without U.S. backing. There are two possible explanations for this otherwise puzzling coyness on the part of U.S. officials. Truman may have regarded Stalin's support of Chiang as so crucial as to warrant compromising Chinese sovereignty over Manchuria. Or, believing he had Stalin's pledge to respect the Open Door, he may have been unwilling to jeopardize other issues. His answer to Stimson's earlier warning that even fifty-fifty control of the railways would make the USSR the dominating power bears repeating: "He said he realized that but the promise [of an Open Door] was perfectly clear and distinct."

Soong flew to Chungking for consultations before proceeding to Moscow. Meanwhile, Hurley presented the message Soong had been permitted to read during his first meeting with Truman. A Soviet diplomat already had given Chiang the text of the Yalta accord. Through Hurley, Chiang suggested that the United States and Britain participate in all agreements between China and the Soviet Union and that Port Arthur be designated a joint naval base of the four powers. Suspicious of Soviet intentions, the Chinese wanted Britain and the United States to act as guarantors. Truman turned down these proposals. After discussions with Chiang and other officials, in some of which Hurley participated, Soong left for Moscow.[12]

Chinese misgivings were fully realized when Soong began negotiations with Stalin and Molotov. Stalin emphasized that all outstanding issues had to be settled before he could sign a treaty of friendship. To Soong's dismay, the Soviet leader began by demanding that China recognize the independence of the People's Republic of Mongolia. At one session, he handed the foreign minister drafts of three treaties: the coveted pact of alliance, one covering the disposition of Dairen and Port Arthur, and another pertaining to railroads. The latter two called for such extreme concessions that Soong tried to give them all back. But at Molotov's prodding, he kept them and transmitted their contents to Chungking.[13]

The part of the Yalta accord pertaining to Outer Mongolia had said only that the status quo "shall be preserved." Outer Mongolia had maintained de facto independence for decades, but China never had acknowledged it. Soong interpreted the Yalta agreement to mean what it said—that his government take no steps to alter the situation. If Chiang agreed to recognize independence by executive act, he told Stalin, the regime would fall.

Stalin's terms for Manchuria were equally onerous. They provided for a Soviet military zone that would include not only Port Arthur and environs but also Dairen, which the Yalta accord had said would be "internationalized." The railroads (and related properties such as coal mines, timberlands, and factories) would be owned and managed by the Soviet Union.

Chiang desired Stalin's support, of course, as well as acknowledgment of China's "full sovereignty" over Manchuria. On other matters, negotiations stood far apart. The Nationalists were unwilling to recognize the independence of Outer Mongolia, Chiang said, although he offered a plebiscite after the war. He wanted Dairen excluded from the Soviet military zone and administered as a free port by the Chinese. Ownership of railroads should remain with China, and management should be vested in a joint Sino-Soviet company. Harriman believed the disputes could not be resolved unless the United States took part in the negotiations. He recommended that the United States prepare its own interpretation of the Yalta accord and present it to Stalin at Potsdam. Although Soong had several sessions with Stalin during which both sides made concessions, differences over Manchuria were too great to be bridged. At bottom, the issue was which phrase in the Yalta accord should prevail—Soviet "preeminent interests," as Stalin defined them, or China's "full sovereignty." Soong left Moscow on July 14 with no agreement in hand.[14]

The U.S. role in Soong's negotiations with Stalin should be made clear. Both Truman and Byrnes had informed the Chinese that the United States would not act as interpreter of the Yalta accord. All they were willing to say was that they supported the agreement, stood for an Open Door, and wished to be consulted before settlements were made. Writers have cited this as evidence that their real purpose was to stall negotiations until such time as the nuclear bomb dealt the United States a stronger hand in negotiations. If so, they neglected to inform Ambassador Harriman, who met with Soong almost daily in Moscow.

In reality, Harriman acted as Soong's adviser. He offered the foreign minister as his own opinions views he knew were congenial to Truman and Byrnes. These he reported in cables marked "Personal and top secret for the President and Secretary of State." He urged concessions on the part of the Chinese. Concerning Port Arthur and Dairen, he told Soong that Chiang "was being unrealistic in not conceding more liberal rights and privileges to the Soviets." "I urged Soong not to come to an impasse with Stalin," he stated in the same cable. "I again pointed out to him the great advantages to the National Government in coming to an agreement with the Soviet Government prior to the entry of Soviet troops into Manchuria and the serious consequences which otherwise might result."[15] The idea that Truman and Byrnes would have allowed Harriman to proffer such advice if their goal was to delay agreement cannot be sustained.

At Potsdam, Stalin brought up Far Eastern matters when he and Molotov visited Truman and Byrnes at the Little White House before the first plenary session. He reaffirmed Soviet readiness to enter the war against Japan by mid-August, providing Sino-Soviet deliberations had been concluded satisfactorily. He reviewed the negotiations, saying that he thought Soong "understood the Russian position better than Chungking." He discussed the assurances he had given Soong about Soviet support for "one government," noninterference in Chinese affairs, and China's sovereignty over Manchuria. When Byrnes asked about differences, Stalin alluded to Port Arthur, Dairen, and the railroads. The Chinese were trying to circumvent Soviet interests, he claimed, emphasizing the reasonableness of the Soviet position.

After an exchange between Byrnes and Stalin regarding the latter's proposal on administration of Dairen, Truman asked what effect this would have on U.S. rights. Stalin replied that the port would be free and open to all nations. The president remarked that this meant the Open Door. Byrnes reverted to the negotiations in general—that agreements conforming to Yalta would be acceptable, but if any exceeded the accord, that "would create difficulties." Stalin denied any such intent, protesting that Soviet desires were "more liberal" than the Yalta agreement because technically it entitled them to demand all the rights held by the czarist government. He said the Chinese were at fault because they did not understand "horse trading" and did not seem to be "aware of the big picture." Neither Truman nor Byrnes disputed Stalin, and both made it clear that the "main interest" of the United States was in a free port at Dairen. Concluding the discussion, Stalin referred to Outer Mongolia with the remark that the Chinese "could not lose what they did not have."[16]

It is only slight exaggeration to say that this conversation revealed all one needed to know about what Truman hoped to achieve through the Sino-Soviet negotiations. Stalin had reaffirmed his promise to enter the war against Japan, which the president very much wanted. "He'll be in the Jap War on August 15th," he wrote in his diary with obvious satisfaction. "Fini Japs when that comes about." With regard to China, the Soviet leader had gone on at length about his commitment to the unification of China under Chiang. This also pleased Truman, who noted that "most of the big points are settled." As for Manchuria, neither the president nor Byrnes raised objection to the Soviet position although they did emphasize the importance they attached to an Open Door at Dairen. The price China would have to pay in Manchuria, let alone in Outer Mongolia, appeared not to faze them. These simply

were not "big points." Stimson dined at the Little White House that
evening and complained in his diary that the large number of guests,
coupled with the noise of a military band outside, left "no opportunity
for business." Despite such obstacles, Truman managed to tell him
briefly about the meeting "and said he thought that he had clinched
the Open Door in Manchuria."[17]

The significance Truman and Byrnes placed upon an Open Door
in Manchuria should be placed in perspective. Although U.S. economic
interests were involved, neither the president nor the secretary of state
seems to have had the remotest idea, or very much concern, about
the potential for trade in the region—which in any case was not large.
Their devotion to the subject came out of immediate and practical
considerations. They did not want to be placed in a position in which
they could be accused of having sacrificed a historic U.S. foreign policy.
Byrnes's papers contain a memorandum by an adviser a week after
the meeting with Stalin, which so accurately describes the political
situation as to be quoted at length:

> It might also be argued that the expedient of a resumption of a special
> Russian position in Manchuria having been conceded at Yalta, the present
> differences between the Russians and the Chinese in regard to the agree-
> ments are of minor importance. But the situation is not likely to be so
> regarded by the American public, a large section of which is profoundly
> interested in China and in safeguarding the American position in China.
> They will be critical of any concessions beyond the Yalta commitments;
> and they will expect reservations safeguarding American interests in the
> face of these commitments.

The memorandum recommended a formal agreement between the United
States and the USSR recognizing the Open Door in Manchuria. According to the author, this would have "considerable political value"
in the likely event that the Sino-Soviet treaties when completed "are
made the occasion for public and press criticism of this administration."
Truman and Byrnes actively pursued this proposal until such time as
they believed the danger has passed.[18]

As for the thesis that Truman sought to delay Soviet entry into the
Pacific war by prolonging Sino-Soviet negotiations until after the bombs,
a message he sent to Chiang from Potsdam on July 23 often is cited.
Truman said: "I asked that you carry out the Yalta agreement, but I
had not asked you to make any concession in excess of that agreement.
If you and Generalissimo Stalin differ as to the correct interpretation
of the Yalta agreement, I hope you will arrange for Soong to return
to Moscow and continue your efforts to reach understanding." The

cable usually is presented as if its recommendation that negotiations be renewed constituted an effort to gain time by restraining the Chinese, who otherwise might accept the terms Stalin offered. The opposite was true. The message actually was a reply to pleas by both Soong and Chiang that the United States intercede with Stalin because they could make no further concessions. Soong's cable to Byrnes had asked that Harriman be informed of Soong's opinion that "I am convinced that we have gone as far as we possibly could in meeting Soviet demands. I tell you this in all candor, and you know how completely frank I have been with you."[19]

On July 25, Chiang cabled Truman that "we have gone to the limit to fulfill the Yalta formula, and may even have already gone beyond the limit that the Chinese people will support." He asked Truman to impress upon Stalin "the eminently reasonable stand we have taken, so that he will not insist on the impossible." In his message of July 23, Truman was not trying to restrain the Chinese—he was telling them once again that they would have to do the best they could with the Soviets. As the previously cited memorandum had warned, the administration would be widely condemned if it became known that Truman and Byrnes had condoned agreements that could be construed as having gone beyond the Yalta accord and compromised the Open Door.[20]

Byrnes actually had prepared the way for the "strategy of delay" myth. After the news from Alamogordo, he had become increasingly impressed with the bomb's potential for affecting diplomatic issues. His aide, Walter Brown, noted on July 20 that Byrnes "hopes Soong will stand firm and then Russians will not go to war. Then he feels Japan will surrender before Russia goes to war and this will save China." On July 28, Byrnes said the same thing to Secretary of the Navy Forrestal: "Byrnes said he was most anxious to get the Japanese affair over with before the Russians got in, with particular reference to Dairen and Port Arthur." He favored Soong's return to Moscow "in order to keep the conversations on the subject going." To neither individual did Byrnes indicate that the president agreed with this view. On the contrary, in reporting a conversation with Byrnes on July 24, Brown wrote that Truman "hopes Soong will return to Moscow and agreement can be reached with Stalin. JFB [Byrnes] still hoping for time, believing after atomic bomb Japan will surrender and Russia will not get in so much on the kill." In a book written in the 1950s, in which he defended himself against charges that he had been "soft" on communism, Byrnes transformed what had been his "hopes" that Soong would "stand firm" into a clever anti-Soviet strategy. However, he neglected to mention any such strategy in an earlier book that covered the same topic.[21]

Truman had the same reasons as Byrnes for exaggerating in his memoirs and elsewhere his fear about Soviet intentions, but he never claimed he wanted to prolong the Sino-Soviet negotiations. Indeed, he wanted them concluded as quickly as possible. What neither Byrnes nor more recent advocates of the "delay" thesis mention is that on the same day he expressed his hopes to Forrestal, Byrnes was directed by Truman to inform Soong that immediate steps should be taken to resume negotiations "in hope of reaching agreement."[22] Unless Soong was blessed with the power of telepathy, he could scarcely be expected to interpret this message as meaning anything other than what it said.

From his diary and what he told others, it seems clear that Truman was more inclined than Byrnes to carry out commitments and to believe Stalin would live up to his. The day the cable was sent to Soong and Byrnes talked with Forrestal, the latter noted that Truman at dinner had said he "found Stalin not difficult to do business with." Trust Stalin or not, there were excellent reasons for wanting a Sino-Soviet accord wrapped up. On the morning of July 23, Truman had told Stimson he was "very anxious" to learn General Marshall's opinion as to whether the Soviets were any longer needed in the war. That afternoon, Stimson put the question to Marshall, who replied that they were not: The buildup of their forces along the Manchurian border already had the desired effect of pinning down Japanese troops. "But he pointed out that even if we went ahead in the war without the Russians and compelled the Japanese to surrender to our terms, that would not prevent the Russians from marching into Manchuria anyhow and striking, thus permitting them to get virtually what they wanted in the surrender terms."[23] If this happened before Sino-Soviet negotiations were concluded, Stalin would be unhindered by any agreement at Yalta about the Far East.

Harriman, rarely accused of optimism about Soviet intentions, stressed the need for a speedy conclusion of negotiations. Having traveled to Potsdam from Moscow immediately following suspension of the Soong-Stalin talks, he was apprehensive about what would happen absent an agreement. "Although it may not be desirable for us at this time to show any concern over the question of Russia's entry into the war against Japan," he wrote, "it would seem there are substantial advantages in the reestablishment of friendly relations between the Soviet Union and China, particularly the agreement that the Soviet Government will support the Chinese National Government as the unifying force in China."[24]

According to Harriman, Stalin would not deviate significantly from the terms he had offered Soong. There were only two ways to prevent the negotiations from breaking down. Either Soong would have to retreat, "contrary to the interests of the United States," or the United States would have to present its own interpretation of the Yalta accord when the talks resumed. On July 31, he recommended that he inform Stalin that Roosevelt at Yalta had insisted Dairen be internationalized as a free port; that the United States would not agree to have it in the Soviet military zone; and that if Stalin refused Chinese administration of the port, the United States proposed to have it run by a four-power international commission.[25]

All of Harriman's proposals pertained to Dairen. As he put it, "the differences regarding the operation of the railroads are not as fundamental." He might have added "to the United States"—Truman and Byrnes had told Stalin that Dairen was a symbol of the Open Door, "the main interest" of the United States. Harriman included the draft of a U.S.-Soviet understanding providing for the Open Door. It was virtually identical to the one alluded to by an adviser as having "political value" if Sino-Soviet agreements "are made the occasion for public and press criticisms of the administration." Whatever Byrnes's predilections, he authorized that Harriman's recommendations and the draft understanding be conveyed as instructions to Harriman on August 5. The secretary stressed obtaining a statement from Stalin about the Open Door so that it might be published at the same time as the Sino-Soviet agreements. "This would go far to dispel misunderstanding," he said, "as our public opinion is much opposed to any arrangements which might be construed to prejudice our historic open door policy."[26]

A summary of the case for concluding rather than prolonging the Chinese-Soviet negotiations is in order. As General Marshall had pointed out, the Soviets could join the war when they chose, regardless of U.S. actions or conclusion of a pact with the Chinese. Once in, they could attain "virtually what they pleased in the surrender terms." Dropping the bombs on Japan constituted no deadline beyond which the Russians would be stymied. It almost certainly would have triggered them into an immediate declaration of war and sent them into Manchuria. A Japanese capitulation before Sino-Soviet agreement was reached would render the Yalta accord inapplicable. The Soviet Union would be under no obligation to recognize China's "full sovereignty" over Manchuria— let alone an Open Door—or to support Chiang's regime.

Marshall's prediction proved accurate. The first atomic bomb was dropped on Hiroshima on August 6, 1945. Two days later, Molotov informed the Japanese ambassador that the Soviet Union would "consider itself at war with Japan" the following day. On August 9, Soviet armies launched a three-pronged invasion of Manchuria, and a second bomb was dropped on Nagasaki. Japan on the tenth issued a conditional acceptance of the Potsdam Declaration. The U.S. reply laid down terms that the Japanese did not accept until the fourteenth. Within this context, Sino-Soviet negotiations resumed.[27]

The second round of talks between Soong and Stalin began on August 7, the day after Hiroshima. Harriman had been correct in believing that Stalin would not modify his demands—if anything, he escalated them. He insisted that Dairen be within the Soviet military zone, which would be larger than that held by czarist Russia. The port and city should be managed by a Soviet official, security maintained by Russian police. At the same time, the wording he proposed for the Sino-Soviet Treaty of Friendship and Alliance had become alarmingly vague about obligations to support Chiang's government.[28]

Soong's position was weak; it became weaker as Soviet troops in Manchuria pushed southward. Stalin pointed out that the longer negotiations dragged on, the greater the danger that Chinese Communist forces would move into Manchuria. Soong probably would have capitulated had not Harriman entered protests against Soviet conditions. Following the instructions he had requested at Potsdam and newer ones cabled from Washington, he urged the Soviets to moderate their terms regarding Dairen, which in the U.S. view far exceeded any reasonable interpretation of the Yalta accord. He argued for precise wording about Soviet obligations in the Treaty of Friendship and submitted a proposal of adherence to the Open Door. On the latter, Stalin at first said "This shall be done," but then did nothing about it.[29]

The Sino-Soviet agreements were signed on August 14, the same day Japan accepted surrender terms. Stalin made a few concessions, but the Chinese conceded a great deal more. Despite U.S. protests, Dairen was included in the Soviet military zone, in return for promise not to exercise military authority there in time of peace. Control of railways and related industries would be in Russian hands. The Treaty of Friendship, again despite U.S. protests, still contained ambiguous language about Soviet responsibilities to support the Nationalist government. Soong justified acceptance to Harriman with the comment that, in the end, it was "a matter of good faith." To Harriman's inquiry about a statement on the Open Door, Molotov replied that Stalin now believed the accords just signed so obviously implied such principles as to render a separate document unnecessary.[30]

When the Sino-Soviet agreements were made public two weeks later, the administration kept a low profile. In a press conference, Byrnes—

without acknowledging any responsibility—referred to the settlements as "an important step forward." The United States had not taken part officially in the negotiations, and the Yalta Far Eastern accord remained a secret. Meanwhile, behind the scenes, Harriman had been instructed to pursue the matter of Soviet adherence to the Open Door. Truman and Byrnes wanted insurance against criticism that they had permitted the Soviet Union to violate a U.S. policy. Instead, doubtless to their relief, press response to the Sino-Soviet treaties was overwhelmingly favorable. Once the threat of negative response had passed, they simply abandoned their efforts to extract a public statement from Stalin.[31]

Roosevelt had purchased Stalin's promise at Yalta to enter the Pacific war for a price China would have to pay. His largest concern was to save American lives in a conflict the military estimated might last eighteen months after defeat of Germany and require an invasion of the Japanese home islands. But the Chinese Nationalists stood to receive something of great value in return for concessions in Manchuria. Stalin offered to recognize Chiang's regime and to refrain from succoring its potent opposition. Roosevelt assumed this would be an attractive offer to the Nationalists because their government's continued existence might depend on it. From the time he took office, Harry Truman carried out the Far Eastern accord. Even though the atomic bombs might render Soviet help in the war less important, Soviet support for Chiang remained crucial. Truman understood this support would not come free. To get it, he was willing to concede Soviet domination of Manchuria provided the USSR agreed to maintain the Open Door—or the appearance of an Open Door—because he was far more worried about domestic reactions than the marginal economic interests involved. The problem was that his and Roosevelt's wartime policies now became hostages to the public's concern for relations with the Soviet Union. Over that he had little control.

NOTES

1. *Foreign Relations of the United States, The Conferences at Malta and Yalta, 1945* (Washington, D.C., 1955), p. 984.

2. For Harriman's views, see Minutes of Secretary's Staff Committee, April 21, Box 304, Notter File; Kennan's cable is in *United States Relations with China,* Department of State Publication 3573, pp. 96–97; Stettinius cable in *FRUS, 1945* (Washington, D.C., 1967), VII, pp. 344–345.

3. *FRUS, 1945,* VII, pp. 869–870.

4. Stimson's reply to Grew memorandum, May 21, is in Vol. 7, Grew Papers; Truman's quotation from Harry S. Truman, *Year of Decisions* (Garden City, N.Y.: Doubleday, 1955), p. 264.

5. *FRUS, The Conference of Berlin (The Potsdam Conference), 1945* (Washington, D.C., 1960), I, pp. 41–44.

6. *FRUS, Potsdam,* I, pp. 45–47.

7. June 6, Stimson Diary.

8. Truman to Hopkins, May 31, *FRUS, 1945,* VII, p. 891.

9. *FRUS, 1945,* VII, pp. 893–894.

10. Memorandum of conversation, June 9; cable to Hurley, June 9; *FRUS, 1945,* VII, pp. 896–898.

11. Grew memorandum of conversation with Soong, June 11, Vol. 7, Grew Papers.

12. *FRUS, 1945,* VII, pp. 901–904.

13. Harriman's reports on his talks with Soong are in *FRUS, 1945,* VII, pp. 911–914, 915–917, 919–928, 932–934.

14. At Potsdam, Clark Kerr submitted to Eden a memorandum on his talk with Soong before the latter left Moscow. The negotiations showed, according to Kerr, that the Soviets "were trying to expand the text of the Agreement to their own advantage." The Chinese government did not care about Outer Mongolia, Soong had told him, which was "nothing but a sandy waste" inhabited by nomads, camels, and "shaggy ponies," but China would suffer loss of prestige if it yielded its claim to sovereignty under Soviet pressure. *Documents on British Policy Overseas* (London: Her Majesty's Stationery Office, 1984), pp. 364–367.

15. Harriman to Truman and Byrnes, July 9, Map Room Files, Truman Papers.

16. *FRUS, Potsdam,* II, pp. 1582–1587.

17. Truman remarks in diary entry, June 17, Robert H. Ferrell, ed., *Off the Record: The Private Papers of Harry S. Truman* (New York: Harper, 1980), p. 53; Stimson account of conversation, July 17, Stimson Diary.

18. Memorandum by John Carter Vincent, July 23, Folder 569(2), Byrnes Papers.

19. Truman cable, July 23, *FRUS, 1945,* VII, p. 950; Soong's message for Harriman is in Hurley to Byrnes, 19 July, Map Room Files, Truman Papers.

20. Chiang message in Hurley to Byrnes, 20 July, Map Room Files, Truman Papers.

21. Walter Brown notes, July 20, 24, Folder 602, Byrnes Papers; entry for July 28, Forrestal Diary, Vol. II. See James F. Byrnes, *All in One Lifetime* (New York: Harper, 1958), pp. 290–292; in his earlier *Speaking Frankly* (New York: Harper, 1947), Byrnes wrote (p. 208) that "I would have been satisfied had the Russians determined not to enter the war," but does not even suggest using Soong to pursue a strategy of delay.

22. *FRUS, Potsdam,* II, p. 1245.

23. Entry for July 23, Stimson Diary.

24. *FRUS, Potsdam,* II, p. 1244.

25. *FRUS, Potsdam,* II, pp. 1246–1247.

26. Byrnes to Harriman, August 5, Map Room Files, Truman Papers.

27. See Harriman to Truman and Byrnes, August 9, for report on Soviet military operations, Map Room Files, Truman Papers.

28. *FRUS, 1945,* VII, pp. 958–959.

29. *FRUS, 1945,* VII, pp. 960–965.

30. Soong remark is in *FRUS, 1945,* VII, pp. 967–969; Molotov explanation about Open Door, Harriman to Truman and Byrnes, August 14, Map Room Files, Truman Papers.

31. *FRUS, 1945,* VII, p. 981.

CHAPTER SEVEN

The Atomic Bomb: A New Dimension

The United States opened a new era in history when its air forces dropped atomic bombs on Hiroshima and Nagasaki in August 1945. This hitherto unimaginable force has since made it possible for the human race to destroy the planet on which it lives. The ghastliness of the situation has stimulated great debate about the origins of the nuclear arms race. Unfortunately, though dressed in academic regalia, many of the contributions to this debate bear less resemblance to historical inquiry than to prosecutors' briefs designed to convict the accused. And since the United States was the first power to possess nuclear weapons, Truman, Byrnes, and other U.S. officials have been duly rounded up as suspects. The case is loaded by the fact that, given the circumstances, almost any alternative can easily appear preferable to the one chosen at a specific time. It should be remembered that Truman and Byrnes were not blessed with hindsight or the minds of philosophers. They were pragmatic leaders of limited vision trying to cope with a situation for which there was no precedent.

The development of the atomic program, which President Roosevelt authorized early in the war, has been treated at length. Initially, the fear was that Germany, where nuclear fission had been discovered in 1938, would be the first nation to construct bombs and use them. As early as 1943, however, recommendations were made within committees formed to study the subject that Japan rather than Germany should be the target. There were two reasons for this suggestion, neither of which had to do with racism. First, if Germany had bombs or shortly would have them, it would retaliate. Second, a dud might provide German scientists with the necessary technical information to construct a workable bomb. The Japanese were a safer bet because it was correctly assumed that they had no viable nuclear program.[1]

Although President Roosevelt discussed nuclear matters with some of his advisers, a few scientists, and Churchill, there is no indication that he had any plan about the bomb's role in the war or after. It was characteristic of him to keep options open—to avoid hard choices until they had to be made. His penchant for telling others what he thought they wanted to hear makes it difficult to determine his state of mind at any time. There are few documents, the last being a memorandum he and Churchill signed at Hyde Park in September 1944. In it they agreed that no steps would be taken to reach international agreement about control and use of atomic energy and that Anglo-American collaboration in developing it "for military and commercial use" should continue after defeat of Japan. "The matter should continue to be regarded as of the utmost secrecy," it stated, "but when a 'bomb' is finally available, it might perhaps, after mature consideration, be used against the Japanese, who should be warned that this bombardment will be repeated until they surrender."[2]

Truman claimed that he first learned about the atomic program from FDR himself during the summer of 1944, not after he became president as he wrote in his memoirs. The timing is of little matter. Merely knowing of the program provided no guide to Roosevelt's intentions, if indeed any had crystallized by the time of his death. Nor would the Hyde Park aide-mémoire, brought to Truman's attention in late June 1945, have made much difference had he known of it earlier. The part of it that rejected an international agreement in favor of secrecy would have been superfluous: Roosevelt had made no overtures to Stalin either in writing or at Yalta. As for the statement about possibly using the bomb against the Japanese, Truman arguably may have been unwise or immoral in acting as he did, but certainly the matter received "mature consideration."

Until the end of his life, Truman professed to no doubts about dropping nuclear bombs on Japan. He regarded them as military weapons, he said, which could save both American and Japanese lives. But things were not that simple. From diary entries and letters, it is clear that he glimpsed the enormity of what was to be unleashed, particularly after he learned the magnitude of the test explosion in New Mexico.[3] It is inconceivable, furthermore, that he did not speculate about the weapon's future role in world affairs with reference to the Soviet Union. Unfortunately, given the fragmentary nature of his testimony on the subject, it is impossible to trace his thinking. Scholars have sought to get around this obstacle by trying to reconstruct his attitudes through the diaries and recollections of others. A tricky process at best, in Truman's case this approach has led to many questionable assertions.

The advisers Truman inherited had markedly differing opinions about atomic matters, and some changed their views over time. Byrnes, as director of the Office of War Mobilization, had been most concerned about how to justify to Congress and the public the enormous expenditures if there were no positive results. Later, as secretary of state, his belief in the bomb as a diplomatic weapon seems to have exceeded Truman's. They undoubtedly talked about the matter, but no records of their conversations have been found. Admiral Leahy, unswervingly anti-Soviet, doubted "the thing" would work. Joseph E. Davies, who enjoyed access to Truman even though holding no official position, was just as staunchly pro-Soviet. Neither Stettinius nor Hopkins appears to have contributed anything on the matter: Stettinius left for San Francisco two weeks after Truman took office, and the desperately ill Hopkins faded from the scene upon returning from Moscow.

Finally, there was Henry L. Stimson, in whose hands rested overall direction of the atomic program. Stimson devoted a great deal of attention to the issues involved, conveyed his ideas to Truman frequently, and best of all, recorded the discussions in his diaries, which have provided the richest source for Truman's views. Stimson was seventy-seven years old when Truman became president. His health was precarious, his energies limited. He left day-to-day management of the War Department to subordinates and spent irregular hours in his office. Freed from the crush of bureaucratic detail, he had time to concentrate on the bomb and its implications. By the time of Roosevelt's death, when it was assumed the weapon would be available in only a few months, he seems to have thought of little else. He began to refer to it privately as "my secret."[4]

Although Stimson had revised his thinking several times, his advice to Truman during the weeks before Potsdam was to postpone controversial issues until the bomb had been "laid on" Japan. The awesome destructiveness of the weapon, he believed, would give the United States great leverage in negotiations with the Soviet Union. He never proposed threatening the Russians—he wanted to use the prospects of sharing basic scientific information as a quid pro quo for concessions on other issues. Presenting his views to the president, he often referred to the secret in such quotable terms as the "master card" or a "royal straight flush." His phrases, as well as his obsession with the bomb, appear in many accounts as though they reflect Truman's own convictions.[5]

Truman unfailingly showed Stimson great deference. He would hear out what the older man had to say, rarely interrupt, and as often as not thank him for taking time. On purely military or procedural matters, he usually gave approval to Stimson's recommendations. On the broader question of dealing with the Soviet Union, however, Truman responded differently, though still with tact. He tended to reply in a vaguely approving manner, indicating without committing himself that he had been thinking along the same lines or that Stimson probably had the right idea.[6]

The secretary may be pardoned for confusing courtesy with agreement, but historians should know better. Far from heeding Stimson's advice to postpone negotiation on controversial issues, Truman did the opposite. He tried vigorously to resolve the most divisive ones of all— Poland, reparations, and the Far East—not only before any atomic bombs could be "laid on" Japan, but even before a test was scheduled.

The truth is that although Truman listened patiently to Stimson's views about how to deal with the USSR, he rarely solicited them. He neither asked the secretary's opinion about sending Hopkins to Moscow nor kept him informed about the negotiations. Stimson had to embarrass Truman into inviting him to attend the Potsdam Conference. Less than a week before the presidential party was to depart, "I asked him to tell me frankly whether he was afraid to ask me to come to those meetings on account of the fear that I could not take the trip. He laughed and said 'Yes', that was just it; that he wanted to save me from over-exertion at this time." Truman apparently wanted to save him from participating in what was being done at the conference. Stimson was excluded from strategy meetings held at the Little White House, and his request that Assistant Secretary of War John J. McCloy be included in the plenary sessions was turned down. Halfway through Potsdam, the secretary had to appeal to Truman that he at least be permitted to "drop in early every morning and talk with him or Byrnes of the events of the preceding day."[7] Stimson's diaries contain a great deal of valuable information, but serve as a poor guide to Truman's thoughts about the role of the atomic bomb in U.S. diplomacy.

Although he had mentioned the subject to Truman after a cabinet meeting held on the day the latter was sworn in, Stimson did not talk at length about nuclear matters until he met with the new president on April 25. Then, using a memorandum written by subordinates, he tried to impress upon Truman the weapon's potential impact on world affairs. The points he raised included relations with the Soviet Union, the possibility of an arms race, and the need for international control to avoid future atomic wars. Solutions had to be found, he said, "to bring the world in a pattern in which the peace of the world and our civilization can be saved."[8] Stimson suggested no policies at this time, either on using the bomb against Japan or its bearings on relations with the USSR. He did ask the president to approve an advisory committee. Truman agreed.

What came to be known as the Interim Committee first met early in May. With Stimson as chairman, it included representatives of the State and Navy departments, three men of scientific background whose prestige stemmed as much from administrative positions at universities and institutes (in other words, "practical" scientists), and Byrnes as President Truman's personal representative. In addition, there was a scientific panel of three physicists, who directed the nuclear projects at Chicago, Berkeley, and Los Alamos, and the distinguished Enrico Fermi, who had presided over the first nuclear chain reaction in 1942.[9]

The Interim Committee examined a number of questions involving the future of nuclear energy and weapons. Two are of particular importance. The first had to do with using a nuclear bomb (or bombs) to shorten the war. There was no real debate over whether this weapon should be used if it became available before Japan surrendered; discussion centered on how it should be employed. Three options were considered: a demonstration in an uninhabited area, to which representatives of Japan and other nations would be invited; bombing a target in Japan, but only after warning so that inhabitants could be evacuated; and bombing with no warning. The first option was rejected on the ground that a dud would make the U.S. threat appear empty, while even an impressive explosion would not force Japanese militarists into accepting surrender. The second had drawbacks: A dud would be just as embarrassing, the Japanese might move large numbers of prisoners of war into the area, and they would make every effort to destroy the mission in flight. The committee's recommendation, concurred in by the scientific panel and conveyed to Truman, was that "the bomb should be used against Japan as soon as possible; that it be used on a war plant surrounded by workers' homes; and that it be used without prior warning."[10]

Viewed in military terms, the committee's advice can hardly be faulted. The greatest possible psychological shock would be administered to Japan if the bomb worked, and there would be no reaction if it did not. Nor would Japanese militarists be able to conceal or minimize the bomb's destructiveness because, as J. Robert Oppenheimer pointed out, the "visual effect" would make it impossible to claim the results were caused merely by a large-scale conventional strike.[11] Still, the idea of using such a weapon on "a war plant surrounded by workers' homes" in retrospect seems callous, even by the standards of World War II. Whether such a recommendation would have been made if Germany had been the target can never be known, even though many of its cities had been routinely bombed to rubble. It is fair to say that feelings against the Japanese as a people and a race made it easier for the committee and for Truman to countenance such an act. Barbarous conduct in China, the attack on Pearl Harbor, and such atrocities as the Bataan death march placed the Japanese apart from the Germans, only some of whom were Nazis. As Truman put it in his diary two weeks before Hiroshima, "The Japs are savages, ruthless, merciless, and fanatic."[12]

The Interim Committee took up the matter of whether to inform the Soviets. Byrnes argued against the idea, claiming that Stalin would ask to be brought "into the partnership." He proposed to push on as rapidly as possible "and at the same time make every effort to better our political relations with Russia." At first the committee accepted Byrnes's argument. In late June, after the scientific panel recommended disclosure, the committee reversed itself. It agreed unanimously that Truman should inform Stalin, but should provide no additional details if asked. When Stimson discussed the committee's suggestion with the president on July 3, the latter said "he thought that was the best way to do it." Truman followed all the committee's recommendations except this one. He told Stalin that the United States had developed a powerful new weapon, but in the face of the latter's seeming indifference, did not go on to specify that it was nuclear.[13]

When news of the nuclear test explosion reached Potsdam, Truman set in motion events that led to the obliteration of Hiroshima and Nagasaki. One question looms in analyzing this decision: How close did he think Japan was to surrender? At one extreme is his own stated view, supported by others who participated in the decision, that he believed an invasion of the Japanese home islands was necessary. At the other is the contention that everyone in authority knew Japan had been trying to surrender for weeks and would have done so if only assurance had been given that the emperor would be retained. Even without such assurance, Japan would have had to give in unconditionally well before the first assault. Truman refused to accept an immediate surrender with qualifications or to wait for the inevitable collapse, according to this interpretation, because he welcomed the opportunity to stage a demonstration of the bomb's destructiveness. This show of force was not to impress the Japanese, who were defeated, but to impress the Soviets so as to render them more "manageable" in Eastern Europe and elsewhere and to end the war before they could move far into Manchuria.[14]

The war had long since been lost for Japan by the summer of 1945. It had been lost since Pearl Harbor, for that matter, provided the United States was willing to fight on. The Japanese did not have the resources, the industrial capacity, or the manpower to prevail over their enemy. The tide of expansion had been halted as early as the spring of 1942 by the battles of Coral Sea and Midway. Thereafter the Japanese were on the defensive, as thrusts through the Central and South Pacific brought the Americans closer to Japan proper. Meanwhile, submarines took an enormous toll on shipping, needed to sustain Japan's war machine.

Through the first six months of 1945, the Japanese position became increasingly untenable. U.S. forces recaptured the Philippines and pierced Japan's inner defensive ring by taking Okinawa, which lay 300 miles from the home islands. Surface vessels as well as submarines tightened the blockade. Air attacks by B-29s, at first ineffective, were systematically destroying cities. In mid-March, the most destructive conventional air attack in history was launched against Tokyo, a fire-bomb raid that left more than 80,000 dead. In April, the Soviet Union announced its intention not to renew the neutrality pact and began transferring troops to the Manchurian border. Germany's surrender in May meant that over the coming months the Allies could concentrate on the Pacific war.

A faction in the Japanese government had been looking for a way to end the war for some time. Baron Kantaro Suzuki, a retired admiral, was appointed premier in April with the understanding that he would try to terminate the war in a manner consistent with honor. The militant faction, representing the army and to a lesser extent the navy, was so formidable that he had to go to lengths to conceal his intentions under a cloud of "fight on to ultimate victory" rhetoric. Suzuki secured the appointment of a like-minded individual, Shigenori Togo, as foreign minister.[15]

Suzuki and Togo sought to enlist the Soviet Union as a mediator to obtain peace, doing so even in the face of reports that the USSR would soon enter the war against Japan. They hoped concessions they were prepared to offer—among them Sakhalin Island, the Kuriles, and a dominant position in Manchuria—would be sufficiently enticing to the Soviets. The Japanese did not know, of course, that Stalin at Yalta already had secured an Anglo-American commitment on these matters in return for his joining the war. Even so, the conditions they proposed were absurd under the circumstances. As late as July 11, Togo instructed the ambassador in Moscow, Naotaki Sato, to inform the Soviets that Japan "has absolutely no idea of annexing or holding the territories occupied as a result of the war." Struggling to remain deferential, Sato could not contain himself. He reminded Togo that "we have already lost Burma and the Philippines and even Okinawa, which is at the very tip of our Empire, has fallen into the hands of the enemy." He ridiculed the notion of offering to give up territories "we have already lost." It was useless to approach the Soviets with "pretty little phrases devoid of all connection with reality." He tried to convince his superiors that a negotiated peace was out of the question.[16]

On July 12, Togo cabled Sato to request that the Soviets receive Prince Fumimaro Konoye, special envoy from the emperor, who would inform them of conditions the Japanese sought and inducements they were willing to offer for Russia's good offices. Although Konoye could not reach Moscow before Stalin and Molotov left for Potsdam, Togo wanted negotiation to begin as soon as they returned. The Soviets refused to accept the mission, stating that its purpose was not clear and no proposals had been made. In the days following, Togo urged Sato to do his utmost to persuade the Soviets to receive Konoye, but refused to divulge particulars because it would be "disadvantageous and impossible from the standpoint of foreign and domestic considerations to make an immediate declaration of specific terms."[17] His reference to "domestic considerations" is important. Togo could not forward proposals because the army refused to accept that Japan was defeated, and there was no agreement over terms.

Much has been made of the Togo-Sato exchanges because they were made available to the U.S. government through code breaking. They have been used to show that Truman prolonged the war even though he knew Japan was trying to end it. The fact is that not one of the intercepted cables states that retention of the emperor was the sole obstacle to surrender. As shown, Togo was unable to inform Sato of any terms because of "foreign and domestic considerations." The Foreign Office also spurned Sato's simple advice: If the government sought peace, "we should inquire what the peace conditions will be."[18] How could U.S. officials interpret the cables as other than an effort to cut a deal with the Soviet Union that would spare Japan the consequences of defeat?

Could Truman have shortened the war by informing the Japanese, directly or through their representatives in Switzerland, that the institution of the emperor would survive in some form? Stimson and Grew advised such a course. But there were several arguments against this, none having to do with opportunity to use atomic bombs. The unconditional surrender formula had been announced by Roosevelt early in 1943, and he had given no indication of modifying it by the time of his death. Truman as recently as May 1945 had publicly declared a commitment to what had become a slogan of the war. Byrnes in particular seems to have advised that any deviation would appear to be a betrayal of FDR and would have serious domestic repercussions. Assistant Secretaries of State Archibald MacLeish and Dean Acheson, abetted by the retired Cordell Hull, argued that the imperial institution had to be abolished if Japan were to be democratized and prevented from taking the path of militarism in the future. Finally, there was the probability that any overture from the United States would appear to Japanese hard-liners as evidence of war-weariness and permit them to argue that resistance would bring further concessions.[19]

Critics who attribute Truman's actions to anti-Soviet motives fail to consider the alternatives. Had the United States tried to end the war by retreating from unconditional surrender, Stalin almost certainly would have seen an attempt to prevent the USSR from obtaining the goals set down in the Yalta accord. During his talks with Hopkins and Harriman, he had stated forcefully his reasons for wanting the institution of emperor abolished. Harriman had assured him that the United States would not deviate from unconditional surrender. To have gone back on this pledge would have invited a charge that the United States was preserving Japan as a counterweight to Russia. That is what anti-Soviet adviser Joseph C. Grew thought should be done. Stalin's accusations of betrayal over negotiations on the Italian front, fresh in everyone's mind, made it unlikely he would have accepted U.S. protests of innocence.[20]

Japan's response to the July 26 Potsdam Declaration also has stirred controversy. The declaration called upon Japan to end the war immediately or face "prompt and utter destruction." It gave assurance that although Japan's war-making potential would be eliminated and "stern justice meted out to all war criminals," there was no intention of enslaving the people or destroying the nation. After the stated objectives had been accomplished and a "peacefully inclined and responsible government" had been freely elected, the document proclaimed, occupation would end and eventual participation in world trade be permitted. The declaration did not state what would be done about the emperor. If the Allies meant to treat him as a war criminal, no responsible Japanese official could even consider surrender. Actually, the final point of the declaration called for unconditional surrender "of all Japanese armed forces" rather than of the nation. Perhaps this signified a willingness to leave the Japanese governmental system intact. The ambiguity was deliberate. If there was to be deviation from unconditional surrender, it must not appear as a sign of eroded American will but as a generous gesture to a defeated enemy.[21]

Japanese leaders began to discuss how to answer the declaration the day after it was released. Foreign Minister Togo, supported by Premier Suzuki, counseled moderation. Togo proposed a noncommittal reply, or none at all, thereby obtaining time to seek clarification of the declaration and to step up efforts to secure Soviet mediation. Military hard-liners insisted on rejection. At this late date, they still professed to welcome an invasion, which would enable Japan to inflict such losses as to gain a negotiated peace. Togo and Suzuki prevailed, or so they thought, in gaining the military's reluctant approval to make no announcement at all.[22]

There followed a disastrous leak to the press, whether or not deliberate not even the preeminent scholar of the subject, R.J.C. Butow, has been able to determine. In making his case to buy time, Suzuki had argued that the proper response to the Potsdam Declaration was to "mokusatsu" it, by which he meant withholding comment for the time. Unfortunately, the term has harsher connotations, among them "to kill with silence" and "to treat with silent contempt." The phrase appeared in the next day's newspapers in the more truculent sense, with one paper purporting to quote the government as saying that the Potsdam Declaration "is a thing of no great value." As the press was government-controlled, the Japanese people and the Allies naturally assumed that the stories represented the official position. If doubt remained, Suzuki eliminated it that afternoon at a press conference. Apparently bowing to the hard-liners, his prepared statement read as follows: "I consider the joint proclamation of the three powers to be a rehash of the Cairo declaration. The government does not regard it as a thing of any great value; the government will just ignore it. We will press forward resolutely to carry the war to a successful conclusion."[23]

The "mokusatsu" incident has caused confusion about the appropriateness of the U.S. response. Some writers, alluding to the term's meanings, have characterized the Japanese position as ambiguous and suggested that the least the United States should have done is sought clarification. One has gone so far as to claim that Truman deliberately interpreted the phrase in its most abusive sense and, despite evidence to the contrary, continued to do so to prolong the war until nuclear bombs could be used. The notion that he had the faintest clue as to what "mokusatsu" meant is amusing, and there is no evidence that he received from an interpreter a list of possible constructions from which to choose. In any event, Suzuki's statement at the press conference would have removed all doubts. Subsequent Japanese newspaper articles and radio broadcasts, presumably approved by the authorities, referred to the Potsdam Declaration as "ridiculous," "unforgivable," "impudent," and "insolent."[24]

Lacking access to the high counsels of the Japanese government, U.S. leaders were not aware of the details surrounding the press leak and Suzuki's subsequent reversal. Even if they had been, the inescapable conclusion would have been that the military had overruled the moderates. Equally important, although the Japanese continued to solicit

Soviet help, they made no overtures to the United States seeking a favorable construction of the Potsdam Declaration with regard to the emperor. This undercut the claim, conveyed to the Office of Strategic Services (OSS) by minor Japanese officials in Switzerland, that Suzuki's behavior at the press conference was for public consumption while his "real" position would be conveyed through other channels. In short, Truman had no good reason to construe the Japanese response as anything other than a flat rejection of the Potsdam Declaration.[25]

Regardless of the Japanese position during the days following receipt of the Potsdam statement, how much longer could they have withstood the destruction of shipping and the pounding from the air? Some have argued that dropping the bombs was superfluous because all Truman had to do was await Japan's collapse. The evidence to support this thesis is conjectural because the situation cannot be replicated. The later views of air force generals such as Curtis LeMay, for instance, can scarcely be taken seriously in light of their commitment to conventional bombing. Most often cited is the Strategic Bombing Survey, conducted after the war, which stated that "Japan would have surrendered even if the atomic bombs had not been dropped, even if Russia had not entered the war, and even if no invasion had been planned or contemplated."[26] But criticizing Truman through a document that did not exist at the time he made his decisions is to use retrospective analysis.

Truman had to proceed on a worst-case basis, and there was reason for him to do so. Advocates of air power had predicted that bombing alone would bring Germany to its knees. Despite years of destruction from the air, the Germans fought on until Hitler's death in his Berlin bunker. Why expect anything less from the Japanese? The recent experience at Okinawa was not encouraging. The United States had committed 300,000 troops to an island of 700 square miles. Still, it took from April 1 to late June to subdue the Japanese, who fought virtually to the last man. And the first large-scale use of kamikazes there raised an alarming specter of heavy losses of forces invading the home islands.

A month before Potsdam, Truman had approved plans for the final push against Japan. The schedule called for invasion of the southern island of Kyushu on November 1 and, assuming success, an assault against the main island of Honshu on March 1, 1946. Heavy losses were anticipated. General Marshall estimated 31,000 casualties, Admiral Leahy double that, during the first thirty days of fighting. There were two factors Truman thought might have sufficient effect to render these operations unnecessary: use of atomic bombs and Soviet entry into the war. But it seems clear he anticipated no early capitulation without either or both. On July 25, the day before he issued the Potsdam Declaration calling upon Japan to surrender, he noted in his diary, "I am sure they will not do that, but we will have given them the chance."[27]

Success of the test explosion did not make Truman's position as clear as later writers have made out. His first reaction was that such bombs alone would cause Japan to give up: "Believe Japs will fold up before Russia comes in. I am sure they will when Manhattan appears over their homeland." A week later he was less certain. Even though by that time he had received a description of the enormous destructiveness, there was no assurance a bomb would explode as had the testing device. He expressed doubts in his diary: "Anyway we 'think' we have found a way to cause a disintegration of the atom." And there was no guarantee bombs would have the desired effect if they did explode. Because of the uncertainty, Truman continued to attach great importance to Stalin's promise to enter the conflict. "I've gotten what I came for," he wrote Bess from Potsdam. "Stalin goes to war with no strings on it. . . . I'll say that we'll end the war a year sooner now, and think of the kids who won't be killed. That is the important thing now." Two days later, listing what he hoped would come out of the conference, he told her: "Then I want the Jap War won and I want both of 'em [the Soviet Union and Great Britain] in it." He wrote both letters after the nuclear test. Far from trying to forestall Soviet participation, he still welcomed it.[28]

Truman has been criticized for not waiting to use the bombs until after the USSR declared war. "Fini Japs when that comes about," he had written. It is possible that Soviet entry would have precipitated early surrender without the bombs because it would have ended Japan's hope of mediation and vastly increased the forces arrayed against it. Even so, and Truman could not be certain, there was no way of telling how long peace would take. Unaware of how the "mokusatsu" reply had come about, he could only assume Japanese resolution remained strong. If war continued for weeks or months because nuclear weapons were not used, he would have been responsible for American lives lost and for prolonging the misery of thousands of prisoners. Meanwhile, conventional bombing might well have taken as many lives as would atomic bombs.

Truman did not, as he later claimed, regard the atomic bomb as just another weapon. "We have discovered the most terrible bomb in the history of the world," he noted two weeks before Hiroshima. "It may be the first destruction prophesied in the Euphrates Valley era, after Noah and his fabulous ark."[29] After three and a half years of war against an enemy he regarded as barbaric, he was willing to do whatever necessary to end the fighting. The most obvious way to do this was to inflict upon Japan a rapid succession of blows to convince even the most recalcitrant that resistance was useless. These blows consisted of the two bombs available and of Soviet entry into the war.

The first bomb was exploded over Hiroshima early on the morning of August 6. Reports of the catastrophe reached Tokyo within an hour, but details were sketchy. At dawn the next morning, word was received that "the whole city of Hiroshima was destroyed by a single bomb." That afternoon the Japanese cabinet met to consider the country's position in light of this development. Moderates considered it the more reason to accept the Potsdam Declaration with the proviso that the emperor be retained. Some thought the bombing might be a blessing, hoping it would permit the military to surrender with honor against superior technology. That was not the case. Hard-liners claimed the bomb probably was not nuclear—that even if it were, the Americans probably lacked enough fissionable materials to make another and that even if they had another bomb, adverse world opinion would prevent them from using it. The hard-liners dismissed as propaganda U.S. broadcasts that the bomb was atomic and that more would be used. They insisted on conditions involving the method of surrender, occupation, and treatment of war criminals the moderates knew would be unacceptable to the United States. The meeting adjourned without decision.[30]

Two days later, the Supreme Council for the Direction of the War met. By this time, Soviet troops had launched an invasion of Manchuria and were making rapid progress against the once-powerful Kwantung army, by now bled of men and equipment. During the meeting, a report arrived that Nagasaki had been destroyed by another bomb. The argument that the United States had no more bombs, or would not use them if it had, disappeared. And there were rumors that Tokyo would be the target on August 12. In the face of all this, the military kept to its position and still talked of a decisive battle for the homeland that would force the Allies to negotiate. Only the emperor's personal intervention at an imperial conference later that day permitted the moderates to win: Japan offered to accept the Potsdam Declaration with the proviso that it "does not comprise any demand which prejudices the prerogatives of His Majesty as a Sovereign Ruler."[31]

U.S. monitors picked up Tokyo's broadcast message and sent it to President Truman early on the morning of August 10. He asked Admiral Leahy to summon Secretaries Byrnes, Stimson, and Forrestal to consider the response. Stimson, supported by Leahy, favored accepting the proposal, to facilitate an orderly surrender and to prevent chaos in Japan. Byrnes disagreed. As usual, he was concerned with political consequences. Anything short of unconditional surrender would result in the "crucifixion of the President." He was well aware that few Americans knew what role the emperor actually played in the Japanese government. For years propaganda had lumped Hirohito with Hitler and Mussolini as leaders of the Axis powers. The Potsdam Declaration had been issued when "we had no atomic bomb and Russia was not in the war," he pointed out, and to retreat now would invite a charge that a major war aim had been betrayed.[32]

A compromise was reached. Byrnes drafted a reply that "the authority of the Emperor and the Japanese government to rule the state shall be subject to the Supreme Commander of the Allied powers." In conformity with the Potsdam Declaration, he added that the "ultimate" form of government would be established "by the freely expressed will of the Japanese people." This placed the Allies in the position of dictating terms and deflecting criticism that the system responsible for the war was remaining.[33]

The proposed reply was transmitted to Britain, China, and the Soviet Union for approval. Chiang Kai-shek accepted it; the British suggested a minor change. But difficulties arose with the Soviets. Molotov gave Harriman "the definite impression that he was quite willing to have the war continue" and told him no answer could come until the following day. When Harriman insisted on haste, Molotov said he would try to speed things and a few hours later gave him the Soviet statement. Harriman found it unsatisfactory because a paragraph appeared to give the Soviets a veto on makeup of the proposed Allied High Command in Japan. In conversation, Molotov said he thought the High Command might consist of an American and a Russian, which Harriman knew Washington would reject. After consultation with Stalin, Molotov's secretary informed Harriman by telephone that there had been a misunderstanding and that the Soviet reply would be altered to meet the ambassador's objections. Harriman so informed Truman, and the Allied reply was transmitted to Japan through the Swiss embassy. Its contents were broadcast in order that the Japanese be apprised of it quickly.[34]

Byrnes's advice and Truman's decision are revealing. Russian troops were sweeping through Manchuria against unexpectedly light opposition. The longer the war lasted, the more territory the Soviets would occupy—and the larger would be their claim to having contributed to Japan's defeat. Byrnes and Truman were alarmed by the implications for the Open Door in Manchuria and for the postwar administration of Japan. Accepting Tokyo's offer would have ended the war in a matter of hours. Nevertheless, Byrnes argued against retaining the emperor, though it meant prolonging the conflict. Even the compromise Truman agreed to assured delay. It not only demanded that the emperor subordinate himself to the Allied commander, but it gave no guarantee that the institution would be preserved in the "ultimate" form of government. Even if the Japanese did not reject the proposal, they were unlikely to accept it without debate. Truman and Byrnes assumed these risks because domestic considerations were of more immediate importance to them than the difficulties the USSR might raise over Manchuria and Japan.

Byrnes's message met bitter resistance in Tokyo. Militants demanded rejection and repeated their contention that only a massive battle on the shores of Japan would bring peace with honor. Even some moderates, Premier Suzuki among them, regarded the conditions as unacceptable. Foreign Minister Togo, suppressing his apprehensions about the statement's wording, insisted that it was the best Japan could get. But in the end, only the emperor's second personal intervention broke the stalemate. Shortly after four o'clock on the afternoon of August 14, Truman learned of Japan's capitulation through an intercepted cable to Bern. Two hours later, the Swiss chargé delivered Tokyo's reply. The war was over.[35]

There has been much debate over the importance the nuclear bomb had on Japan's decision to surrender. Writers who minimize it emphasize the cumulative effects of battlefield defeats, conventional bombing, naval blockades, and Soviet entry as the "real" reasons. The two bombs would not have sufficed absent these factors. But surely they caused the war to end when it did—not weeks or months later. Only an hour after the attack on Hiroshima, when informed that a new type of bomb had destroyed the city, Hirohito said that "we must put an end to the war as speedily as possible so that this tragedy will not be repeated."[36] His influence turned the final decision. The argument that the United States possessed only one such bomb, or would be deterred by world opinion from dropping another, evaporated in the fireball over Nagasaki. And what many writers neglect to point out is that the first bomb almost certainly caused the USSR to enter the war when it did. Stalin and Molotov had told Truman that although Soviet troops would be ready by mid-August, they would not attack until the conclusion of a Sino-Soviet treaty.

The USSR carefully acted as though the bomb had nothing to do with its decision. Molotov told Harriman that "although at one time" it was thought they could take no action before August 15, "the Soviet Government had now strictly lived up to its promise to enter [the] Pacific War 3 months after the defeat of Germany." The wording of the Soviet declaration was galling. It stated that after Japan's rejection of the Potsdam Declaration, the other Allies had appealed to Russia to join the conflict and that "Loyal to its Allied duty the Soviet

Government has accepted the proposal." No such proposal was ever made. At Potsdam, Truman and Byrnes had refused Molotov's request for a formal invitation to enter the war, partly because they suspected the Soviets would use it to proclaim their generosity in responding to the plea of the embattled Allies. Their suspicion was confirmed.[37]

The USSR's early entry, which no one believed stemmed from desire to be a good ally, heightened U.S. doubt about Soviet intentions in Manchuria. So did the impression Harriman received from Molotov that the Soviets were willing to have the war drag on. Also, Stalin was quickly and craftily using the Russian military advances to his advantage in the Sino-Soviet negotiations then taking place in Moscow. On August 10, he warned T. V. Soong that the Chinese Communists would get into Manchuria if he continued to balk.

Truman and Byrnes apparently failed to realize that *their* actions after Hiroshima must have seemed threatening to Soviet interests. Why the need for such haste in replying to Tokyo's first overture, if not to restrict the USSR in Manchuria and minimize its contribution to Japan's defeat? And the sudden decision to retain the emperor must have seemed ominous, for it raised the possibility that the United States intended to keep Japan intact as a hedge against Russia's position in the Far East. Whatever the bomb's effect on Japan, it caused both the Soviet Union and the United States to act in ways that seemed to justify the suspicion each held about the other.

NOTES

1. The most thorough account is Richard G. Hewlett and Oscar E. Anderson, Jr., *A History of the United States Atomic Energy Commission,* Vol. I, *The New World, 1939/1946* (University Park: The Pennsylvania State University Press, 1962). See also Martin J. Sherwin, *A World Destroyed: The Atomic Bomb and the Grand Alliance* (New York: Knopf, 1975). His most recent views are in "How Well They Meant," *Bulletin of Atomic Scientists* 41 (August 1985), pp. 9–15.

2. The Hyde Park agreement is printed in Sherwin, *A World Destroyed,* p. 284.

3. On July 18, two days after the first test explosion, Truman noted in his diary: "I fear that machines are ahead of morals by some centuries and when morals catch up perhaps there'll be no reason for any of it. I hope not. But we are only termites on a planet and maybe when we bore too deeply into the planet there'll [be] a reckoning—who knows?" See Robert H. Ferrell, ed., *Off the Record: The Private Papers of Harry S. Truman* (New York: Harper, 1980), p. 55.

4. See Sherwin, *A World Destroyed,* Chapters 7 and 8. "My secret" is in entry for May 15, Stimson Diary.

5. When Stimson on June 6 raised the issue of trading information for concessions, Truman said "he had been thinking of that and mentioned the same things that I was thinking of, namely the settlement of the Polish, Rumanian, Yugoslavian, and Manchurian problems." See entry for June 6, Stimson Diary. The phrases quoted are in entries for May 14 and 15.

6. When Stimson retired from office in September, Truman indicated his respect in a letter to Bess. "Pinned a medal on Stimson yesterday. If anyone in government was entitled to one it is that good man." Robert H. Ferrell, ed., *Dear Bess: The Letters from Harry to Bess Truman, 1910-1959* (New York: Norton, 1983), p. 523.

7. Entries for July 2, 23, Stimson Diary.

8. Entries for April 23, 24, May 15, Stimson Diary.

9. Hewlett and Anderson, *The New World,* pp. 344-346.

10. Hewlett and Anderson, *The New World,* pp. 356-360.

11. Notes on the Interim Committee Meeting, May 31, 1945, reprinted in Sherwin, *A World Destroyed,* pp. 296-305. Oppenheimer quotation is on p. 302.

12. Diary entry for July 25, Ferrell, *Off the Record,* pp. 55-56.

13. Byrnes statements in Sherwin, *A World Destroyed,* p. 301; Truman remark in Stimson Diary, July 3.

14. The most extreme version of this interpretation is Gar Alperovitz, *Atomic Diplomacy: Hiroshima and Potsdam; The Use of the Atomic Bomb & the Confrontation with Soviet Power* (New York: Simon & Shuster, 1965; expanded and updated edition, Elisabeth Sifton Books, 1985).

15. Robert J. C. Butow, *Japan's Decision to Surrender* (Stanford, Calif.: Stanford University Press, 1954), pp. 58-72.

16. Togo to Sato, July 11, and Sato to Togo, July 12, Folder 571, Byrnes Papers.

17. Togo to Sato, July 12, Folder 571, Byrnes Papers.

18. Sato to Togo, July 20, Folder 571, Byrnes Papers.

19. Hewlett and Anderson, *The New World,* p. 381; on July 16, Hull had Grew cable Byrnes via the map room warning against a public announcement that the emperor would be retained: "The militarists would try hard to interfere. Also should it fail the Japs would be encouraged while terrible repercussions would follow in the United States. Would it be well first to await the climax of allied bombing and Russia's entry into the war?" Vol. 7, Grew Papers.

20. On May 28, Stalin told Harriman and Hopkins that the Japanese wanted a conditional surrender "in order to retain intact their military cards and, as Germany had done, prepare for future aggression." *Foreign Relations of the United States, The Conference of Berlin (The Potsdam Conference), 1945* (Washington, D.C., 1960), I, p. 44.

21. The Potsdam Declaration is reprinted in Harry S. Truman, *Year of Decisions* (Garden City, N.Y.: 1955), pp. 390-392.

22. Butow, *Japan's Decision,* p. 144.

23. Butow, *Japan's Decision,* pp. 144-149.

24. "Truman interpreted this [mokusatsu] as a rejection of the proclamation, taking the Japanese term to mean 'ignore' or 'regard as unworthy of comment.'"

Gar Alperovitz, *Atomic Diplomacy,* p. 233. Phrases used by Japanese press in Butow, *Japan's Decision,* p. 146. The British interpreted the Japanese reply as a "categorical rejection." One memorandum warned that if the declaration were broadcast too often, the Japanese would conclude that the Allies were "anxious" for peace and would offer better terms if Japan held out longer. It cited a Japanese broadcast contrasting the "softening attitude of the Allies shown at Potsdam" with the "stiffening attitude of Japan." *Documents on British Policy Overseas* (London: Her Majesty's Stationery Office, 1984), pp. 1251–1252.

25. OSS Memorandum for the President, August 2, Conway File, Truman Papers.

26. United States Strategic Bombing Survey, *Japan's Struggle to End the War* (Washington, D.C., 1946), p. 13.

27. For casualty estimates, see *FRUS, Potsdam,* I, 905, 907; William D. Leahy, *I Was There* (New York: Whittlesey House, 1950), p. 384. Truman, in *Year of Decisions,* p. 417, wrote that Marshall had told him it might cost half a million lives to defeat Japan. Several recent articles dispute this figure: Rufus E. Miles, Jr., "Hiroshima: The Strange Myth of Half a Million American Lives Saved," *International Security* 10 (Fall 1985), pp. 121–140; and Barton J. Bernstein, "A Postwar Myth: 500,000 U.S. Lives Saved," *Bulletin of Atomic Scientists* 42 (June/July 1986), 38–40. Whatever the numbers, there is no doubt Truman thought casualties would be high. At Potsdam, he spoke to Churchill of "the terrible responsibilities that rested upon him in regard to unlimited effusion of American blood." Churchill memorandum of conversation, July 18, *Documents on British Policies Overseas,* p. 370. Truman quotation on Potsdam Declaration in Ferrell, *Off the Record,* p. 56. And see Forrest C. Pogue, *George Marshall: Statesman* (New York: Viking, 1987), pp. 19, 25. As Pogue points out, Marshall advocated using the weapon: "There is no evidence that at any time his thinking or plans were influenced by any possible political effect use of the bomb might have on the Russians." Truman relied on Marshall's advice on such matters more than anyone else's.

28. Ferrell, *Off the Record,* pp. 54, 55; Ferrell, *Dear Bess,* pp. 519, 520.

29. Ferrell, *Off the Record,* p. 55.

30. Lester Brooks, *Behind Japan's Surrender: The Secret Struggle That Ended an Empire* (New York: McGraw-Hill, 1968), p. 167; Butow, *Japan's Decision,* pp. 150–153.

31. Butow, *Japan's Decision,* pp. 158–178.

32. Byrnes remarks in Walter Brown's notes, August 10, Folder 602, Byrnes Papers; see also Stimson's Diary, August 10.

33. Byrnes reply reprinted in Butow, *Japan's Decision,* p. 245.

34. Truman, *Year of Decisions,* pp. 428–432.

35. Butow, *Japan's Decision,* Chapter 9; Truman, *Year of Decisions,* p. 435.

36. Brooks, *Behind Japan's Surrender,* p. 170.

37. The Soviet declaration is reprinted in Butow, *Japan's Decision,* pp. 153–154.

CHAPTER EIGHT

The Coalition Unravels

Wartime coalitions usually unravel when the common threat is over. The demise of the Grand Alliance was unusual only in how rapidly one of the partners came to be regarded by the others as an adversary. At Yalta, Stalin had seemed reasonable, inclined to meet his allies partway on matters such as Poland. But Soviet behavior after the conference led U.S. officials to question whether he valued cooperation or meant to get what he could. This stimulated a reevaluation of the Yalta Far Eastern accord, but the consensus was that nothing much could be done. President Truman's confidence that he could deal with Stalin on a personal basis was shaken by the close of the Potsdam Conference. Though he welcomed Stalin's renewed pledge to join the Pacific war, he suspected his ally's assurances as to the modesty of Soviet goals. The USSR's actions, beginning with its early declaration of war in the Far East, seemed to confirm the worst. Subsequent disputes in that area, failure to resolve European issues left over from Potsdam—all these problems began to affect a working relationship. Over everything, the atomic bomb cast its shadow.

Trouble began immediately after Japan's surrender. On August 15, 1945, Truman sent the Allies copies of General Order No. 1, a directive the emperor was to issue to Japanese forces in the field informing them how and to whom they must surrender. Stalin replied the following day, asking for revisions. He wanted Soviet troops to accept surrender in both the Kuriles and the northern half of Hokkaido, one of Japan's home islands. He justified the former as being in conformity with the Yalta accord, the latter because Russian public opinion would be "seriously offended" if Soviet troops had no zone in Japan. Truman approved Soviet occupation of the Kuriles, but stipulated: "I should like it understood that the United States desires air base rights" on one of the islands "for military and commercial purposes." Stalin's bid for an occupation zone in Japan he dismissed by saying that arrangements already had been made.[1]

Truman's reply, apparently drafted by Admiral Leahy, is puzzling. He undoubtedly regarded Stalin's suggestion of a Soviet zone in Japan as provocative, a wedge to attain full partnership in administering Japan. Yalta provided for acquisitions of territory and concessions in Manchuria as payment for Soviet participation in the war. That Stalin would insist on collecting what was due—and probably more—few could doubt. Occupation of Japan was not included. Truman's attitude toward Soviet desires in Europe was tempered by awareness of the USSR's enormous sacrifices in the war against Hitler. But a six-day campaign against weakened Japanese forces warranted no such consideration. The president's curt reply probably was intended to emphasize this fact.

But how does one interpret Truman's peremptory request for a military air base in the Kuriles? Surely he must have known Stalin would refuse such rights to any nation, let alone one possessing atomic weapons. Assuming he understood the implications of what he was asking, Truman the poker player may have been trying to warn Stalin that the United States would match any Soviet effort to raise the stakes. In any case, it was a blunder.

Stalin answered on August 22. Regarding Truman's refusal of his request for a Soviet zone in Hokkaido, he stated that "I have to say to you that I and my colleagues did not expect such an answer from you." He showed more indignation over what he repeatedly referred to as Truman's "demand" for an air base in the Kuriles. Reminding the president that no such provision was made at Yalta or Potsdam, he said that "demands of such a nature are usually laid before a conquered "state" or allies so weak as to be unable to refuse. The Soviet Union fit neither category. Because the United States did not explain its motives, he concluded, "I have to tell you frankly that neither I nor my colleagues understand what circumstances prompted such a demand to be made of the Soviet Union." He neglected to mention that no provision was made either at Yalta or at Potsdam for a Soviet zone in the Japanese home islands.[2]

Secretary Byrnes stepped in at this point. He resented what he regarded as Leahy's interference in foreign affairs. A week before, during the debate over surrender terms, he told an aide that Leahy "still thought he was Secretary of State, just as he was under Roosevelt, and he had to show him differently."[3] The United States at the time was trying to secure from Stalin a statement acknowledging the Open Door in Manchuria. There also was concern as to whether the Soviet leader would honor his pledge to support the Chinese Nationalist government. Antagonizing him over such a matter as an air base was folly and had invited Stalin's charge that the administration was trying to deviate from agreements. Byrnes let Truman know he was displeased at not being consulted, and he persuaded him to back off. The secretary drafted a reply in which he simply ignored Stalin's protest about being denied a zone and pretended that the request for an air base had been misconstrued. All the United States wanted was access to a base "for emergency use during the period of occupation of Japan." That of course was not what the original message had stated. Byrnes sidestepped Stalin's complaint about the tone of the request by saying it did not refer to any Soviet territory because the Kuriles remained Japanese pending disposition at the peace conference. Stalin chose to drop the issue. He replied that it was now clear that he had "misunderstood you," and he consented to emergency landing rights during the occupation of Japan.[4]

Soviet landings in the Kuriles raised speculation that the action represented the fulfillment of a secret accord. Stalin's radio announcement that the islands and the southern half of Sakhalin would become Soviet possessions added to the uncertainty. In a press conference on September 4, Byrnes resorted to evasion. He admitted that Soviet moves had been sanctioned at Yalta after negotiations he said he "remembered well." But he insisted the arrangements were provisional, until the peace settlement. Actually, Byrnes could not have remembered the negotiations at all because he had left Yalta before they took place. To emphasize the temporary nature of what had been done, he added that he intended to review the situation with Molotov in London when the Council of Foreign Ministers met that month.[5]

Byrnes was the first U.S. official to reveal what Roosevelt had denied: Some agreements made at Yalta had been kept hidden from the public. He defused the matter temporarily by limiting his remarks to immediate issues. A few newspapers tried to play up the "secret deal" aspect, but got little mileage from it at the time. Even this minor furor must have made obvious how embarrassing to the administration full disclosure of the Yalta Far East accord might be, particularly to Byrnes after his much-advertised role as "the Yalta expert."

The Council of Foreign Ministers, as established at Postdam, was to consist of the five permanent members of the UN Security Council—France and China, in addition to the Big Three—and meet quarterly. As proposed by the State Department, the council would deal only with European peace treaties and territory. Byrnes succeeded in having

its purview broadened to include any matter of "worldwide significance." He had great faith in his negotiating ability, loved the spotlight,
and welcomed the opportunity to function independently. The arrangement suited Truman as well. He had boasted that he was "no diplomat,"
and at Potsdam he frequently had expressed his impatience with what
he regarded as haggling.

In addition, Truman was becoming increasingly preoccupied with
domestic affairs, which also led him to grant Byrnes a relatively free
hand in foreign policy matters. Since V-J Day, a host of divisive issues
had arisen that threatened to swamp the administration. Demobilization
was particularly explosive. Public clamor to "bring the boys home"
made a shambles of plans for orderly transition. Truman reluctantly
agreed to accelerate the process, even though he complained it amounted
to "disintegration" rather than demobilization of the armed forces. Still,
people criticized delays, and phrases such as "no boats, no votes"
became popular. Strikes flared across the country as labor and management fought for advantage when existing arrangements lapsed. There
were disputes over wartime economic controls. Some wanted them
phased out gradually to prevent pent-up consumer demand from causing
inflation; others considered their retention unwarranted interference
with market forces. Truman was bound to displease some groups no
matter what he did on these and many other aspects of reconversion.

The president himself stirred controversy. Less than a week before
the foreign ministers' meeting, he sent a special message to Congress
urging enactment of a twenty-one point social and economic program.
Included were recommendations providing for full employment, increased unemployment compensation, permanent farm price supports,
rigorous fair employment practices, and housing legislation. Later he
augmented this package by calling for reforms such as a comprehensive
health program. Opposed by a coalition of conservative Republicans
and Democrats, Truman achieved little of what later would be called
his Fair Deal despite extensive personal lobbying of congressmen. He
also failed to get legislation providing for universal military training
and for unification of the armed services.[6]

Although the domestic situation absorbed much of his energies, it
is difficult to tell whether it affected Truman's attitude toward the
Soviet Union. He undoubtedly regarded rapid demobilization and rejection of universal military training as weakening his hand, for instance, but it is just as likely that his efforts to woo conservatives
influenced him in the direction of firmness. What is clear is that during
this time he refrained from politically exploiting difficulties with the
Soviets as he might have done. On the contrary, he repeatedly told
subordinates that he wanted to minimize friction as much as possible.

Every account of the Council of Foreign Ministers meeting in London addresses one question: To what extent did Byrnes and Truman consider possession of the bomb would influence negotiations? Evidence is fragmentary. Shortly before leaving for London, Byrnes told Assistant Secretary McCloy and Secretary Stimson that he disagreed with their wish to share research data with the Soviets. The Russians could not be trusted, he said, and he hoped America's monopoly would make them more willing to compromise. Stimson wrote that Byrnes wanted "to have the implied threat of the bomb in his pocket" and referred to negotiating by "having this weapon rather ostentatiously on our hip." Ignoring Stimson's qualifying "so to speak" phrase, scholars have cited his disapproving phrases as though they actually were uttered by Byrnes. Whether Truman believed the bomb would make the Soviets tractable at the conference is not known. But it is known he disagreed with Byrnes about sharing data. According to Stimson, Truman told him "we must take Russia into our confidence," and he said the same thing in a cabinet meeting a week later.[7]

What has been referred to as "atomic diplomacy" consisted at most of a general feeling that respect for the newly acquired weapon would cause the Soviets to be accommodating. There would be no threats nor any suggestion that acquiescence on other matters would influence America's willingness to share information. Indeed, Byrnes instructed members of the London delegation not to discuss the subject. This probably did influence Soviet behavior, albeit in the direction opposite that intended. Failure to approach the Soviets on nuclear energy, separately or at the conference, may have convinced them that the United States meant to use blackmail. Concessions would be interpreted as showing fear and might embolden the United States to reopen all the wartime agreements.

Toward the end of the conference, Byrnes told Stettinius he had thought Molotov would raise the question of sharing. If he had, Byrnes would have replied that the United States could give nothing out until a "complete arrangement" had been made. At the same time, he would have said that "I can pledge to you that the United States will never use this bomb at any time unless it is within the United Nations Charter signed at San Francisco and we will only use it in the case of an aggressor to keep the peace."[8] Perhaps he should have volunteered this information at the outset.

The London Conference began on September 11 and was a disaster for the administration and for Byrnes. If Truman shared his view that the bomb would make the USSR obliging, both were mistaken. Molotov seemed intent on demonstrating indifference. He delayed negotiation for days, claiming he had other commitments. Approaching him at a reception one evening, Byrnes asked when he would complete his "sightseeing" so that they could "get down to business." Molotov responded by asking whether the secretary had "an atomic bomb in his side pocket." Byrnes replied in the same vein. Molotov did not know U.S. southerners, he said, who kept weapons in their hip pockets. "If you don't cut out all this stalling and let us get down to work, I am going to pull an atomic bomb out of my hip pocket and let you have it." Molotov laughed.[9]

The council took up some matters left over from Potsdam, such as reparations from Italy, disposition of the latter's colonies, and Italy's conflict with Yugoslavia over the city of Trieste. Most vexatious was the matter of peace treaties with the former Axis satellites, particularly Romania and Bulgaria. Molotov used harsh language on every issue. He accused the United States of denying Italian reparations to the Soviet people and of reneging on a promise to support a trusteeship for an Italian colony in Africa. He was especially abusive about Bulgaria and Romania. In those two countries, he said, the United States supported anti-Soviet elements against democratic governments that conformed to the Declaration on Liberated Europe. If the United States refused to deal with Bulgaria and Romania, the Soviet Union would not cooperate on a peace treaty for Italy.[10]

The idea that after Hiroshima and Nagasaki the United States used "atomic diplomacy" to reduce Soviet influence in Eastern Europe has little support in the available evidence. The puppet regimes installed in Bulgaria and Romania were even more repressive than Poland's Warsaw government. Although Washington withheld recognition before and after Potsdam, it did little more than issue statements of commitment to the Declaration on Liberated Europe. In August, the U.S. representative in Bulgaria, Maynard B. Barnes, on his own initiative requested that elections be put off until the Allied Control Commission worked out an equitable formula. Byrnes reprimanded him. Nor was that all. To the astonishment and delight of State Department officials, the Bulgarian government did postpone elections. Yet to Barnes's recommendation that Washington make proposals to reform the electoral laws, Byrnes replied that the department was "anxious that no subsequent steps be taken which might distract from that victory [postponement]." All this took place after atomic bombs were dropped.[11]

Byrnes at London was equally reluctant to offend the Soviets over the two Balkan states. When differences surfaced, Byrnes met privately with Molotov to smooth them over. He stated his case, according to an aide, "in a pleading manner." Appealing to Molotov on a personal level, he tried to explain why domestic considerations dictated his official stance. After Yalta, he had acted as FDR's "missionary of peace" in explaining to Congress and the American people such agreements as the Declaration on Liberated Europe. His explanations had been "warmly received." Now, through "an honest misunderstanding," there was growing concern at home that the declaration was being violated. Appearing to condone these violations by recognizing the regimes in Bulgaria and Romania would embarrass him personally, as well as the administration. Byrnes's appeal resembled an explanation to a fellow senator: Give us something we can live with. Molotov was unmoved.[12]

Byrnes's public statements about representative government and free elections perhaps were provocative because they clashed with the USSR's need for "friendly" neighbors. But the secretary's remarks were for domestic consumption. He made this clear to Molotov when he suggested that Bulgaria and Romania be reorganized by using Poland as a precedent. There, a few non-Communists were added to the Warsaw regime to create the facade of a coalition government. That is all Byrnes wanted: token changes that would permit him to recognize Communist-dominated regimes while protecting himself against charges that he had abandoned the Declaration on Liberated Europe. He emphasized this when he extended recognition to the Hungarian government on the basis of its promise to hold free elections, the prospects for which at the time appeared small.[13]

Molotov's refusal to accept even cosmetic reorganizations led Byrnes to make a remarkable offer. At another private meeting, he told Molotov that "he had been doing a lot of thinking" and was reminded of Stalin's statement at Yalta about Russia's having been invaded through Poland twice within twenty-five years. To dispel such fears, he said, he was prepared to recommend to the president and Congress "a twenty-five year treaty between the principal powers for the demilitarization of Germany." The Soviet Union then could let "the small neighboring countries go along their paths of peace and democracy." Molotov replied that this was a new idea and he would think it over. The proposal shows how desperate Byrnes was to reach agreements: The chance of getting such a treaty through the Senate would have been remote, its value to the Soviets dubious. He must have had second thoughts; he did not pursue the matter.[14]

When it appeared the deadlock over Romania and Bulgaria would wreck the conference, Byrnes was ready to give in. He was prevented from doing so by John Foster Dulles, whom he had invited to join the U.S. delegation. Byrnes told Dulles that in the face of Soviet intransigence, "we better start thinking about compromise." Dulles would have none of it. He likened acceptance of the regimes in the Balkan states to appeasement of Hitler. If Byrnes went ahead, he threatened to leave the conference and denounce what he regarded as a sellout. The havoc Dulles might wreak on administration foreign policy and Byrnes's reputation was awesome. The secretary capitulated.[15]

Molotov's behavior at London reaffirmed an interpretation of Soviet conduct that Byrnes and Truman had expressed before—that Stalin led a "soft" faction in Moscow, while Molotov represented the militants. Byrnes, an aide noted, "has no confidence in building peace with M[olotov] . . . sees only solution for next meeting to be held in M[oscow] where he can deal with Stalin." The following day Byrnes emphasized the importance of bypassing Moscow. "He saw no hope in stopping M except by appealing to Stalin. He thinks Stalin wants peace and JFB is fearful for the world if Stalin should die."[16] When Molotov reversed himself on an agreement to permit Chinese and French participation in discussion of the peace treaties, Byrnes cabled Truman to appeal directly to Stalin. Even after the latter supported Molotov's position, which led to the breakup of the conference, Byrnes believed in the importance of dealing with Stalin personally.

The secretary's assumption about Soviet factionalism as explanation for Molotov's truculence was convenient but deluding. Byrnes seems never to have entertained the possibility that Molotov's disparaging references to nuclear bombs, as well as his abrasive manner, may have been intended as signals that the Soviets would surrender nothing out of fear and that they expected hard bargaining as usual. The conference failed not because of a division in the Kremlin, but because Byrnes offered little for what he wanted beyond appeals for righteous conduct. As a member of the Soviet delegation complained to a U.S. counterpart, Byrnes acted like a professor instead of a "practical" man. "When is he going to start trading?" the Russian wanted to know.[17]

What could Byrnes have traded? As no decision had been made within the administration about atomic energy, it lacked value as a carrot or a stick. Molotov's bid for trusteeship over the Italian colony of Tripolitania—present-day Libya—was nonnegotiable. The British and French would have withdrawn from the conference sooner than accept what they regarded as a threat to their Mediterranean interests, and Foreign Secretary Bevin warned Byrnes that Molotov was after uranium deposits in the Belgian Congo. The U.S. contract for the uranium, Byrnes told an aide, was "no stronger than the battleship that guards it." Should the Soviets obtain Tripolitania, "they would be in a position to head us off from this uranium."[18] Finally, Byrnes had no authority to negotiate over Molotov's proposal that a four-power control council administer Japan, a prospect Truman opposed. Indeed, during the conference Truman issued public statements making clear that General

Douglas MacArthur, as Supreme Commander of the Allied Forces, was subject to no authority save the United States government. Byrnes thought it was "bad because it made Stalin think were acting in Japan just as he was acting in the Balkans." The secretary considered dangling an economic package before the Soviets, but thought better of it. If leaked, it might appear that he was trying to bribe the Russians into doing what the Declaration on Liberated Europe stated they ought to be doing anyway.[19]

Byrnes made the best of a messy situation. Publicly he proclaimed his desire to work with the Soviet Union in establishing a lasting peace, but emphasized that he would not compromise principles. He was trying to place blame for the conference's failure on Molotov, of course, and with few exceptions, the U.S. press accepted his version. Truman shared Byrnes's view that Stalin represented the moderate group within the Kremlin, and he seems also to have agreed that Molotov was the villain. Still, there is evidence that the president was disappointed in Byrnes.[20] Immersed in efforts to get his Fair Deal through Congress, he had given the secretary virtually free rein. Byrnes the "fixer," who before the conference cockily told a reporter it would take him about three weeks to make the Soviets "see some sense," had come away empty-handed.[21]

Meanwhile, Truman authorized a cabinet debate on atomic energy. It probably was less important than later was assumed. He was prompted by a memorandum of September 11 by Stimson, soon to retire as secretary of war. To Stimson, who had agonized over the matter for months, the memorandum was his legacy on what he believed was the most dangerous problem confronting the world. Before Potsdam, he had advocated withholding information from the Soviets until their society became more liberal. Now he urged "a direct and forthright approach" to them as quickly as possible. Unless such an approach were made, the Soviets would conclude that the United States and Britain intended to form "an Anglo-Saxon" atomic bloc against them. This would "stimulate feverish activity" by the Soviets to obtain their own weapons, resulting in "irretrievably embittered relations" and a disastrous arms race.[22]

After securing British and Canadian approval, Stimson thought it best to inform the USSR that the United States was prepared to negotiate arrangements "to control and limit the use of the atomic bomb" and "to direct and encourage the development of atomic power for peaceful and humanitarian purposes." He stressed the importance of dealing directly with the Soviets, warning that they were unlikely to take seriously an international conference relegating the Soviet Union to just one of many attending nations. As a gesture of faith, the United

States should be prepared to share basic scientific information, though not technical data on bomb construction. Stimson acknowledged there were risks, but accepted them: "The chief lesson I have learned in a long life is that the only way you can make a man trustworthy is to trust him; and the surest way to make him untrustworthy is to distrust him and show your distrust."[23]

At a cabinet luncheon on September 18, Truman alluded to Stimson's departure. He announced that the regular Friday cabinet meeting on September 21 would be entirely on atomic matters. He said his "present disposition was to disclose the principles of atomic energy to the Russians and others but not the method of making the bomb," and he asked the secretary if he could attend to "help out." A flattered Stimson, who had intended to leave Washington on Thursday, replied that "of course I would be there if I could walk on my two legs."[24] Those who would attend had less than three days to formulate their ideas on a complex matter of great magnitude. Why such short notice? If Stimson's September 11 memorandum had convinced Truman of the need to move quickly, he could have given the participants an additional week by informing them at once. If Stimson's presence were the desideratum, he could have been invited to Washington from his Long Island residence. Events scheduled before and after the meeting suggest that Truman set the agenda as a tribute to Stimson, rather than because he thought anything new might result. He provided a suitable forum for Stimson to state his views on a matter he cared deeply about, views the president had indicated he shared.[25]

Friday afternoon began with a ceremony in the Rose Garden, during which Truman awarded Stimson the Distinguished Service Medal. The cabinet session began immediately afterward. Truman opened it by calling on Stimson. The secretary repeated the gist of his memorandum discursively, at one point tracing the historical "friendship" between the United States and Russia back to the Civil War and the purchase of Alaska. He illustrated his theme about making people trustworthy by examples drawn from his experiences in the Philippines decades earlier.

Following Stimson's presentation, everyone from the secretary of labor to the postmaster general spoke, although few offered more than feelings about whether the Soviets could be trusted. Dean Acheson, the newly appointed undersecretary of state, made a cogent argument in support of Stimson, as did Undersecretary of War Robert P. Patterson. Secretary of Commerce Henry A. Wallace endorsed full cooperation with the Soviet Union. Secretary of the Navy James Forrestal led the opposition, saying that the United States should retain its advantage and "exercise a trusteeship over the atomic bomb on behalf of the United Nations." He was supported with varying fervor by Secretary of the Treasury Fred M. Vinson and Attorney General Tom Clark. Attitudes ranged across the spectrum. Truman said little, but twice interrupted to remind those who opposed giving away secrets that only scientific information was at issue, not the bomb. He invited those who wished to submit their views in writing.[26] He adjourned the meeting so Stimson could get to the Washington airport for another ceremony, including a nineteen-gun salute and a band that played "Auld Lang Syne"[27]

Truman's relations with Stimson over the five months preceding the meeting provides ironic commentary on the thesis that Truman "reversed" FDR's policy of cooperation with the Soviet Union and pursued coercive atomic diplomacy. He had rejected Stimson's earlier advice to play nuclear aces and trump cards, only to adopt the older man's final recommendation that he provide the Soviets with scientific information to win their trust.

Those who opposed Stimson's approach at the cabinet meeting said nothing Truman had not heard from Byrnes, Forrestal, and Leahy. He devoted several pages of his memoirs to the session, concluding with what one student rightfully labeled "inane" comments about how much he liked to see "this kind of interchange of opinion" because it showed that "honest men can honestly disagree." Acheson later summed it up more accurately. Because no one had a chance to prepare, he wrote, "the discussion was unworthy of the subject." Truman's account of it was intended to impress readers that he had solicited opinion from all quarters before reaching a decision. By omitting mention of his agreement with Stimson and the circumstances of the discussion, he exaggerated the meeting's significance.[28]

The sessions produced one unanticipated consequence, which provided a glimpse of how divisive the nuclear issue might become. Allegations in the press that the cabinet had split over Wallace's recommendation that "the bomb" be turned over to the USSR stirred speculation and criticism. Truman denied that any such discussion had taken place. Debate had been limited to the matter of exchanging basic scientific data. His emphasis on this distinction, he would learn, failed to satisfy those who opposed giving any nuclear information to the Soviets.[29]

Truman on October 3 submitted his proposals on nuclear energy to Congress. Drafted by one of Acheson's assistants, the message stressed that "the discovery with which we are dealing involves forces of nature too dangerous to fit into any of our usual concepts." In the domestic field, he recommended that Congress pass legislation granting control over nuclear development to an Atomic Energy Commission, its members to be appointed by the president with advice and consent of the Senate. On the international level, he said it was necessary to work out as rapidly as possible arrangements that nuclear energy would become "a powerful and forceful influence towards the maintenance of world peace instead of an instrument of destruction." He acknowledged the difficulties, but pointed out that the alternative would be an arms race "which might well end in disaster." He promised to report the outcome of discussions held and submit agreements requiring congressional action.

Although lacking in detail, several paragraphs indicated that Truman meant to proceed along the lines Stimson and others had suggested. He pointed out that the principles of nuclear energy were widely known and that scientists agreed that "foreign research can come abreast of our present theoretical knowledge in time." Because the matter could not be delayed until the United Nations was prepared to deal with it, he proposed discussions first with Britain and Canada, then with "other nations," to assure cooperation rather than rivalry. He emphasized that talks would not involve bomb production, but be limited to the terms under which "international collaboration and exchange of scientific information might safely proceed."[30]

Readers were quick to translate: Truman intended to approach the Soviets ("other nations") directly and share research with them before controls were set up. It was the first subject raised at his next press conference. What kind of information would be made available, a reporter asked, and under what circumstances? Truman replied that he would give out nothing relating to what he called the "know-how" to build a bomb. "The scientific knowledge that resulted in the atomic bomb is already world-wide knowledge" and "all the great scientists in every country know it."[31] Such remarks went beyond what he had said in his message to Congress, which was that other nations could acquire this knowledge "in time." He was trying to defuse allegations that his proposals would compromise security.

Despite Truman's efforts, critics raised the same objection Byrnes and Forrestal had offered within the administration. Because the United States was far ahead on research, they complained, "exchange" of information would be one way. Distinction between scientific and technical data they saw as spurious—both were necessary to build a bomb. Whatever knowledge the United States made available would hasten the day when the USSR could begin constructing weapons. On the matter of control, they doubted the Soviets would enter agreements providing for on-site inspection necessary to verify compliance. If no guarantees were obtained, the United States would have squandered some of its lead in a futile hope of inspiring trust.[32]

Truman gave a foreign policy speech in New York City on October 27, Navy Day, and enunciated twelve "fundamentals" of U.S. diplomacy, most of which were statements favoring such innocuous goals as the spread of freedom and democracy throughout the world. Only one, concerning governments "imposed upon any nation by the force of a foreign power," could be interpreted as applying to specific conditions—Bulgaria and Romania. He said that in some cases the imposition of such governments could not be prevented, but the United States would not recognize them. The theme of his address was forbearance. He asked the public to remain patient during efforts to advance the fundamentals because "we recognize that we have to operate in an imperfect world."

Referring to the Soviet Union, he stressed "the special problems of other nations" and "their own legitimate urge towards security as they see it." With regard to nuclear energy, he announced his intention to meet with the British and Canadians and later other nations to facilitate "free exchange" of scientific information. He repeated assurances that the "processes of manufacturing the atomic bomb" would not be subject to discussion. No nation need feel threatened by U.S. weapons, he said, which "we regard as a sacred trust." Soviet leaders apparently regarded the speech as conciliatory. It was given wide coverage in the press, and a *New York Times* correspondent in Moscow reported its reception was "most encouraging here."[33]

Invitations were sent Prime Ministers Clement Attlee and Mackenzie King for talks in Washington to begin November 11, 1945. Attlee had proposed such a meeting in September; he became more urgent after Truman's October message. He said he was under strong parliamentary pressure. The bomb had "overshadowed" everything at the London Conference, he pointed out, and would continue to do so until the three partners made their intentions known. Although he did not say so to Truman, he also sought to determine Britain's place in the relationship. The president's statements that discussions would relate only to exchange of scientific information were meant to placate U.S. public opinion, of course, but did this mean the British would be excluded from full nuclear partnership? He also wanted to consult on other matters. At the London Conference, Byrnes had made little effort to coordinate policies and, as a member of the British delegation recalled, "took over and sailed off in a way that terrified us."[34] The prime minister worried that British interests would suffer if the United States pursued an independent course toward the Soviet Union.

Preparation for the meeting was haphazard. Truman apparently thought Byrnes would handle it, but the secretary procrastinated. As late as mid-October, he opposed disclosure. He told Secretaries Forrestal and Patterson that he was "most strongly opposed to imparting any of this [atomic] information to the Russians." It was all very well for scientists to say that science knew no boundaries, but "that did not apply either to Mr. Molotov or Mr. Stalin."[35] He ignored appeals by Acheson and others to begin drafting proposals and took no heed of a memorandum from Patterson in the same vein. A week before the meeting, Vannevar Bush, director of the Office of Scientific Research and Development, met with Byrnes and was astonished to learn that nothing had been done. When he argued the need for a program, Byrnes asked him to submit his ideas. He did so, drafting them over an exhausting weekend, and presented them on November 5. As Byrnes knew Bush supported Stimson's approach, his casual behavior suggests that he had undergone no conversion, but was disinclined to argue the matter.[36]

Attlee and King arrived in Washington on Saturday, November 10. Talks began that day, and by Sunday evening the conferees had agreed on essentials. So far as can be determined, a slightly amended version of Bush's memorandum served as Truman's position paper. Its author again was shocked when Byrnes called him in on Monday morning and asked him to prepare a draft of the conference communiqué. How could he, Bush asked, when he had not attended the sessions? Outlining the understandings, Byrnes assured him they so nearly resembled his recommendations that his absence from the meetings posed no obstacle. Byrnes also had the State Department Counselor, Benjamin V. Cohen, work up a draft, which differed from Bush's. Discussion resulted in a third version that incorporated most of Bush's ideas. The British and Canadians had prepared their own documents, however, and several lengthy sessions were spent wrangling over phrasing.[37]

Finally, on Thursday morning November 15, a copy was ready for a press conference Truman had called. In the presence of Attlee, King, and congressional leaders, Truman read the Agreed Declaration to the assembled correspondents. The document consisted of nine articles, six of them general statements about the enormity of the problem, the need to avoid nuclear war, and the signatories' desire to cooperate with other nations in building a peaceful world. Three of them constituted the document's core. Number six stated that because military application of atomic energy rested upon the same methods and processes required for industrial use, no technical information would be released before controls were in place. Number seven announced the signatories' intent to recommend that the United Nations create a commission to study and make proposals on exchange of basic scientific information, control of atomic energy for peaceful purposes, elimination of nuclear weapons, and effective safeguards to prevent violations.

Number eight said the UN commission should proceed by stages, the completion of one being necessary before proceeding to the next.[38]

The agreement omitted a crucial element of the Stimson plan—an approach to the Soviets before going to the UN—which Bush had endorsed in his November 5 memorandum. As no notes were taken at the Truman-Attlee-King meetings, the reason for the omission is not clear. According to newspaper reports, evidently inspired by a leak within the British delegation, Attlee opposed sharing until the Soviets made a satisfactory statement about their objectives. Nothing in the declaration precluded conferring with the Russians, however, and Truman all along had said that is what he intended to do.[39]

Separate negotiations were held to determine rules for collaboration among the three Western powers. Agreements were reached for "full and effective cooperation," but Attlee failed to get a guarantee that the United States would provide technical data for industrial use. The three also discussed policy toward Japan, China, and Korea. Truman insisted these matters be kept off the agenda to avoid the appearance of "ganging up," which is what the Soviets alleged. After responding favorably to Truman's message to Congress of early October, they began to paint the conference as an effort to form an anti-Soviet nuclear bloc. *Pravda* started using such phrases as "atomic diplomacy" and "atomic imperialism." Three days before the meeting, Molotov gave a militant speech warning the Western powers against using nuclear weapons as a threat and promising that the Soviet Union would acquire nuclear energy on its own.[40]

When the conference ended, Secretary Byrnes went on network radio to extoll the virtues of a policy he had opposed for months. He scoffed at "the suggestion that we are using the atomic bomb as a diplomatic or military threat against any country," labeling such claims "untrue and unwarranted." The agreement with Britain and Canada he characterized as a bold, generous act. Although the United Sttes would retain its monopoly for a while, this need not be long. America was prepared to share scientific information as a start and to provide technological data for peaceful purposes as soon as safeguards could be set.[41]

Byrnes's address, like the declaration, made no mention of inviting Moscow to cosponsor a resolution at the UN. Turman had endorsed this procedure in conversation, but seemed to retreat at a press conference on November 20. Possibly he hesitated out of deference to the British. But pressure to carry out the Stimson plan was building. In his message to Congress, Truman had stated that he intended to consult "other nations" after Britain and Canada. Everyone assumed he meant the USSR. State Department officials warned that failure to approach the Soviets would confirm their allegations and leave the administration vulnerable to accusation that it had reneged on a commitment. In Congress, bipartisan support was growing for a joint resolution calling upon the president to initiate talks with the Soviets on the proposed UN resolution. Sometime during the last week in November, it is not clear when, the decision was made to confer with the Russians. Byrnes, still anxious to resolve European problems pending since the London meeting, on November 23 asked the Soviets to sponsor a foreign ministers' conference in Moscow. When they agreed, he proposed an agenda with atomic energy at the top.[42]

Byrnes later claimed that the idea for a meeting leaped unbidden into his mind as he sat in his State Department office on Thanksgiving Day. Perhaps it did, but he had talked of the need to meet with Stalin since midway through the London Conference. Still believing that Stalin spoke for moderates within the Kremlin, he intended to circumvent what he thought was the Molotov faction. Whether he had changed his mind about atomic disclosure or simply decided to make the best of the situation can only be guessed. The result was the same. He now hoped the prospects of nuclear sharing would cause the Soviets to make concessions at Moscow they were unwilling to make earlier. His newly acquired enthusiasm left him unwilling to be sidetracked. He asked for the conference without notifying the British, spurned their pleas for consultation, and when they balked, he informed them he was prepared to go alone.[43]

Truman's initiative on atomic energy was developed within a shifting context. Many people had supported disclosure, and some even criticized the administration for not moving more rapidly. But the optimistic mood of the Yalta period had dissipated. Opinion polls since V-E Day indicated growing distrust of the Soviet Union. In September, a National Opinion Research Center poll revealed that 85 percent of the respondents opposed sharing nuclear secrets with the USSR. There was similar disillusion in the press and Congress. Nor was that all. FDR and Truman had exercised great latitude at the wartime conferences. One result was to diminish the Senate's participation in foreign policy. Powerful senators intended to reassert their prerogative now that the emergency had ended. They wanted consultation, not briefings about what had been done.[44]

Truman recognized the political realities. He sought to deflect charges that he intended to give away "the bomb" by repeatedly minimizing the significance of sharing basic research. He met frequently with congressional leaders to keep them informed and gain their support. Byrnes did not respond to the warning signals. He prepared for the Moscow Conference as if it were a one-man show and angered key senators with his cavalier disregard for their opinions. He seems to have believed that with atomic energy to sweeten the pot, he could negotiate settlements at Moscow that would enhance his own prestige and make criticism of the administration appear as obstructionism.

NOTES

1. Truman to Stalin, August 18, State Department Decimal Files 740.0019 PW/8-1945.

2. Stalin to Truman, August 22, State Department Decimal Files 740.0019 PW/8-2345.

3. Entry for August 10, Walter Brown's notes, Folder 602, Byrnes Papers.

4. Byrnes memorandum to Truman, August 25, State Department Decimal Files 740.0019 PW/8-2545; Truman to Stalin, August 27, 740.0019 PW/8-2745. Stalin's reply to Truman, August 30, is in Harry S. Truman, *Year of Decisions* (Garden City, N.Y.: Doubleday, 1955), p. 443.

5. *New York Times,* September 5, p. 1.

6. For Truman, reconversion, and the origins of the Fair Deal, see Alonzo L. Hamby, *Beyond the New Deal: Harry S. Truman and American Liberalism* (New York: Columbia University Press, 1973); his edited volume, *Harry S. Truman and the Fair Deal* (Lexington, Mass.: D. C. Heath, 1974); Robert J. Donovan, *Conflict and Crisis: The Presidency of Harry S. Truman, 1945–1948* (New York: Norton, 1977); and Donald R. McCoy, *The Presidency of Harry S. Truman* (Lawrence: University Press of Kansas, 1984).

7. Stimson Diary entries, August 12 to September 3, September 4 and 12.

8. September 28, Calendar Notes, Stettinius Papers.

9. Entry for September 13, Walter Brown notes, Folder 602, Byrnes Papers.

10. *Foreign Relations of the United States, 1945* (Washington, D.C., 1967), II, pp. 263–267, 291–298, 300–310.

11. *FRUS, 1945,* IV, pp. 303–317; and see Lynn Etheridge Davis, *The Cold War Begins: Soviet-American Conflict over Eastern Europe* (Princeton, N.J.: Princeton University Press, 1974), pp. 306–313.

12. Entry for September 16, Walter Brown's notes, Folder 602, Byrnes Papers; for notes on Byrnes-Molotov meetings on September 16, 19, 20, see *FRUS, 1945,* II, pp. 194–202, 243–247, 267–269.

13. For election prospects in Hungary, see Davis, *The Cold War Begins,* pp. 318–319.

14. Entry for September 20, Walter Brown's notes, Folder 602, Byrnes Papers.

15. Robert L. Messer, *The End of an Alliance: James F. Byrnes, Roosevelt, Truman, and the Origins of the Cold War* (Chapel Hill: University of North Carolina Press, 1982), pp. 132–133.

16. Entries for September 20, 21, Walter Brown's notes, Folder 602, Byrnes Papers.

17. Messer, *Alliance,* p. 133.

18. Entry for September 24, Walter Brown's notes, Folder 602, Byrnes Papers.

19. Entry for September 26, Walter Brown's notes, Folder 602, Byrnes Papers; two days later Byrnes told Stettinius the same thing and that the British, Chinese, and Australians were offended: "We were going off in a unilateral way as the Russians were going off in the Balkans." Calendar Notes, September 28, Stettinius Papers. Byrnes's economic package is discussed in Terry H. Anderson, *The United States, Great Britain, and the Cold War, 1944–1947* (Columbia: University of Missouri Press, 1981), pp. 90–91.

20. For Byrnes's public statement, see *Department of State Bulletin* XIII (October 7, 1945), pp. 507–512; Truman expressed dissatisfaction with Byrnes to both Henry A. Wallace and Joseph Davies; see John M. Blum, ed., *The Price of Vision: The Diary of Henry A. Wallce* (Boston: Houghton Mifflin, 1973), pp. 523–524; and entry for December 8, Davies Journal.

21. Byrnes quotation in Robert G. Kaiser, *Cold Winter, Cold War* (New York: Stein and Day, 1974), p. 172.

22. Stimson memorandum, *FRUS, 1945,* II, pp. 40–44.

23. Stimson reviewed the memorandum with Truman on September 12 and noted in his diary that the president said he was "in full accord" with each statement. Entry for September 12, Stimson Diary.

24. Truman's "present disposition" remark is in entry for September 18, Forrestal Diary, Vol. III; his request to Stimson and the latter's reply are in entry for September 18, Stimson Diary.

25. It is interesting to note that Truman scheduled the session while Byrnes was in London, especially in view of the fact that Acting Secretary Dean Acheson, who would sit in for him, was "evidently strongly on our side," according to Stimson. Stimson earlier had received Truman's permission to send Acheson a copy of the September 11 memorandum. See entry for September 13, Stimson Diary.

26. Truman's account of the meeting is in *Year of Decisions* (Garden City, N.Y.: Doubleday, 1955), pp. 525–527; Forrestal's in entry for September 21, Forrestal Diary, Vol. III.

27. Stimson's account of the ceremonies before and after the cabinet session are in entry for September 21, Stimson Diary.

28. "Inane" is in Herbert Feis, *From Trust to Terror: The Onset of the Cold War, 1945–1950* (New York: Norton, 1970), p. 97; Acheson's comment in his *Present at the Creation: My Years in the State Department* (New York: Norton, 1969), p. 174.

29. Truman, *Year of Decisions,* p. 529.

30. *Public Papers of the Presidents: Harry S. Truman, 1945* (Washington, D.C., 1961), pp. 362–366.

31. *New York Times,* October 9, 1945, p. 1; Truman, *Year of Decisions,* pp. 533–534.

32. For a sampling of criticism, see John Lewis Gaddis, *The United States and the Origins of the Cold War, 1941–1947* (New York: Columbia University Press, 1972), pp. 254–257.

33. *Public Papers of the Presidents: Harry S. Truman, 1945,* pp. 381–382; *New York Times,* October 30, Section 1, p. 8.

34. Attlee to Truman, October 16, *FRUS, 1945,* II, pp. 58–59.

35. Entry for October 16, Forrestal Diary, Vol. III.

36. Richard G. Hewlett and Oscar E. Anderson, Jr., *A History of the United States Atomic Energy Commission,* Vol. I, *The New World, 1939/1946* (University Park: The Pennsylvania State University Press, 1962), pp. 459–461; and see James L. Gormly, "The Washington Declaration and the 'Poor Relation': Anglo-American Atomic Diplomacy," *Diplomatic History* 8 (Spring 1964), pp. 125–143.

37. Hewlett and Anderson, *The New World,* pp. 462–464.

38. The declaration is reprinted in Truman, *Year of Decisions,* pp. 542–544.

39. *New York Times,* November 12, 13, 14.

40. Lisle A. Rose, *After Yalta* (New York: Charles Scribner's Sons, 1973), p. 145; and Hewlett and Anderson, *The New World,* p. 461.

41. *New York Times,* November 17, p. 4.

42. Hewlett and Anderson, *The New World,* pp. 470–471.

43. James F. Byrnes, *Speaking Frankly* (New York: Harper, 1947), p. 109; *FRUS, 1945,* II, pp. 580–589.

44. Gaddis, *Origins of the Cold War,* p. 257.

CHAPTER NINE

The Adversaries

Relations with the Soviet Union were in disarray by late autumn 1945. Little progress had been made on disputes remaining from Potsdam, and new ones arose with dismaying frequency. President Truman professed not to be disturbed. Now that the war was over, he told Stettinius, "it was inevitable that we should have real difficulties but we should not take them too seriously." They could be worked out "amicably if we gave ourselves enough time."[1] But time ran against the administration. What Truman considered difficulties to be resolved through negotiation, others saw as a pattern of Soviet expansionism to be opposed. Truman and Byrnes faced the task of trying to work out compromises within an atmosphere increasingly hostile to compromise.

Among problems since V-J Day, two stood out. Stalin at Yalta had agreed to support Chiang's government in China and to recognize China's "full sovereignty in Manchuria." These pledges had been ratified by Sino-Soviet treaties in August. The USSR violated the agreements. Its forces in Manchuria plundered industrial and mining equipment China could not afford to lose. The Soviets collaborated with Chinese Communists in obstructing Chiang's efforts to gain control over the region. U.S. transports carrying Nationalist troops were prevented from entering Dairen and other ports, and obstacles were thrown up against movement overland.[2]

Unwilling to risk clashes, the United States did nothing more than register protests. Truman had conceded that the USSR would dominate Manchuria, but hoped Stalin would maintain the appearance of an Open Door. If he did not, the administration would be charged with having betrayed a U.S. policy of long standing. A larger consideration, the future of China, prevented the president from being assertive in

Manchuria. He was afraid Stalin might throw support behind the Communists against Chiang's fragile regime. Should that happen, as Assistant Secretary of War John J. McCloy put it, "then we are in a real mess."[3] Truman tried to defuse the situation by pressuring Chiang to admit Communists to the government.

Soviet behavior in Iran also appeared ominous. The USSR and Britain in 1941 had sent troops to forestall a German takeover, and U.S. units later participated. The three nations had agreed that occupying forces would leave within six months of war's end. The Soviets had sealed off the northern provinces of Azerbaijan and Kurdistan, and reports indicated they were fomenting Communist-dominated separatist movements. For once acting in concert at the London Conference, Byrnes and Bevin extracted from Molotov a pledge that all troops would be evacuated by early March 1946. Through October and November the Soviets did nothing to comply. Indeed, they intensified efforts to create puppet regimes, and the Red Army barred entry to the two provinces by Iranian troops.[4]

Russian actions could not be considered in isolation. Since Potsdam, the Soviets had tried to acquire a trusteeship over Tripolitania and joint control of the Turkish Straits, and they were demanding bases and territorial cessions from Turkey. London warned that Soviet efforts to have British troops withdraw from Greece would bring a Communist takeover. An individual whom Byrnes had sent to report on the Balkans put it all together in a report he submitted in early December 1945. Russian control of Bulgaria and Romania "will doubtless be used as a means of bringing pressure to bear on Greece, Turkey, and the Straits, and could be converted without great effort into a springboard for aggression in the Eastern Mediterranean region."[5]

Some Soviet policies could be justified on grounds of national security or reconstruction needs. But only individuals as optimistic as Joseph Davies could regard Soviet behavior with complacency. The USSR appeared to be probing in all directions. Would compromises satisfy Stalin's appetite or whet it? Suspicion was compounded by the idea that the United States faced not merely a government pursuing historical objectives, but an aggressive, ideological enemy with whom accommodation would be difficult, if not impossible. Officials such as Harriman, Forrestal, and Leahy believed this with varying degrees of intensity, and it was frequently expressed in Congress and the press.[6]

Patrick J. Hurley, U.S. ambassador to China, then added a new ingredient. Home on leave, he had expressed to Truman and Byrnes his desire to resign because of exhaustion and poor health. He was confident Chinese unity could be attained, but said he was not up to the task. By late November, the president and secretary believed they had persuaded a rested Hurley to return to China. Instead, just before he was scheduled to leave, he resigned and issued a blistering statement charging Foreign Service officers in China with sabotaging his efforts. He went further when he appeared before the Senate Foreign Relations Committee a week later. He claimed that a "considerable" portion of the State Department "is endeavoring to support Communism in general as well as specifically in China."[7]

Byrnes went before the committee to answer Hurley and denied that officials in Washington or China were trying to subvert U.S. policies. Byrnes was put on the spot when asked if secret arrangements about China had been made at Yalta. He could not remember everything done at the conference, he said, but it was possible agreements were made that affected China "in some way or another." He offered to provide committee members with copies of the Yalta communiqué so they could judge. Byrnes had known about the Far Eastern accords since before Potsdam and knew there was no reference to them in the communiqué. He avoided embarrassing revelations, as he had in September when questioned about Soviet occupation of the Kuriles. But in so doing, he mortgaged his credibility.[8]

The fragmentary evidence concerning Truman's thinking at the time suggests he was beginning to regard Byrnes as a liability. After Hurley's resignation, Truman asked recently retired Army Chief of Staff George C. Marshall to serve as his representative in China. To assure everyone that policy remained constant, Truman wanted to issue a statement of support for Chiang. Byrnes, worried that such a message would complicate negotiations in Moscow, argued for a more evenhanded approach. Following a meeting during which Byrnes stated his objections to the president and Marshall, Leahy noted that "for the first time I sense a feeling that Secretary Byrnes is not immune to the communistically-inclined advisers in his Department." Whether Truman shared Leahy's opinion is unknown, but he instructed the admiral rather than the State Department to draft the message.[9] "The President is all right," Leahy confided to an aide. "He's behind Chiang. But those 'pinkies' in the State Department can't be trusted. . . . The President told me the other day he now understands why F.D.R. didn't trust the State Department." Leahy saw "pinkies" everywhere, but there is no question Truman thought Byrnes and the department out of line. After another meeting, he informed Leahy of his "surprise and displeasure at the attitude of Secretary Byrnes, expressed yesterday toward the Central Government of China."[10] Truman expressed his dissatisfaction to others and may have sounded out Marshall about taking Byrnes's place.

Byrnes's approach on nuclear matters bothered Truman. The secretary's new enthusiasm for using nuclear energy to bargain apparently blinded him to the domestic danger. Truman knew his efforts to minimize the importance of sharing research had failed to persuade those who opposed giving anything. Senators Tom Connally, chairman of the Foreign Relations Committee, and ranking Republican Arthur Vandenberg—both members of the Special Committee on Atomic Energy—had stalked out of the meeting held to proclaim the Anglo-American-Canadian declaration of November 15. They were angry that Congress had not been consulted and angrier at what the administration had agreed to. Byrnes had ignored them while drafting proposals for Moscow, and he waited until just before leaving to inform them of plans. Worse, the document he read to them went beyond the declaration they already thought went too far. The latter provided that completion of one stage of exchange was necessary before proceeding to the next. Byrnes's paper contained no such qualification. There were heated exchanges.[11]

While Byrnes was en route to Moscow, Connally and Vandenberg convened the Special Committee on Atomic Energy, which voted unanimously to meet with the president. On December 14, committee members expressed their complaints. They opposed agreements without safeguards at every stage. Pointing out that Byrnes had named scientist James B. Conant to the delegation, they wanted to know whether the secretary intended to permit Conant to disclose any information. Truman said no: Byrnes's negotiations would be exploratory, no commitments would be made before clearance with Washington, and no information would be given.[12]

The senators asked Truman to send Byrnes instructions stressing the need for effective controls before disclosure. The president appeared sympathetic, but refused to commit himself. He believed that sharing research posed no threat to security and hoped it would make the Soviets cooperative. Next day, he had Acheson inform Byrnes of the meeting, but added nothing to the original proposals. Byrnes replied that he would adhere to the declaration of November 15. Actually, he first submitted at the conference the proposal that deviated from the declaration in not providing for stages. He rectified this later by offering a paragraph that he said "had been omitted by mistake."[13]

Byrnes was powerless to resolve substantive differences between the administration and its critics. Still, his conduct must have added to Truman's doubts. Byrnes took pride in his ability as a conciliator, yet he had infuriated important senators. His treatment of Vandenberg was inexplicable. The senator possessed an ego in need of constant feeding. He had shown flexibility in the past, provided sufficient flattery were lavished upon him. Byrnes's lack of deference wounded his pride and confirmed his suspicions that the secretary was an appeaser.[14] Possibly Byrnes thought if he negotiated an attractive package, criticism of one part would appear as nit-picking.

What effect the nuclear question had in Moscow is impossible to judge. Molotov, in an obvious attempt to show that the subject could not be used to gain advantage on other issues, insisted it be placed last on the agenda. There was little debate when it was discussed. Molotov suggested only two important changes. He said the proposed UN Commission on Atomic Energy should be answerable to the Security Council rather than the General Assembly, as Byrnes proposed, because the former had power to act and sat in continuous session. Byrnes assumed his real concern was that the Soviets had veto power in the council. Molotov asked that the provision about stages be omitted as something the commission should decide. Byrnes accepted Molotov's first point, but rejected the second on grounds that moving in stages appeared in the Truman-Attlee-King declaration. Molotov withdrew it. The three foreign ministers agreed to invite the other permanent members of the Security Council, and Canada, to sponsor a resolution calling for an atomic commission at the UN's first session in January. Except for Molotov's amendment on accountability, the U.S. recommendations were accepted.[15]

Stalin's behavior confirmed Byrnes's view that Molotov was an obstacle to cooperation. Not only had he refused to consider nuclear matters first, but Byrnes got the impression that members of the Soviet delegation had been ordered to refrain from mentioning the subject until it was raised formally. Nor did Soviet scientists approach Conant, as Byrnes thought they would. Then, at a banquet on Christmas Eve at the Kremlin, Molotov returned to his stand. Proposing a toast to Conant, he asked whether the American had a nuclear bomb in his coat pocket. Stalin admonished Molotov and praised Conant and his fellow scientists. Byrnes's interpreter, Charles Bohlen, later wrote: "From that moment on the Soviets gave the atomic bomb the serious consideration it deserved."[16]

That Molotov's offhand remark, if it was such, caused Stalin to reevaluate his thinking is doubtful. More likely he had given the nuclear issue "serious consideration" all along. One of the Soviet Union's major wartime goals was to create buffer states for defense in depth against any threat. Then, as a British diplomat put it, "plump came the Atomic Bomb. At a blow the balance which had now seemed set and steady was rudely shaken."[17] Territory provided scant protection against bombers carrying nuclear weapons. Molotov's demand that atomic energy be moved to the bottom of the agenda, which Stalin undoubtedly approved, was to show that the Soviets were not intimidated. The point made, Molotov's sarcasm toward Conant served no purpose. Stalin habitually spoke more soothingly than his foreign minister, which was why U.S. officials had developed the idea of a split within the Kremlin. Regardless of whether the incident was staged, Stalin's intervention probably had no significance.

Soviet negotiators often had argued interminably over fine points in agreements. Assuming Stalin had experienced no revelation when Molotov offered his jibe, how explain the USSR's readiness to accept the U.S. approach to nuclear exchange and control? Byrnes assumed it was because the proposal was so desirable. "History will not disclose action by any government," he wrote, "comparable to this generous offer."[18] No one seems to have considered that Soviet acquiescence might have stemmed from indifference—not to the subject of nuclear energy and weapons, but to the nature of the proposed system.

The USSR would have benefited from scientific information first, technological data for industrial use later. Under the plan, the United States would keep its monopoly on weapons until verifiable controls were set up and functioning. Truman had referred to this power as a "sacred trust" that threatened no one. Stalin might assume the United States would not launch an atomic war over the composition of an East European government, but what if a major conflict developed? Or what if a rabid anti-Communist succeeded Truman? Even in the unlikely event that Stalin would have permitted inspection teams to rove about, Soviet security would rest on nothing more substantial than assurances. And should the program bog down, the United States would have gained time to make more bombs.

What Americans regarded as an act of unprecedented generosity must have struck the Soviets as a scheme to ensure their permanent inferiority. They could never be certain the United States had destroyed all its bombs or turned them over to the UN. The latter prospect was not as attractive as Americans thought, as the United States and its allies dominated the Security Council and the General Assembly. Stalin could not have been enamored of the plan even if it were possible to satisfy every doubt. In a world free of nuclear weapons, the United States would remain the only nation with the ability to construct them. That lead would be critical in a protracted war. It would have been self-defeating to have rejected the plan, and Stalin may have been willing to cooperate as long as he thought it in Soviet interests. Given his suspicion about the motives of others, he may also have concluded that Soviet security required an independent nuclear capacity.

Negotiation on other matters followed a familiar pattern. Molotov tried to place Byrnes and Bevin on the defensive by raising questions about British and American conduct in several parts of the world. Byrnes tried to explain U.S. actions; Bevin was less apologetic—during one exchange, he said he resented being "put on the carpet." At the opening session, Molotov suggested changes in the agenda. All were provocative. He wanted to add the questions of U.S. and British troop withdrawals from North China and Greece and said they should discuss British military presence in Indonesia. He asked that the matter of transferring control of Manchuria to China be deleted because the USSR had a "special agreement" with the Nationalist government.[19]

Justification for his last point contained elements of bleak humor. The Soviets would have been out of Manchuria, he said, and were there only because the Chinese government had asked them to stay. Thus there were no differences. He neglected to mention why the request was made. Because the Soviets had collaborated with Chinese Communists to prevent Nationalist forces from entering Manchuria, withdrawal would have left the area in Communist hands. Chiang bought time by asking the Russians to remain, hoping that eventually they would live up to their commitments.[20]

The foreign minister's tactics brought results. He said if Britain and the United States wanted to keep Iran on the agenda, they would have to include Greece and Indonesia. Bevin argued that the situations were not analogous because, unlike Iran, there were no treaties covering those areas to which the Soviet Union was a party. Afraid of trouble, Byrnes suggested that "questions of evacuating troops from Greece, Iran, and Indonesia be eliminated from the agenda but be discussed informally." Molotov pointed out that this would shorten the agenda, and he proposed to shorten it further by eliminating Manchuria. Byrnes agreed.[21]

Byrnes's wish to hold the conference in Moscow so he could talk with Stalin appeared to pay off, particularly with regard to Bulgaria and Romania. Before Potsdam, the United States had refused to recognize their governments because they did not conform to the Declaration on Liberated Europe. Byrnes at Moscow proposed that representatives of all major parties be admitted and pledges be made to hold free elections within six months. He told Molotov privately that to make certain Washington was accurately informed, he had asked a well-known newspaper editor, Mark Ethridge, to visit the two countries. Although Ethridge held "liberal political views" and a "sympathetic attitude" toward the Soviet Union, his findings left him unable to recommend recognition. Byrnes said he had withheld the report because he wanted to show it to Molotov first. Molotov agreed to read it, but replied that Byrnes's negative attitude "obviously" had prejudiced Ethridge. A few days later, Molotov denounced the proposals as interference in the affairs of sovereign nations. Attacking as usual, he said that whatever problems existed had been stirred up by U.S. and British representatives. He refused to discuss Ethridge's report, asking why the editor had not been sent to Greece where "the situation was worse."[22]

When Byrnes discussed Bulgaria and Romania with Stalin, he remarked that he had had "a difficult time with Mr. Molotov on this subject." Smiling, Stalin said this was news. Byrnes brought up the Ethridge report, warning that he had promised the American public and press to publish it and that he would have to do so "unless some solution could be found here." In that case, Stalin replied, he would have Ilya Ehrenburg—"also an impartial man"—publish his views. Byrnes backed away with the limp response that two reports would be "unfortunate," as they would promote divisiveness.

The sparring over, Stalin got down to cases. He denied reports in the Western press that the USSR exercised influence through its troops in Bulgaria and Romania. "Such action would be regarded as unworthy of the Soviet Union and as interference in internal affairs." To resolve the issue in a "practical sense," he offered proposals. Opposition parties had boycotted recent elections in Bulgaria, he said, showing disloyalty and forfeiting any right to consideration. Although the elections had created a popular government, he volunteered to advise it to add two members of the "loyal" opposition. He suggested that Romania admit two ministers and that an Anglo-American-Soviet commission be named to work out details. Both regimes would be encouraged to hold free elections and to guarantee civil liberties.[23]

Stalin's suggestions were embodied in the protocol after negotiation among the foreign ministers. Regarding the additional portfolios, in both cases individuals would be selected on the basis of willingness to "work loyally with the government." Disagreement was disloyalty.[24] This was a far cry from the U.S. proposals of coalitions from all major parties. At the London Conference, Byrnes had indicated he would accept a gesture when he asked that the "Polish precedent" be followed in Bulgaria and Romania. Two new ministers in each government fell short even of that, but he thought it the best he could get. Stalin's offer must have seemed reasonable after Molotov's tactics.

Stalin was less intransigent about Iran, and Byrnes thought their talks an "encouraging combination of frankness and cordiality." Stalin denied the Soviets had either territorial or political ambitions in Iran. Concern was for safety of the Baku oil fields, across the border on Russian soil. Byrnes asked why the USSR had prevented Iranian troops from entering Azerbaijan: Surely 30,000 Soviet troops had nothing to fear from 1,500 Iranians. Stalin answered it was not a military threat, but sabotage directed by a hostile Iranian government. Because of this danger, he could not promise to meet the March 2 deadline, but said he would begin withdrawing troops the moment he felt secure.[25]

In his account of discussions about Iran published in 1947, Byrnes wrote that Stalin had assured him "We will do nothing to make you blush." If that is what Byrnes thought, he undoubtedly regarded the statement as a promise of good behavior. Notes at the session indicate he was mistaken. Stalin's remark followed Byrnes's assertion that disagreement would prove embarrassing if the Iranian issue were raised at the UN in January. "No one had any need to blush," he replied, "if the question was raised in the Assembly." Rather than a pledge, this was a declaration that Soviet policy would not be influenced by what Stalin may have interpreted as a threat.[26]

Byrnes was gratified by Stalin's willingness to compromise several issues that had impeded postwar cooperation. Agreement was reached as to which nations should draw up peace treaties with former Axis satellites, resolving a dispute that had caused the London Conference to founder. Together with prospects for Anglo-American recognition of Bulgaria and Romania, this smoothed the way for a general peace conference to end the war in Europe. Stalin abandoned his claim to a share in governing Japan. He agreed to participate in the Far Eastern Commission based in Washington and an Allied Council in Japan. Both were advisory; their recommendations were not binding on the United States or General MacArthur. Whether Stalin had imagined he would receive a share of power in Japan, or used the issue to bargain for U.S. recognition of Soviet domination in Eastern Europe, is unknown.[27]

Byrnes had reason to be satisfied. He had secured acceptance of proposals on nuclear energy and on Japan. Stalin's agreement to make token changes in Bulgaria and Romania offered a way out. Accepting the offer was no more cynical than Truman's recognition of Poland's Communist-dominated government. Though he had not obtained a date for Soviet departure from Manchuria, he could console himself that the Soviets had reaffirmed their support for a unified China under Chiang. He had gotten nothing on Iran other than Stalin's protestations of innocence, but failure appeared nowhere in the protocol or communiqué. George F. Kennan, who attended the sessions, characterized Byrnes's performance: "His main purpose is to achieve some sort of agreement, he doesn't much care what. The realities behind this agreement, since they concern only such people as Koreans, Rumanians and Iranians, about whom he knows nothing, do not concern him. He wants an agreement for its political effect at home."[28]

Before leaving Moscow, Byrnes arranged to address the nation over radio December 30, the day after he was to land in Washington.

Temperamentally unsuited for the role of spear carrier, he undoubtedly wished to show he was the architect of, and spokesman for, foreign policy. But he also had more pragmatic reasons for addressing the country. Just as Roosevelt had sent him home early from Yalta to help prepare a favorable reception, Byrnes wanted to state the most positive case for the Moscow Conference before critics in Congress and the press had their turn. He was aware that he had enemies in the administration such as Leahy, who could disparage his work to the president and who might leak information to the press.

Truman's version of what happened next has been accepted until recently by scholars, despite Byrnes's denials. According to Truman, he had become concerned about Byrnes's reliability when Vandenberg and Connally told him they had gotten the impression during their briefing that Byrnes intended to give away atomic information before safeguards were established. Truman denied this and had Acheson send a cautionary message to Byrnes in Moscow. The latter acknowledged it on December 17, but did not communicate again until Christmas Eve in a brief cable Truman regarded as unhelpful. The president was in Independence, Missouri, when he learned that Byrnes intended to make a public report before meeting with him. Truman did not know the results before receiving a copy of the communiqué that evening. "I did not like what I read," he wrote. "There was not a word about Iran or any other place where the Soviets were on the march. We had gained only an empty promise of further talks."[29]

Returning to Washington on December 28, Truman met Vandenberg, who had telephoned to express his alarm over the communiqué's provisions on nuclear energy. Noting that the paragraph about stages appeared as the last of four points, Vandenberg professed to see this as making it possible to divulge information before controls were set up. Truman again denied he had such intent and mollified the senator by inviting his help in drafting a press release. After the meeting, Truman proceeded to the presidential yacht *Williamsburg* for a cruise down the Potomac. Next day, while the ship was at Quantico, he claimed to have overheard a telephone conversation between Byrnes and press secretary Charles Ross about the scheduled radio broadcast. According to Truman, he told Ross to inform Byrnes he had "better" report at Quantico before doing anything. When the secretary arrived that afternoon, Truman took him into his stateroom, where he told the secretary "that I did not like the way in which I had been left in the dark." Byrnes tried to place the blame on subordinates, but then admitted responsibility for the oversight.[30]

After Byrnes departed, Truman wrote, he began reading documents the secretary had left. They confirmed his worst fears. The results of the conference "were unreal." Byrnes "had taken it upon himself to move the foreign policy of the United States in a direction to which I could not, and would not, agree." Determined to set him straight, Truman composed a "My Dear Jim" memorandum in longhand, which he claimed he read to Byrnes on January 5. He defended compromises at Potsdam when "we were anxious for Russian entry into the Japanese War," but that situation no longer obtained. He was certain that the Soviets intended to seize the Turkish Straits. Unless they were confronted with "an iron fist and strong language," another war was in the making because the only language they understood was "how many divisions have you?" The United States should take unyielding positions on issues and insist on the return of ships from the USSR and settlement of Lend-Lease payments. He ended with the much-quoted phrase "I'm tired of babying the Soviets." According to Truman, Byrnes "accepted my decision" and neither asked to be replaced nor tendered his resignation.[31]

Truman's reconstruction of these events was self-serving, contained factual inaccuracies, and reflected on his reputation. The charge that he had received only two communications from Byrnes during the Moscow Conference is demonstrably incorrect. No fewer than twenty-seven messages came from Moscow, some of which are marked "shown to president." Byrnes's defense is convincing. He made no effort to talk with Truman by phone from Moscow because he assumed conversation would be tapped. Because cables had to be sent in code, he forwarded them to the State Department for decoding and for Acheson to convey to the president. Truman had been criticizing Byrnes to subordinates for some time, yet none recorded complaints from Truman about being kept uninformed during the conference. Besides, if he had wanted more information, he could have requested it.[32]

Truman's condemnation of the agreements Byrnes negotiated was unfair was well. He absolved himself of responsibility by claiming that "I only saw you for a possible thirty minutes the night before you left." Again, Byrnes's rebuttal is believable. Ordinarily he met with the president every Monday and Thursday and saw him other times. For three weeks before the conference, he claimed, most conversations were devoted to that subject. As for the "thirty minutes" on the last evening, "I called upon him only to ask if he had any last minute instructions or suggestions to make. . . . Had he indicated any desire for me to remain longer, I would gladly have remained."[33] In any case, if Truman did neglect to inform Byrnes about what he regarded as limits on issues, he failed to exercise his responsibility as chief executive. Nowhere did he allege that the secretary violated written or oral instructions. Regarding Iran, which seemed to disturb Truman most, the

Soviets had made clear more than two weeks before the conference that they considered the matter settled and saw no grounds for "renewed consideration of the question."[34] Had Truman wanted Byrnes to force the issue, he had ample time to instruct him accordingly.

Although Truman undoubtedly expressed dissatisfaction to Byrnes on at least two occasions, he probably did not read him the "My Dear Jim" memorandum as written. At the least, it is unlikely Byrnes's ego would have permitted him to accept such a tongue-lashing. In his recollection of the situation, he said he would have resigned at once. Perhaps the document was not intended for Byrnes. Truman had a habit of working out his frustrations by talking tough about what he "really" wanted to do in his diary and in memoranda to himself. If he intended the paper to have contemporary significance, it may have been as insurance that could be shown to critics as evidence that Byrnes had appeased the Soviets against Truman's wishes.[35]

His litany of complaints against Russian behavior—ending with "I'm tired of babying the Soviets"—is significant, regardless of his motives for composing the memorandum. It indicates a reversion to the position he took during his first days in office: The way to deal with the Soviets was to stand up to them, using blunt language they could not fail to understand. He sought to conceal this change by claiming that concessions made before and during Potsdam were motivated solely by his desire to get the USSR into the war. Any concessions Byrnes made at London or Moscow were, by implication, unnecessary and amounted to "babying." Truman conveniently ignored those months when he believed Stalin was an "honest" horse trader with whom he could do business. What caused Truman to change his views and attempt to rewrite the past? The evidence suggests that domestic considerations influenced him as much as did Soviet actions.

Truman had shared two assumptions with Byrnes before the Moscow Conference. Both thought the Kremlin was split by factions, with Molotov representing the "hards" and Stalin the "softs." The latter was "a moderating influence in the present Russian government," Truman told Stettinius. "It would be a real catastrophe if Stalin should die at the present time."[36] This belief made it desirable to hold a conference where Byrnes could circumvent Molotov by talking with Stalin. Also like Byrnes, Truman considered the nuclear proposals generous, in return for which Stalin as a "smart political boss" should be willing to sweeten the pot on other issues. Prospects seemed good that negotiation in a give-and-take atmosphere would produce agreement.

Stalin did not conform to expectation. He softened Molotov's language and offered minor concessions. His gratitude, if any, for the invitation to cosponsor a UN resolution for an atomic energy commission produced no dividend. He had permitted the addition of six non-Communist members to the Warsaw regime, a few of whom were well-known figures. Willingness to accept only two nonentities each in the governments of Bulgaria and Romania, a "fig leaf" as George Kennan put it, left Truman vulnerable regarding the Declaration on Liberated Europe. Probably most important was Stalin's failure to offer anything of value on Iran, then receiving wide notice in the press. Even a vague statement of good intentions in the communiqué, far from solving the problem, would have spared Truman the embarrassment of appearing to countenance aggression.

There can be no doubt that Soviet behavior angered Truman and roused his suspicions, but that does not explain his wholesale condemnation of the conference. What he understood, as Byrnes did not, was that public and congressional hostility toward the Soviet Union had created a new situation. Agreements that once might have been accepted as necessary compromises with a wartime ally now appeared as capitulations. His conversion stemmed in part from determination to avoid the label of "appeaser," even if it meant repudiating some of his own stated objectives.

Truman's most unwarranted charge was that Byrnes had obtained "no more than a general promise" that the Soviets "would be willing to sit down and talk again about the control of atomic energy." The agreement Byrnes negotiated followed in every respect the Truman-Attlee-King declaration of November 15. Both permitted the sharing of scientific knowledge before controls were established. Opposition to this approach, spearheaded by Vandenberg and Connally, had grown despite Truman's repeated assurances that such disclosures posed no threat. Truman surrendered during the first week of January when he agreed to seek revision of the Moscow accord on atomic energy. The alteration, accepted by Britain and the USSR, provided that no information of any kind would be given out before safeguards were in place and that all recommendations by the UN atomic energy commission must be approved by Congress. Rather than admit he had succumbed to pressure, Truman humiliated Byrnes by making it appear the revision was necessary to correct inadequacies in the agreement.[37]

Few scholars have recognized the significance of this retreat on what Truman called "the Number One problem of the world." Since September, he had advocated Stimson's recommendation that theoretical information be given without compensation to the Soviets to assuage their fear of "an Anglo-Saxon" atomic bloc. Failure, Stimson had warned, would result in "irretrievably embittered relations" and stimulate a catastrophic arms race. Whether sharing information would have had the effect he predicted is moot. The important point is that Truman believed it would and had defended this approach in public. He must have understood that reneging would confirm Soviet suspicions and strengthen the USSR's determination to acquire its own nuclear capability.

Truman had cause to be angered by Byrnes's disregard for protocol, but his response had more complicated origins. He had ambivalent feelings about the South Carolinian, as seen in his reference to "my able and conniving Secretary of State" only four days after appointing him. By November, he was using the word "conniving" but without the "able." Given this attitude, he was derelict if he failed to establish clear latitudes for Byrnes's negotiation in Moscow. It is difficult to escape the conclusion that although Truman hoped the conference would be successful, he was prepared to place responsibility for failure—or what others saw as failure—on Byrnes. His professed outrage over the Bulgarian and Romanian compromises rings hollow coming from the man who told Hopkins to inform Stalin that what happened in Eastern Europe "made no difference to U.S. interests" except as it affected peace and to ask him for a gesture toward Poland "whether he means it or not."[38] Regarding the conference, Truman's motto appeared to be "The Buck Stops with Jimmy Byrnes."

Partly Byrnes was a victim of the times: His reputation as the Yalta expert, once a source of strength, had become an embarrassment. He contributed to his predicament. After defending his action at London on the ground that he refused to compromise principle for the sake of agreement, he appeared to do just that in Moscow. He offended senators, with the result that they scrutinized every phrase in the accord for signs of appeasement. And regardless of reasons, his decision to make a public report about the conference without talking with Truman was inexcusable. This crafty man seems to have been blinded by hubris.

Byrnes's stock fell even lower during the months following the Moscow Conference. Columnists were speculating on how long he would last even before he again became embroiled in controversy over what had been done at Yalta. He was in London attending the opening session of the UN General Assembly when Acheson publicly denied there was any agreement providing for Russian acquisition of the Kuriles. The Soviets refuted this claim by publishing the relevant portion of the Yalta Far Eastern accord. Upon his return to Washington, Byrnes was asked for an explanation at a press conference on January 29, 1946. He said the Soviets were correct, but tried to distance himself by insisting he had been unaware of the agreement until after V-J

Day. Although he was not certain, he said, he thought Truman learned of it at about the same time.[39]

This was nonsense. The accord was common knowledge to those around the president. In the presence of Grew and Leahy, Truman had handed T. V. Soong a replication of it for use in negotiations with Stalin. Byrnes was not yet secretary but knew he would be, and during that time he was in constant touch with Truman and others. It is inconceivable they failed to apprise him. His statements destroyed what credibility he had. When questioned about the Kuriles in September, he said he remembered clearly what had been agreed to at Yalta. In December, he told a Senate committee there were no secret agreements about the Far East. Now he claimed he had known of them only a few months. He further alienated Truman by placing him in the position of seeming incompetent if he had not learned of them earlier—or of deceiving Congress and the public if he had.[40]

Truman held his own press conference the next day. He said he had known about the Yalta accord since before Potsdam, but had withheld it because British and Soviet approval was necessary. He tried to diminish the document by referring to it merely as a "wartime understanding," as though any commitment was temporary. A revealing exchange took place when he was asked whether he supported "the State Department's policy." Truman replied sharply that the president set foreign policy and the State Department carried it out. His remark was interpreted as evidence of displeasure with Byrnes.[41]

Assertion of presidential responsibility for foreign policy was technically correct, but in practice Truman had delegated great authority to his secretary of state. That would be the case no longer. Although Byrnes fell in step with the administration's firm line, his role in shaping policies diminished. Truman probably would have replaced him with Marshall as soon as decently possible, but the latter was in China trying to work out an accommodation between Chiang and the Communists. In any case, the president now asserted control over foreign policy.

Less than two weeks after this press conference, Stalin made a speech that to Truman must have validated his decision to stop "babying" the Soviets. The Russian leader said that World War II had been caused by "monopoly capitalism," of which Nazi Germany and Japan were but extreme examples. Soviet might had defeated this evil— he minimized the role of the United States and Britain—but the USSR remained at risk so long as such forces existed. The Soviet Union had no choice but to adopt a program of unassailable strength against "capitalist encirclement." It must increase its military power and industrial strength, and—ominous in the atomic age—it must "in the

very near future . . . surpass the achievements of science" outside
Russia.[42] Some Americans interpreted the speech as a time-dishonored
example of using foreign threats to gain support for domestic sacrifices.
To others, it was a declaration of World War III.

Truman did not concur with the apocalyptic view of Stalin's address,
but regarded it as a challenge to be answered. Two weeks later, he
approved a speech by the now militant Byrnes warning the Soviets
against actions that might lead to "situations where no power intends
war but no power will be able to avert war." Truman's underlinings
and marginal comments show his enthusiasm for Byrnes's most truculent phrases, especially those announcing U.S. determination to resist
aggression. He returned his copy with this comment: "Jim, I've read
it and like it."[43]

Four months earlier, Truman had said that difficulties with the Soviet
Union were to be expected and could be solved "amicably" if given
enough time. He still sought accommodation, but believed it could be
attained only from a position of strength and willingness to employ
that strength. Soviet actions, particularly in Iran, had influenced him,
but he was also affected by domestic pressure to get tough. The Grand
Alliance of World War II was dead, and in its place arose a condition
that became known as the Cold War. Barring a change in leadership
on both sides, what followed was predictable, if not inevitable.

NOTES

1. October 22, Calendar Notes, Stettinius Papers.

2. *Foreign Relations of the United States, 1945* (Washington, D.C., 1967),
VII, pp. 1031–1045.

3. Memorandum of meeting, November 6, inserted in Forrestal Diary, Vol.
III.

4. *FRUS, 1945,* VIII, pp. 413–415.

5. Mark Ethridge memorandum, December 7, *FRUS, 1945,* V, p. 637.
Truman told press secretary Charles Ross that the Soviets "have 500,000 men
in Bulgaria and some day they are going to move down and take the Black
Sea straits. . . . There's only one thing they understand." "Divisions?" Ross
asked. Trumen nodded and said, "We can't send any divisions over to prevent
them from moving from Bulgaria. I don't know what we're going to do." Entry
for December 17, Ayers Diary.

6. See John Lewis Gaddis, *The United States and the Origins of the Cold
War, 1941–1947* (New York: Columbia University Press, 1972), pp. 273–274.

7. Herbert Feis, *The China Tangle: The American Effort in China from
Pearl Harbor to the Marshall Mission* (New York: Atheneum, 1965), Chapters
24, 25, and 36.

8. *Department of State Bulletin* XIII (December 9, 1945); United States Senate, Committee on Foreign Relations, *Hearings on the Investigation of Far Eastern Policy,* 79th Congress, 1st Session, 1945, pp. 123–124, 233.

9. As quoted in Robert L. Messer, *The End of an Alliance: James F. Byrnes, Truman, and the Origins of the Cold War* (Chapel Hill: University of North Carolina Press, 1982), p. 147.

10. George Elsey memorandum, November 30, Elsey Papers.

11. *FRUS, 1945,* II, pp. 92–96.

12. Richard G. Hewlett and Oscar E. Anderson, Jr., *A History of the United States Atomic Energy Commission,* Vol. I, *The New World, 1939/1946* (University Park: The Pennsylvania State University Press, 1962), p. 474.

13. Acheson to Byrnes, December 15, *FRUS, 1945,* II, pp. 609–610; Byrnes remark about the "mistake" is on p. 698.

14. While the Moscow Conference was going on, Vandenberg wrote to a friend of the "Truman-Byrnes appeasement policy which I cannot stomach," as quoted in Lisle A. Rose, *After Yalta* (New York: Charles Scribner's Sons, 1973), p. 138.

15. *FRUS, 1945,* II, pp. 736, 762, 815–824.

16. Charles Bohlen, *Witness to History* (New York: Norton, 1973), p. 249.

17. *FRUS, 1945,* II, pp. 82–84.

18. James F. Byrnes, *Speaking Frankly* (New York: Harper, 1947), p. 265.

19. Bevin's remark is in *FRUS, 1945,* II, p. 614; notes of the first session on pp. 610–621.

20. Forrest C. Pogue, *George Marshall: Statesman* (New York: Viking, 1987), p. 77; and see Feis, *China Tangle,* Chapter 33.

21. *FRUS, 1945,* II, p. 616.

22. *FRUS, 1945,* II, pp. 644–645.

23. All quotations from *FRUS, 1945,* II, pp. 750–758.

24. *FRUS, 1945,* II, pp. 821–822.

25. *FRUS, 1945,* II, pp. 680–687.

26. Byrnes, *Speaking Frankly,* p. 120; *FRUS, 1945,* II, pp. 751–752.

27. *FRUS, 1945,* II, p. 819.

28. George F. Kennan's diary notes for December 19, reprinted in *Memoirs, 1925–1950* (Boston: Little, Brown, 1967), pp. 287–288.

29. Harry S. Truman, *Year of Decisions* (Garden City, N.Y.: Doubleday, 1955), pp. 546–553.

30. Truman, *Year of Decisions,* p. 550. But see Folder 641, Byrnes Papers, for memorandum of telephone message from the president about *Williamsburg,* December 29, beginning "Happy to hear of your safe arrival. Suggest you come down today or tomorrow to report on your mission." The message belies Truman's version.

31. The memorandum is reprinted in Truman, *Year of Decisions,* pp. 551–552.

32. For the figure of twenty-seven messages, see Messer, *Alliance,* p. 160; on December 20, Truman had Acheson cable Byrnes "to clear up a point" about the latter's reports on two previous sessions, evidence that *at the time*

Truman felt he was being sufficiently informed; *FRUS, 1945,* II, pp. 707–708. Byrnes's response to Truman's allegations is in a paper "Draft October 23" [nd], Folder 640, Byrnes Papers. There is another version, written in response to Jonathan Daniels, *Man of Independence* (Philadelphia: Lippincott, 1950) in Folder 573, Byrnes Papers.

33. "Draft October 23," Folder 640, Byrnes Papers.

34. Harriman to Byrnes, November 30, *FRUS, 1945,* VIII, pp. 468–469.

35. "Those who know of the cordial relations that had existed between Senator Truman and me for a number of years are not apt to believe now that he read 'the riot act' to me," Byrnes wrote. "They would know that had any such thing occurred and had the president made the statement he is quoted as having made, he would have had my resignation then." Folder 573, Byrnes Papers.

36. October 22, Calendar Notes, Stettinius Papers.

37. Truman quotation is in *Year of Decisions,* p. 550; compare Truman-Attlee-King agreement, *Public Papers of the Presidents, Harry S. Truman, 1945* (Washington, D.C., 1961), pp. 472–475, with Moscow communiqué, *FRUS, 1945,* II, pp. 815–824. For revision of the Moscow accord, see Rose, *After Yalta,* pp. 160–161.

38. Entry for May 22, Truman Diary.

39. Messer, *Alliance,* pp. 169–171.

40. *FRUS, 1945,* VII, pp. 896–897; as further evidence that the exact wording of the Far East accord was available to those around Truman, see John J. McCloy's report on the accord to Forrestal and Stimson, June 10, inserted in Forrestal Diary, Vol. III. Former aide George Elsey recently told an interviewer that as early as April, at Leahy's instructions, he hand-carried the official text to Byrnes at the Shoreham Hotel, where the latter and Ben Cohen studied it. Mark Gallicchio, "The Cold War Begins in Asia: American East Asian Policy and the Fall of the Japanese Empire," to be published by Columbia University Press in 1988. Professor Gallicchio generously made the galleys available to me.

41. See *New York Times* and *Washington Post,* February 1, 1946.

42. *Vital Speeches* XII (March 1, 1946), pp. 300–304.

43. Byrnes's speech is in *Department of State Bulletin* XIV (March 10, 1946), pp. 355–358; Truman's comment is quoted in Messer, *Alliance,* p. 188. Truman told aides that he had advised Byrnes to "stiffen up" and "try for three months not to make any compromises." Entry for February 28, Ayers Diary.

Epilogue

President Truman's decision to stop "babying" the Soviets seemed justified by events during the first months of 1946, especially resolution of the Iranian crisis. Conclusions he had reached were given theoretical support in what became an influential analysis of Soviet behavior that George F. Kennan submitted from Moscow. And public opinion made "standing up to" the Soviets politically advantageous. Polls continued to reveal hardening attitudes, which Republicans made clear they intended to exploit in an election year.

In mid-February, the Canadian government announced it had arrested twenty-two individuals on charges of obtaining information on the atomic bomb for the Soviet Union. They had operated under control of agents posing as diplomatic personnel. Truman had learned of the spy ring from Prime Minister Mackenzie King the previous fall, but was unaware of its extent until he received a detailed report in December. What effect the revelation had on his attitude toward the Soviets is unclear, but it could hardly have been favorable. Public disclosure, of course, provided ammunition for those urging a tougher policy.[1]

Iran grew more dangerous as the Soviets failed to remove their troops by the agreed deadline of March 2. Instead, they sent reinforcements into the northern provinces. Accurate information was difficult to obtain, but the most alarming interpretation was that the USSR was preparing to invade the rest of Iran, Turkey, and Iraq. At the peak of the crisis, Truman told Averell Harriman that the possibility existed of war with the Soviet Union.[2]

The United States put pressure on Russia to withdraw. In his speech of February 28, Secretary Byrnes alluded to Iran when he stated that no power had the right to maintain forces "in the territories of other sovereign states without their approval and consent freely given." He said that if other members of the Security Council upheld the UN Charter, no nation "can safely break the peace." Moscow was asked to explain its actions in messages of March 6 and 8, and the United States supported Iran in bringing the matter before the Security Council over Soviet objection. When the Turkish ambassador died, Truman had his body sent home aboard the battleship *Missouri,* escorted by other vessels. This task force remained in the eastern Mediterranean. On March 24, the Soviets promised to leave in five or six weeks provided "nothing unforeseen" took place, but a day later moved troops closer to Teheran. Finally, on April 14 they announced that "evacuation would be completed unconditionally by May 6."[3]

Truman later boasted that the Soviet Union pulled out because he had given Stalin an ultimatum. His claim has been challenged: Nothing resembling an ultimatum has been found in the files, and a number of former officials have denied knowledge of any such message. Actually, Truman did have a strong statement conveyed orally to Stalin on April 4 by the new ambassador, Walter Bedell Smith. Smith told the Soviet leader that although Truman and Byrnes believed him to be a man of his word and the American people hoped this was so, it would be mistaken to think the United States was "either divided, weak or unwilling to face our responsibilities. If the people of the United States were ever to become convinced that we are faced with a wave of progressive aggression on the part of any powerful nation or group of nations, we would react exactly as we have in the past."[4]

Truman's use of the term "ultimatum" was technically incorrect, but Smith's words certainly constituted a warning. Evidence suggests, without proving, that they influenced the Soviet decision. Most important is that Truman thought so. It confirmed his belief that the Soviets respected strength and despised weakness—and should be treated accordingly. His demonstration of resolve was not to damage Soviet-U.S. relations, but to place them on a realistic basis. To show that he meant to keep doors open, he had Smith invite Stalin to visit the United States.

On February 22, in response to a State Department request, George Kennan sent a five-part cable stating his interpretation of Soviet behavior and his recommendations for America's response. Soviet conduct did not rely on analyses of specific situations, he said. Rather, "it arises mainly from basic inner-Russian necessities which existed before recent war and exist today." What he called "the Kremlin's neurotic view" derived from a sense of insecurity that Communist leaders shared with the czars because both systems were backward and artificial. They wanted to prevent Russians from learning about the outside world and

Westerners from learning about Russia. Marxist dogma, which must not be underestimated, provided a "fig leaf of their moral and intellectual respectability," enabling them to justify their fear of foreigners and harsh treatment of the Soviet people.

"Capitalist encirclement," with which there could be no lasting peace, compelled the Soviets to pursue two goals: Transform Russia into an impregnable bastion and try to set capitalist powers against one another. Any steps promoting these ends were justifiable, indeed necessary, without regard for other considerations. Kennan analyzed a number of official and unofficial methods the Kremlin would use. These included expanding the limits of Soviet power, exploiting organizations such as the UN, weakening Western influence in colonial areas, and manipulating Communist parties and "progressive" groups in other countries.

Despite the array of instruments the Soviets possessed, Kennan believed "the problem is within our power to solve." His recommendations stressed the need to maintain Western cohesion, combat Soviet propaganda, educate the public, and improve the "health and vigor of our own society." All these were long-term tasks. What probably seemed most significant at the time, in light of Iran, was his first point. Soviet power, he said, "is neither schematic nor adventuristic." Although "impervious to logic of reason . . . it is highly sensitive to logic of force." It usually retreated "when strong resistance is encountered at any point. Thus if the adversary has sufficient force and makes clear his readiness to use it, he rarely has to do so. . . . There need be no prestige-engaging showdowns."[5] The USSR's retreat from Iran appeared to validate his analysis.

The effect of this message, in Kennan's words, "was nothing less than sensational." Truman read it, Forrestal reproduced and circulated it among top military personnel, and its author was invited to head a newly created policy-planning group. Kennan correctly observed that six months earlier, his advice would have met with disapproval—six months later, it would have seemed redundant. At the time, it provided both an explanation of otherwise inexplicable behavior and a prescription for responding that corroborated Truman's experience. Best of all, it placed entire blame on the Soviets. Kennan's analysis provided the basis for what became known as the "containment" policy.[6]

Truman's conversion brought neither new initiatives nor efforts to undo agreements. Five weeks after he wrote in his angry "My Dear Jim" memorandum that he would not recognize Romania or Bulgaria until their governments were "radically" altered, for instance, he recognized Romania on terms Byrnes had negotiated. What had changed was the way he perceived Soviet-U.S. relations. He no longer regarded disputes as inevitable results of competing national interests that could be resolved on a give-and-take basis. Now he viewed them as stemming from Communist Russia's need to extend its sphere and to weaken and divide those who stood in its way. He gave public indication of this attitude when he sat nodding approval as Winston Churchill delivered his "iron curtain" speech in Fulton, Missouri, on March 5.[7] Truman still sought coexistence, but believed it could be achieved only by dealing with the Soviets from positions of strength they were bound to respect. He had acquired his militance reluctantly.

NOTES

1. Richard G. Hewlett and Oscar E. Anderson, *A History of the United States Atomic Energy Commission,* Vol. I, *The New World, 1939/1946* (University Park: The Pennsylvania State University Press, 1962), pp. 480, 501; Lisle A. Rose, *After Yalta* (New York: Charles Scribner's Sons, 1973), pp. 137–138.

2. *Foreign Relations of the United States, 1946* (Washington, D.C., 1970), VII, p. 340; *New York Times,* March 13, 14, 15, 1946; Herbert Feis, *From Trust to Terror: The Onset of the Cold War, 1945–1950* (New York: Norton, 1979), pp. 82–83.

3. Kuross Samii, "Truman Against Stalin in Iran: A Tale of Three Messages," *Middle Eastern Studies* 23 (January 1987), pp. 95–107. See also Robin DeNardo, "The Battle for Azerbaijan, 1946," unpublished seminar paper written under direction of A. Goldschmidt, The Pennsylvania State University, March 1987.

4. Smith's talk with Stalin is in *FRUS, 1946,* VI, pp. 732–736. Because he thought the session might become "stormy," Smith reported, he went alone. In a survey of the considerable literature on this subject, Samii, in "Truman Against Stalin," points out that those who have argued most strenuously that Truman misrepresented his actions omit mention of the meeting and collateral evidence indicating the importance he attached to Smith's message.

5. *FRUS, 1946,* VI, pp. 696–709.

6. George F. Kennan, *Memoirs, 1925–1950* (Boston: Little, Brown, 1967), pp. 292–295.

7. There can be no doubt that Truman was fully briefed on what Churchill intended to say; see John Lewis Gaddis, *The United States and the Origins of the Cold War, 1941–1947* (New York: Columbia University Press, 1972), pp. 306–309.

Selected
Bibliography

The literature on the origins of the Cold War is voluminous. Sources listed are limited to those cited in this work or those found particularly useful.

MANUSCRIPT COLLECTIONS

Clemson University: James F. Byrnes Papers
Harvard University: Joseph C. Grew Papers
Library of Congress: Joseph E. Davies Papers; Cordell Hull Papers; William D. Leahy Papers
National Archives: Harley Notter File; State Department Files, Record Group 59 (cited by file number)
Princeton University: Bernard M. Baruch Papers; John Foster Dulles Papers; John Foster Dulles Oral History Project; James V. Forrestal Papers; George F. Kennan Papers; Harry Dexter White Papers
Franklin D. Roosevelt Library: Oscar Cox Papers; Harry L. Hopkins Papers; Isador Lubin Papers; Henry Morgenthau Papers; Franklin D. Roosevelt Papers; Samuel I. Rosenman Papers; Map Room File; Official File; President's Secretary's File; Soviet Protocol Committee File
Harry S. Truman Library: Dean Acheson Papers; Eban A. Ayers Papers; William L. Clayton Papers; Clark M. Clifford Papers; Conway File; George Elsey Papers; Richard C. Patterson, Jr., Papers; Samuel I. Rosenman Papers; Charles Ross Papers; John M. Snyder Papers; Harry S. Truman Papers; Map Room File; Oral History; OSS Memoranda; President's Secretary's File
University of Virginia: Edward R. Stettinius, Jr., Papers
Yale University: Henry L. Stimson Papers

UNPUBLISHED MATERIAL

DeNardo, Robin. "The Battle for Azerbaijan, 1946." Seminar paper, The Pennsylvania State University, March 1987.

Gallicchio, Mark. "The Cold War Begins in Asia: American East Asian Policy and the Fall of the Japanese Empire." To be published by Columbia University Press in 1988.

Manser, Richard L. "Roosevelt and China: From Cairo to Yalta." Doctoral dissertation, Temple University, 1987.

Szymczak, Robert. "The Unquiet Dead: The Katyn Forest as an Issue in American Diplomacy and Politics." Doctoral dissertation, Carnegie-Mellon University, 1980.

GOVERNMENT PUBLICATIONS

Documents on British Policy Overseas. Series I, Volume I, 1945. London: Her Majesty's Stationery Office, 1984.

Public Papers of the Presidents: Harry S. Truman, 1945–1946. Washington, D.C.: 1961–1962.

United States Department of State. *Department of State Bulletin.* Volumes XIII and XIV, 1945–1946. Washington, D.C.:

———. *Foreign Relations of the United States* (FRUS). Annual Volumes, 1941–1946. Washington, D.C.: 1958–1970.

———. *Foreign Relations of the United States: The Conference of Berlin (The Potsdam Conference), 1945.* 2 volumes. Washington, D.C.: 1960.

———. *Foreign Relations of the United States: The Conferences at Cairo and Teheran, 1943.* Washington, D.C.: 1961.

———. *Foreign Relations of the United States: The Conferences at Malta and Yalta, 1945.* Washington, D.C.: 1955.

United States Senate. *Hearings on the Investigation of Far Eastern Policy.* 79th Congress, 1st Session, 1945.

United States Strategic Bombing Survey. *Japan's Struggle to End the War.* Washington, D.C.: 1946.

Woodward, E. L. *British Foreign Policy in the Second World War.* 5 Volumes. London: Her Majesty's Stationery Office, 1970–1976.

ARTICLES

Ash, Timothy Garton. "From World War to Cold War." *The New York Review of Books* XXXIV (June 11, 1987), pp. 44–50.

Bernstein, Barton J. "A Postwar Myth: 500,000 U.S. Lives Saved." *Bulletin of Atomic Scientists* 42 (June/July 1986), pp. 38–40.

Boyle, Peter G. "The British Foreign Office View of Soviet-American Relations, 1945–1946." *Diplomatic History* 3 (Summer 1979), pp. 307–320.

Buhite, Russell D. "Soviet-American Relations and the Repatriation of Prisoners of War, 1945." *The Historian* XXXV (May 1973), pp. 384–397.

Gaddis, John Lewis. "The Emerging Post-Revisionist Synthesis on the Origins of the Cold War." *Diplomatic History* 7 (Summer 1983), pp. 171–190.

Herring, George C., Jr. "Lend-Lease to Russia and the Origins of the Cold War." *Journal of American History* XVI (June 1969), pp. 93–114.

Kimball, Warren F. "Naked Reverse Right: Roosevelt, Churchill, and Eastern Europe from Tolstoy to Yalta—and a Little Beyond." *Diplomatic History* 9 (Winter 1985), pp. 1–24.

Levine, Steven I. "A New Look at American Mediation in the Chinese Civil War: The Marshall Mission and Manchuria." *Diplomatic History* 3 (Fall 1979), pp. 349–375.

Maddox, Robert J. "Amerikanische Geschichtsrevisionisten und der Beginn des Kalten Krieges." *Osteuropa* 27 (May 1977), pp. 427–434.

_____. "Roosevelt and Stalin: The Final Days." *Continuity: A Journal of History* 6 (Spring 1983), pp. 113–122.

_____. "The Rise and Fall of Cold War Revisionism." *The Historian* XLVI (May 1984), pp. 416–428.

_____. "Reparations and the Origins of the Cold War." *Mid-America* (October 1985), pp. 125–135.

_____. "Truman, Poland, and the Origins of the Cold War." *Presidential Studies Quarterly* XVII (Winter 1987), pp. 27–41.

Miles, Rufus E., Jr. "Hiroshima: The Strange Myth of Half a Million Lives Saved." *International Security* 10 (Fall 1985), pp. 121–140.

Miscamble, Wilson D. "Anthony Eden and the Truman-Molotov Conversations, April 1945." *Diplomatic History* 2 (Spring 1978), pp. 167–180.

Orzell, Laurance J. "A Painful Problem: Poland in Allied Diplomacy, February-July, 1945." *Mid-America* 59 (October 1977), pp. 147–169.

Samii, Kuross. "Truman Against Stalin in Iran: A Tale of Three Messages." *Middle Eastern Studies* 23 (January 1987), pp. 95–107.

Schlesinger, Arthur M., Jr. "Origins of the Cold War." *Foreign Affairs* XLVI (October 1967), pp. 22–52.

_____. "West European Scholars Absolve Yalta." *Wall Street Journal* (June 16, 1987), p. 30.

Sherwin, Martin J. "How Well They Meant." *Bulletin of Atomic Scientists* 41 (August 1985), pp. 9–15.

Woods, Randall B. "Conflict or Community? The United States and Argentina's Admission to the United Nations." *Pacific Historical Review* XLVI (August 1977), pp. 361–386.

BOOKS

Acheson, Dean. *Present at the Creation: My Years in the State Department.* New York: Norton, 1969.

Alperovitz, Gar. *Atomic Diplomacy: Hiroshima and Potsdam, The Use of the Atomic Bomb & the American Confrontation with Soviet Power.* New York:

Simon & Schuster, 1965, updated and expanded version by Elisabeth Sifton Books, 1985.

Anderson, Terry H. *The United States, Great Britain, and the Cold War, 1944–1947.* Columbia: University of Missouri Press, 1981.

Backer, John N. *The Decision to Divide Germany.* Durham, N.C.: Duke University Press, 1978.

Blum, John Morton. *From the Morgenthau Diaries: Years of War, 1941–1945.* Boston: Houghton Mifflin, 1967.

———. *The Price of Vision: The Diary of Henry A. Wallace.* Boston: Houghton Mifflin, 1973.

Bohlen, Charles E. *Witness to History, 1929–1969.* New York: Norton, 1973.

Brooks, Lester. *Behind Japan's Surrender: The Secret Struggle That Ended an Empire.* New York: McGraw-Hill, 1968.

Buhite, Russell D. *Patrick J. Hurley and American Foreign Policy.* Ithaca, N.Y.: Cornell University Press, 1973.

———. *Decisions at Yalta: An Appraisal of Summit Diplomacy.* Wilmington, Del.: Scholarly Resources, 1986.

Butow, Robert J. C. *Japan's Decision to Surrender.* Stanford, Calif.: Stanford University Press, 1954.

Byrnes, James F. *Speaking Frankly.* New York: Harper, 1947.

———. *All in One Lifetime.* New York: Harper, 1958.

Calvocoressi, Peter, and Guy Wint. *Total War.* New York: Penguin, 1979.

Campbell, Thomas M., and George C. Herring. *The Diaries of Edward R. Stettinius, Jr.* New York: New Viewpoints, 1975.

Chase, John L. "Unconditional Surrender Reconsidered." In *Causes and Consequences of World War II,* Robert A. Divine, ed. Chicago: Quadrangle, 1969.

Churchill, Winston S. *Triumph and Tragedy.* Boston: Houghton Mifflin, 1953.

Ciechanowski, Jan. *Defeat in Victory.* Garden City, N.Y.: Doubleday, 1947.

Clemens, Diane Shaver. *Yalta.* New York: Oxford, 1970.

Cochran, Burt. *Harry Truman and the Crisis Presidency.* New York: Funk & Wagnalls, 1973.

Dallek, Robert. *Franklin D. Roosevelt and American Foreign Policy, 1932–1945.* New York: Oxford, 1979.

Daniels, Jonathan. *Man of Independence.* Philadelphia: Lippincott, 1950.

Davis, Lynn Etheridge. *The Cold War Begins: Soviet-American Conflict over Eastern Europe.* Princeton, N.J.: Princeton University Press, 1974.

Deane, John R. *Strange Alliance.* New York: Viking, 1947.

DeSantis, Hugh. *The Diplomacy of Silence: The American Foreign Service, the Soviet Union, and the Cold War, 1933–1947.* Chicago: University of Chicago Press, 1980.

Dilks, David, ed. *The Diaries of Sir Alexander Cadogan, 1938–1945.* New York: G. P. Putnam's Sons, 1972.

Divine, Robert A. *Roosevelt and World War II.* Baltimore, Md.: The Johns Hopkins University Press, 1969.

Donovan, Robert J. *Conflict and Crisis: The Presidency of Harry S Truman, 1945–1948.* New York: Norton, 1977.

Eden, Anthony. *The Memoirs of Anthony Eden: The Reckoning.* Boston: Houghton Mifflin, 1965.

Feis, Herbert. *The China Tangle: The American Effort in China from Pearl Harbor to the Marshall Mission.* New York: Atheneum, 1965.

_____. *Churchill-Roosevelt-Stalin: The War They Waged and the Peace They Sought.* Princeton, N.J.: Princeton University Press, 1957.

_____. *From Trust to Terror: The Onset of the Cold War, 1945–1950.* New York: Norton, 1970.

Ferrell, Robert H. *Harry S. Truman and the American Presidency.* Boston: Little, Brown, 1983.

_____, ed. *Off the Record: The Private Papers of Harry S. Truman.* New York: Harper, 1980.

_____, ed. *Dear Bess: The Letters from Harry to Bess Truman, 1910–1959.* New York: Norton, 1983.

Gaddis, John Lewis. *The United States and the Origins of the Cold War, 1941–1947.* New York: Columbia University Press, 1972.

Gimbel, John. *The American Occupation of Germany: Politics and the Military, 1945–1949.* Stanford, Calif.: Stanford University Press, 1968.

Hamby, Alonzo L. *Beyond the New Deal: Harry S. Truman and American Liberalism.* New York: Columbia University Press, 1973.

_____, ed. *Harry S. Truman and the Fair Deal.* Lexington, Mass.: D. C. Heath, 1974.

Hammond, Thomas T., ed. *Witnesses to the Origins of the Cold War.* Seattle: University of Washington Press, 1982.

Harbutt, Fraser J. *The Iron Curtain: Churchill, America and the Origins of the Cold War.* New York: Oxford, 1986.

Harriman, W. Averell, and Ellie Abel. *America and Russia in a Changing World.* Garden City, N.Y.: Doubleday, 1971.

_____. *Special Envoy to Churchill and Stalin, 1941–1946.* New York: Random House, 1975.

Herken, Gregg. *The Winning Weapon: The Atomic Bomb in the Cold War, 1945–1950.* New York: Knopf, 1980.

Herring, George. *Aid to Russia, 1941–1946.* New York: Columbia University Press, 1973.

Hewlett, Richard B., and Oscar E. Anderson, Jr. *A History of the United States Atomic Energy Commmission.* Vol. I, *The New World, 1939/1946.* University Park: The Pennsylvania State University Press, 1962.

Hillman, William. *Mr. President.* New York: Farrar, Straus, & Young, 1952.

Horowitz, David. *Free World Colossus.* Rev. ed., 1971. New York: Hill and Wang, 1965.

Hull, Cordell. *The Memoirs of Cordell Hull.* 2 vols. New York: Macmillan, 1948.

Irye, Akira. *The Cold War in Asia.* Englewood Cliffs, N.J.: Prentice-Hall, 1974.

Issacson, Walter, and Evan Thomas. *The Wise Men, Six Friends and the World They Made: Acheson, Bohlen, Harriman, Kennan, Lovett, McCloy.* New York: Simon & Schuster, 1986.

Kaiser, Robert B. *Cold Winter, Cold War.* New York: Stein and Day, 1974.

Kennan, George F. *The Decision to Intervene.* Princeton, N.J.: Princeton University Press, 1958.

————. *Memoirs: 1925–1950.* Boston: Little, Brown, 1967.

Kimball, Warren. *Swords or Plowshares?: The Morgenthau Plan for Defeated Germany.* Philadelphia: Lippincott, 1976.

————, ed. *Churchill and Roosevelt: The Complete Correspondence.* Princeton, N.J.: Princeton University Press, 1984.

Kuklick, Bruce. *American Policy and the Division of Germany: The Clash with Russia over Reparations.* Ithaca, N.Y.: Cornell University Press, 1972.

Kuniholm, Bruce Robellet. *The Origins of the Cold War in the Near East: Great Power Conflict and Diplomacy in Iran, Turkey, and Greece.* Princeton, N.J.: Princeton University Press, 1980.

Lane, Arthur Bliss. *I Saw Poland Betrayed.* Indianapolis, Ind.: Bobbs-Merrill, 1948.

Larson, Deborah Welch. *Origins of Containment: A Psychological Explanation.* Princeton, N.J.: Princeton University Press, 1985.

Leahy, William D. *I Was There.* New York: Whittlesey House, 1950.

Levantrosser, William F., ed. *Harry S. Truman: The Man From Independence.* New York: Greenwood Press, 1986.

Lukacs, John. *A New History of the Cold War.* 3d ed. New York: Anchor, 1966.

————. *1945: Year Zero.* Garden City, N.Y.: Doubleday, 1978.

Lundestad, Geir. *The American Non-Policy Towards Eastern Europe: Universality in an Area Not of Essential Interest to the United States.* Oslo: Universitetsforlaget, 1975.

McCagg, William O., Jr. *Stalin Embattled, 1943–1948.* Detroit: Wayne State University Press, 1978.

McCoy, Donald R. *The Presidency of Harry S. Truman.* Lawrence: University Press of Kansas, 1984.

McNeill, William H. *America, Britain and Russia.* London: Oxford, 1953.

Maddox, Robert J. *The Unknown War with Russia: Wilson's Siberian Intervention.* San Rafael, Calif.: Presidio Press, 1977.

————. *The New Left and the Origins of the Cold War.* Princeton, N.J.: Princeton University Press, 1973.

Mastny, Vojtech. *Russia's Road to the Cold War: Diplomacy, Warfare, and the Politics of Communism, 1941–1945.* New York: Columbia University Press, 1979.

Mee, Charles L., Jr. *Meeting at Potsdam.* New York: M. Evans, 1975.

Messer, Robert L. *The End of an Alliance: James F. Byrnes, Roosevelt, Truman, and the Origins of the Cold War.* Chapel Hill: University of North Carolina Press, 1982.

Miller, Richard Lawrence. *Truman: The Rise to Power.* New York: McGraw-Hill, 1986.

Murphy, Robert. *Diplomat Among Warriors.* New York: Pyramid Books, 1964.

Paterson, Thomas C. *Soviet-American Confrontation.* Baltimore, Md.: The Johns Hopkins University Press, 1973.

Perkins, Frances. *The Roosevelt I Knew.* New York: Viking, 1946.

Phillips, Cabell. *The Truman Presidency: The History of a Triumphant Succession.* New York: Macmillan, 1966.

Pogue, Forrest C. *George Marshall: Statesman.* New York: Viking, 1987.

Rose, Lisle A. *After Yalta.* New York: Charles Scribner's Sons, 1973.

_____. *Dubious Victory: The United States and the End of World War II.* Kent, Ohio: Kent State University Press, 1973.

Rosenman, Samuel I., ed. *The Public Papers and Addresses of Franklin D. Roosevelt. Vol. XIII.* New York: Harper, 1950.

Sainsbury, Keith. *The Turning Point: Roosevelt, Stalin, Churchill, and Chiang Kai-shek, 1943: The Moscow, Cairo, and Teheran Conferences.* New York: Oxford, 1985.

Samii, Kuross A. *Involvement by Invitation: American Strategies of Containment in Iran.* University Park: The Pennsylvania State University Press, 1987.

Sherwin, Martin J. *A World Destroyed: The Atomic Bomb and the Grand Alliance.* New York: Knopf, 1975.

Sherwood, Robert. *Roosevelt and Hopkins: An Intimate History.* New York: Harper, 1950.

Smith, Gaddis. *American Diplomacy During the Second World War, 1941–1945.* 2d ed. New York: Knopf, 1985.

Smith, Walter Bedell. *My Three Years in Moscow.* Philadelphia: Lippincott, 1950.

Snell, John L. *The Wartime Origins of the East-West Dilemma over Germany.* New Orleans: Houser, 1959.

Stettinius, Edward R., Jr. *Roosevelt and the Russians: The Yalta Conference.* New York: Doubleday, 1949.

Stimson, Henry L., and McGeorge Bundy. *On Active Service in Peace and War.* New York: Harper, 1948.

Thomas, Hugh. *Armed Truce: The Beginnings of the Cold War.* New York: Atheneum, 1987.

Thorne, Christopher. *Allies of a Kind: The United States, Great Britain, and the War Against Japan, 1941–1945.* New York: Oxford, 1978.

Truman, Harry S. *Year of Decisions.* Garden City, N.Y.: Doubleday, 1955.

Tsou, Tang. *America's Failure in China, 1941–1950.* Chicago: University of Chicago Press, 1963.

Ulam, Adam. *The Rivals: America and Russia Since World War II.* New York: Viking, 1971.

Unterberger, Betty Miller. *America's Siberian Intervention.* Durham, N.C.: Duke University Press, 1956.

Vandenberg, Arthur H., Jr., ed. *The Private Papers of Senator Vandenberg.* Boston: Houghton Mifflin, 1952.

Ward, Patricia D. *The Threat of Peace: James F. Byrnes and the Council of Foreign Ministers, 1945–1946.* Kent, Ohio: Kent State University Press, 1979.

Wheeler-Bennett, John, and Anthony Nichols. *The Semblance of Peace: The Political Settlement After the Second World War.* London: Macmillan Ltd., 1972.

Williams, William Appleman. *The Tragedy of American Diplomacy.* Rev. and enl. ed. New York: Dell, 1962. Original ed., 1959.

Yergin, Daniel. *Shattered Peace: The Origins of the Cold War and the National Security State.* Boston: Houghton Mifflin, 1977.

Index